D0075475

Postmodern Political Communication

Recent Titles from the
PRAEGER SERIES IN POLITICAL COMMUNICATION
Robert E. Denton, Jr., General Editor

A Shining City on a Hill: Ronald Reagan's Economic Rhetoric, 1951–1989
Amos Kiewe and Davis W. Houck

The Cold War As Rhetoric: The Beginnings, 1945–1950
Lynn B. Hinds and Theodore O. Windt, Jr.

Presidential Perspectives on Space Exploration: Guiding Metaphors from Eisenhower to Bush
Linda T. Krug

Political Campaign Communication, Second Edition
Judith S. Trent and Robert V. Friedenberg

Ethical Dimensions of Political Communication
Edited by Robert E. Denton, Jr.

Cordial Concurrence: Orchestrating National Party Conventions in the Telepolitical Age
Larry David Smith and Dan Nimmo

Political Empiricism: Communication Strategies in State and Regional Elections
Rita Kirk Whillock

Contemporary Apocalyptic Rhetoric
Barry Brummett

Televised Presidential Debates: Advocacy in Contemporary America
Susan Hellweg, Michael Pfau, and Steven Brydon

Vietnam-on-the-Potomac
Moya Ann Ball

The Political Pundits
Dan Nimmo and James E. Combs

POSTMODERN POLITICAL COMMUNICATION

The Fringe Challenges the Center

EDITED BY ANDREW KING

Praeger Series in Political Communication

PRAEGER

Westport, Connecticut
London

Library of Congress Cataloging-in-Publication Data

Postmodern political communication : the fringe challenges the center
/ edited by Andrew King.
    p.   cm. — (Praeger series in political communication)
    Includes bibliographical references and index.
    ISBN 0–275–93840–9 (alk. paper)
    1. Communication—Political aspects—United States. 2. Rhetoric—
Political aspects—United States. 3. Marginality, Social—United
States. 4. United States—Politics and government—1981–1989.
5. United States—Politics and government—1989–   I. King, Andrew,
1947–   II. Title: Postmodern political communication.
III. Series.
P95.82.U6P69   1992
302.2'0973–dc20   91–45612

British Library Cataloguing in Publication Data is available.

Library of Congress Catalog Card Number: 91–45612
ISBN: 0–275–93840–9

First published in 1992

Praeger Publishers, 88 Post Road West, Westport, CT 06881
An imprint of Greenwood Publishing Group, Inc.

Printed in the United States of America

∞™

The paper used in this book complies with the
Permanent Paper Standard issued by the National
Information Standards Organization (Z39.48–1984).

10 9 8 7 6 5 4 3 2 1

Contents

Series Foreword
  Robert E. Denton, Jr.   vii

Introduction: The Great Power Shift
  Andrew King   xi

1 What Is Postmodern Rhetoric?
   Andrew King   1

2 Postmodern Forerunners
   Andrew King   13

3 The Higher Culture as the Site of Struggle
   Andrew King   23

4 Marginalization, the Body, and Empowerment: The
   Rhetoric of the Obese and Little People in America
   Kenneth Zagacki   31

5 The Reciprocal Power of Group Identities and Social
   Styles: A Note on a Specimen Deviant Youth Group
   Calvin Morrill and William Bailey   57

6 Sanctuary Confronts the Court: An Unrepentant
   Prophet
   Jeanne E. Clark   71

CONTENTS

7   Chicano Utopianism in the Southwest
     Richard J. Jensen and John C. Hammerback   85

8   The Goddess of Democracy as Icon in the Chinese
     Student Revolt
     Kenneth C. Petress   99

9   Ma Anand Sheela: Media Power through Radical
     Discourse
     Catherine Ann Collins   115

10   Understanding Fandom Rhetorically: The Case of
     "Beauty and the Beast"
     Kari Whittenberger-Keith   131

11   Purchasing Identity: Advertising and the Embrace
     and Celebration of Self
     Charles Urban Larson   153

12   A Critical Look at the Postmodern Future
     Andrew King   169

     Selected Bibliography   177

     Index   185

     About the Editor and Contributors   187

Series Foreword

Those of us from the discipline of communication studies have long believed that communication is prior to all other fields of inquiry. In several other forums I have argued that the essence of politics is "talk" or human interaction.[1] Such interaction may be formal or informal, verbal or nonverbal, public or private but it is always persuasive, forcing us consciously or subconsciously to interpret, to evaluate, and to act. Communication is the vehicle for human action.

From this perspective, it is not surprising that Aristotle recognized the natural kinship of politics and communication in his writings *Politics* and *Rhetoric*. In the former, he establishes that humans are "political beings [who] alone of the animals [are] furnished with the faculty of language."[2] And in the latter, he begins his systematic analysis of discourse by proclaiming that "rhetorical study, in its strict sense, is concerned with the modes of persuasion."[3] Thus, it was over twenty-three hundred years ago that politics and communication go hand in hand because they are essential parts of human nature.

Back in 1981, Dan Nimmo and Keith Sanders proclaimed that political communication was an emerging field.[4] Although its origin, as noted, dates back centuries, a "self-consciously cross-disciplinary" focus began in the late 1950s. Thousands of books and articles later, colleges and universities offer a variety of graduate and undergraduate coursework in the area in such diverse departments as communication, mass communication, journalism, political science, and sociology.[5] In Nimmo and Sander's early assessment, the "key areas of inquiry" included rhetorical analysis, propaganda analysis, attitude change studies, voting studies, government and the news media, functional and systems analyses, technological changes, media technologies, campaign techniques, and research techniques.[6] In a survey of the state of the field in 1983, the same authors and Lynda Kaid found additional, more specific areas of concern such as the presidency, political polls, public opinion, debates, and advertising to name a few.[7] Since the first study, they also noted a shift away from the rather strict behavioral approach.

Today, Dan Nimmo and David Swanson assert that "political communication has developed some identity as a more or less distinct domain of scholarly work."[8] The scope and concerns of the area have further expanded to include critical theories and cultural studies. While there is no precise definition, method, or disciplinary home of the area of inquiry, its primary domain is the role, processes, and effects of communication within the context of politics broadly defined.

In 1985, the editors of *Political Communication Yearbook: 1984* noted that "more things are happening in the study, teaching, and practice of political communication than can be captured within the space limitations of the relatively few publications available."[9] In addition, they argued that the backgrounds of "those involved in the field [are] so varied and pluralist in outlook and approach, . . . it [is] a mistake to adhere slavishly to any set format in shaping the content."[10] And more recently, Swanson and Nimmo called for "ways of overcoming the unhappy consequences of fragmentation within a framework that respects, encourages, and benefits from diverse scholarly commitments, agendas, and approaches."[11]

In agreement with these assessments of the area and with gentle encouragement, Praeger established in 1988 the series entitled "Praeger Studies in Political Communication." The series is open to all qualitative and quantitative methodologies as well as contemporary and historical studies. The key to characterizing the studies in the series is the focus on communication variables or activities within a political context or dimension. Scholars from the disciplines of communication, history, political science, and sociology have participated in the series.

Postmodern Political Communication is about the nature of discourse, power, and the politics of visible but largely disenfranchised groups. The very notion of "postmodern" seems to be an oxymoron. Modern speech is contemporary speech. It changes as society changes. Its style, form and content mirrors the media and pace of daily life.

However, postmodernism challenges the traditional focus of political discourse from the elite leader to the emerging voices of commonfolk. It concentrates on speakers and groups who have historically been denied access to traditional media and mass audiences. The authors in this volume believe that we are witnessing a new kind of citizen politics. There is a major shift from politics based upon social class issues to issues based upon age, gender, religion and ethnicity. With this shift is a corresponding shift in the locus of power from the nation-state to more local arenas.

A postmodern perspective broadens the definitions and parameters of political discourse and notions of power. It invites examination of rhetoric outside formal institutions and traditional positions of leadership. In essence, postmodernism acknowledges the realistic function of rhetoric. In the words of Kenneth Burke, rhetoric "is rooted in an essential function of language itself, a function that is wholly realistic, and is continually born anew; the use of language as a symbolic means of inducing cooperation in beings that by nature respond to symbols."[12]

The following collection of essays provides an innovative and informative look at contemporary social discourse. It covers a broad range of topics and social groups. Equally important, however, is the articulation of the goals, assumptions, and yields of a postmodern rhetorical perspective.

I am, without shame or modesty, a fan of the series. The joy of serving as its editor is in participating in the dialogue of the field of political communication and in reading the contributors' works. I invite you to join me.

Robert E. Denton, Jr.

NOTES

1. See Robert E. Denton, Jr., *The Symbolic Dimensions of the American Presidency* (Prospect Heights, IL: Waveland Press, 1982); Robert E. Denton, Jr. and Gary Woodward, *Political Communication in America* (New York: Praeger, 1985, Second Edition, 1990); Robert E. Denton, Jr., and Dan Hahn, *Presidential Communication* (New York: Praeger, 1986); and Robert E. Denton, Jr., *The Primetime Presidency of Ronald Reagan* (New York: Praeger, 1988).

2. Aristotle, *The Politics of Aristotle*, trans. Ernest Barker (New York: Oxford University Press, 1970), p. 5.

3. Aristotle, *Rhetoric*, trans. Rhys Roberts (New York: The Modern Library, 1954), p. 22.

4. Dan Nimmo and Keith Sanders, "Introduction: The Emergence of Political Communication as a Field," in *Handbook of Political Communication*, Dan Nimmo and Keith Sanders, eds. (Beverly Hills, CA: Sage, 1981), pp. 11–36.

5. Ibid., p. 15.

6. Ibid., pp. 17–27.

7. Keith Sanders, Lynda Kaid, and Dan Nimmo, eds. *Political Communication Yearbook: 1984* (Carbondale, IL: Southern Illinois University, 1985), pp. 283–308.

8. Dan Nimmo and David Swanson, "The Field of Political Communication: Beyond the Voter Persuasion Paradigm" in *New Directions in Political Communication*, David Swanson and Dan Nimmo, eds. (Beverly Hills, CA: Sage, 1990), p. 8.

9. Sanders, Kaid, and Nimmo, p. xiv.

10. Ibid., p. xiv.

11. Nimmo and Swanson, p. 11.

12. Kenneth Burke, *A Rhetoric of Motives* (Berkeley, CA: University of California Press, 1969), p. 43.

Introduction: The Great Power Shift

Andrew King

This book deals with outsiders, groups struggling to seize power. These are the peoples of the margin; those who must shout to be heard above the din of the official media. A question poses itself immediately. Why study marginal groups at all? Are not marginal groups of less importance by definition? Ought not scholars study the great questions and the big events performed by the big people?

The answer is beguilingly simple. It is simply the case that much important political behavior is carried on outside the boundaries of our formal institutions. Political discourse is not circumscribed by the presidency, the Congress, the courts, or the state governments. As power increasingly flows beyond our traditional political agencies, much of the future is taking shape through the struggles of disinherited groups. New forums, new voices, and new rules of the game are emerging. We must engage these new voices or be ambushed by history.

There is more complex but less beguiling answer. That answer is that we have lost our way on the journey toward the light. We are no longer sure which events are the import ones or which are the voices that carry authority. We have beaten back the darkness, but we are lost in civilizational gloom. We have lost our grip on the center. The essence of modernity and progress (we were once told) was the breakdown of local, religious, ethnic, and other power centers of the folk culture and the concentration of authority within national political institutions. Post-modernism is witnessing the return of power from the nation-state to local arenas and attempts to restore community in the teeth of an inexorable globalism. In addition to the redistribution of power there is a loss of faith. With the decay of the Enlightenment belief in progress and individual autonomy we have lost our sense of mission. With the abandonment of the modern era's obsession with structural and historical determinism, we have retreated to a humbler objective. We seek to understand the ways in which ordinary people make sense of their day-to-day lives. After decades of ridiculing folk culture as provincial superstition, even intellectuals seek the grail of community. We believe that we are witnessing the rise of a new kind of citizen politics at a time when traditional political conflicts are moving beyond the old production-based class issues and more toward divisions based on age, gender, family, community, religion, and ethnicity.

This book represents the work of rhetoricians rather than political scientists. It is fitting that students of persuasive language rather than political theorists or sociologists should contribute to the work. The history of human discourse has been a dialogue between the center and the margin over the character and quality of modern life. One can speak of it as a cycle of emerging, dominant, dying, and muted voices carrying on the long struggle over whose voice should prevail and whose rule will be honored.

Then too, from Greco-Roman times until the middle of the eighteenth century, the study of rhetoric has been at the heart of educational instruction in Western civilization. Dismembered in the full flush of the modern era, rhetoric became an adjunct of written composition and belles lettres. During the nineteenth century it disappeared from the academy. In the early twentieth century it reappeared in departments of public speaking. Public speaking was an "applied skill" and thus a pariah among the arts and humanities. In imitation of earlier practices in English departments, students of rhetoric became historians of speakers and explicators of speeches—all the while, calling themselves rhetorical critics. Discourse was studied apart from context and taxonomy and aesthetics replaced analysis. Individual speakers were celebrated as fountainheads of eloquence while the collective making of meaning was largely ignored. Often rhetorical scholars concentrated on an analysis of stock arguments in a way that parodied the Enlightenment ideal of the moral and rational unity of the human species.

While rhetoricians in speech departments fought for academic respect, rhetoricians in English departments remained at the outermost margins of power. Despite the brilliant work of scholars such as Corbett and Kinneavey, rhetoricians were viewed as ink-stained wretches groaning beneath student compositions. Literary scholars were the aristocrats of the discipline, and while rhetoricians squatted in nameless cellars, the literati rose to the purple. Rhetoricians housed in classics departments fared better, but they were few.

The 1970s changed everything. The field seemed to experience a vast expansion. Sensing rich interior marrow, ravenous scholars began gnawing at the rhetorical bone. Semioticians and poststructuralists helped thrust rhetoric to the center of humane studies in the 1980s. The proletarianization of the rhetorician ceased, and the study of discourse became a new emblem proclaiming the unity of the arts and sciences. The fresh interest in rhetoric eroded boundaries between disciplines, generated a new interdisciplinary vocabulary, and shook established methodologies to their foundations. Richard McKeon's old dream of rhetoric as the architectonic of the arts and sciences seemed on the verge of realization.

The restoration of rhetoric to a commanding position in the circle of humane study has brought significant change. First, it has contributed to a suspicion of the universal and a new respect for the provincial and the local. We have a deeper understanding of the connection between the rules governing particular kinds of discourse and the sites in which they were produced. Second, we have begun to think more carefully about the political dimensions of doing scholarship. The image of the lonely scholar seeking to satisfy an attack of intellectual curiosity is in retreat. We now view membership in a scholarly community as a burden that carries with it a certain power to define social reality. To form conceptions of the world is a moral act and so is the activity of dismissing some problems and fastening upon others. We are continually making decisions that limit or provoke debate or promote particular perspectives and denigrate others.

Armed with a fresh focus and a renewed sense of mission, the writers in this book concentrate on the emergence of voices outside the center. In analyzing the dialogue between the center and the periphery, they ask how discourse is related to the order it imposes and they attempt to assess the cost of these struggles. Traditionally, rhetoricians have gravitated to power. When they have not scrutinized powerful leaders or agents of institutional structures, they have selected fully mounted communities such as organized religion, the polis, or the national state. The groups studied here are relatively powerless, and their efforts at community formation are either rudimentary or fraught with great difficulty. They typically lack resources, allies, political legitimacy, and expertise. As a compensatory strategy some have developed a high degree of rhetorical expertise and an ability to use the media.

THE NATURE OF POWER

Power in the Information Society has a fugitive and mercurial quality that is still not fully understood. In feudal and early modern times, power rested with the persons who controlled physical resources, land, or machines. Today it resides with those who have specialized knowledge. Leadership has become fluid, and "assigned" leaders constantly defer to those who possess the expertise to solve particular problems. Ironically this situation has strengthened the role of major institutions while at the same time undermining their legitimacy.

One of the first great modern institutions was the United States Department of Agriculture. With its constellation of mighty land grant colleges, it functioned as a vast problem-solving entity. It set about the systematic production of organized knowledge and carried out its application to a huge variety of formerly intractable problems. Today, a far greater panoply of research-driven institutions has eclipsed the old civic, religious, and military institutions of Western civilizations. The problem, as so many thinkers from Jürgen Habermas to Kenneth Cmeil and Kathleen Jamieson have pointed out, is that the new experts lack the legitimacy of the older leadership class. These "experts" do not pretend to embody the aspirations of the citizenry as did the amateur citizen orator of earlier times. Thus, the expert's authoritative voice has no mandate from the people. It resonates with data and pragmatic application, but not with moral authority. Ironically, institutions are physically powerful as never before, but they are in danger of losing their mandates. As this book will argue, the old folk culture is not dead, but merely beginning to assert itself in new ways, filling the void left by the death of the culture of civic humanism and the orator-tribune of the people.

Skinheads, ethnonationalists, little people, and other groups of the margin are featured in this book. These are the people that history has elected not to memorialize. In the idiom of the martyred son of Nancy Hanks, their discourse has generally been "little noted" and it has been "not long remembered."

History has celebrated the powerful. It has been two decades since J. D. Plumb asserted that 'history' was born as a weapon of dynastic legitimation. Historians traced the divine origins of ruling families, celebrated the inevitability of conquerors, and disseminated and solemnized the retrospectively constructed myths of great leaders. If the selection of significant events and great personalities seems increasingly arbitrary today, only yesterday the task seemed a relatively straightforward one. Has "Battle and King" ever really lost its grip on the popular mind? Even when it has been displaced by a history of "peoples," no one has pretended that all events are equal candidates in the construction of historical narrative. World historical personalities have left their claw marks on the landscape, and great events tower above the ordinary affairs of men and women. Even those who dealt with the humble events of the so-called ordinary masses felt it necessary to argue that these struggles were to be viewed as manifestations of higher forces or of the march of ruling ideas through the world.

Authoritative answers to problems of historical selection were issued by the German historian Leopold von Ranke. His scientific history identified political, military, and religious groups as the primary agents of change. The grand patterns of history were defined by these elites. Matching events and trends in a seamless narrative, Ranke's "scientific history" promised a usable and authoritative past.

Unfortunately Ranke's method was bypassed by social scientists such as Dilthey, Weber, and Thomas, who selected biography as the fundamental unit of time. The virtuosity and prestige of these three thinkers undermined the consensus on an objective history. Their challenge shook the idea of an objective history to its fundament, and the sociologists began to argue that the shape and content of time is symbolically and subjectively constructed. In brief, the meaning of history does not lie in wait to be ambushed, but is created through human interaction and thus is subject to constant negotiation.

This perspective, a broad variant of what sociologists call "symbolic interaction," has guided the choice of case histories for this book. The perspective is evident in the fluidity of the rhetorical analysis and a concentration on process rather than structure and on the mutual negotiation of meaning as opposed to the exemplary force of great texts or the galvanizing power of the great orator. Above all, it moves us far from the hand-wringing of intellectuals who speak condescendingly of the atomized masses and the decay of citizenship. The great humanist may be in the shade, but at the level of quotidian experience, dialogue is alive and well. Likewise, citizenship is being carried on in other arenas. If the national state and its institutions are tattered, loyalty and belonging are not moribund. They have been bestowed elsewhere. In short, the quest for community goes on, but the big news is being written on the margin. Nearly two decades ago a brilliant rhetorical scholar, Ernest Bormann of the University of Minnesota, set out to study this grass roots, bottom-upward discourse. More than once he was attacked by scholars who objected to his method of analysis on the grounds that it lacked boundedness, precision, and rigor. Now that Bormann has been vindicated and his objects and methods of study have become commonplace, it is apparent that there was another reason for the savagery of the attack. Bormann turned his back on the great orator as an object of reverence and veneration. At a time when professors were urging students to consult their inner genius, Bormann had already concluded that rhetorical invention was a profoundly social process. Perhaps his Dakota roots inspired this fundamentally democratic approach to the study of discourse. Bormann's work has immediate social application. He did not treat symbols as aesthetic expression, but studied the ways in which they reflected and affected group hierarchy, group aspirations, and individual happiness. Although we have not made direct use of his method for the case studies, we have been guided by his spirit. Professor

Bormann's healthy suspicion of large institutions and abstract world thinkers helped to inspire confidence in the belief that by attending to the voices on the margin we are studying the seedbed of postmodern experience.

Postmodern Political Communication

Chapter One

What Is Postmodern Rhetoric?

Andrew King

Is there a distinctive postmodern discourse, or is the term a mere shibboleth? Does postmodern discourse possess generic characteristics? Does it have an inner logic and a special moral syntax? Can it be understood through the medium of conventional rhetorical analysis? Surely postmodern discourse challenges our traditional conceptions of speakers, texts, messages, and situations. Will critics be able to assess its meaning and importance? The answer is not yet clear. For the present the continental divide that yawns between traditional ways of evaluating discourse and postmodern critical practice seems unbridgeable. For example, in a recent issue of *Western Journal of Communication*, critics Michael Leff and Michael McGee disagreed on such fundamental questions as the meaning of history, the definition of text, the job of the critic, and the salience of rhetoric itself as a humane study.[1]

What is "decentered" discourse and how do its conceptions of speaker, text, message, audience, and situation differ from the classical models we have long and lovingly elaborated? Is the speaker an autonomous moral agent? Must meaning be pursued through an endless and joyless regression of texts? Are audiences mere aggregates? What happens to the authority of a critic who is both antihistorical and antiuniversalist in outlook?

THE SPEAKER

Postmodernism means a change of focus from the rhetoric of the elite speaker to the rhetoric of the emerging or subaltern voice. The elite speaker, the Ciceronian orator-statesman, has long been our model.

Until yesterday rhetorical scholars have fixed upon the great orator as an object of study. Great orators were treated as autonomous moral agents, and their speeches became the canonical texts, the exemplary works that shaped history. Speakers such as Demosthenes, Cicero, William Pitt, FDR, and Churchill were viewed as "world-historical personalities" who seized the tides of events at the flood and rode them to dramatic adventures. Hardly less important than the words of those who succeeded were the words of those who failed. The doomed words of Cato the Younger and Edmund Burke were also valued because they pointed out a moral or illuminated a historical precept.

The people who uttered significant words were emphatically the people of the center. They were generally members of a privileged elite, embedded in the central institutions of their communities. As embodiments of order, they seemed to function as conduits between the sacred realm of heaven and the sublunar polity. They were custodians of the great centering words, words such as nation, state, race, people, country, community, region, culture, folk, law, nature, progress, and destiny. Furthermore, the study of these great individuals lent an air of legitimacy to rhetorical scholarship. It reaffirmed the Enlightenment metaphysic of radical individualism and moral progress. In addition a kind of nobility of association gilded the critic who adopted this perspective.

Postmodern discourse, on the other hand, is the discourse of emerging voices. These are the voices that literary critics call subaltern voices, that feminists have named the muted voice, that folklorists denominate the voice of the trickster or coyote, and that linguists call the code-switcher's voice. It is the voice of the periphery, not of the center. It is the voice of the silent ones who are struggling to speak. It may be the ultimate postmodern voice—the anonymous voices of crowds, the muffled roar of rumor and of threats, or even insults and obscenities gouged on public walls.

Postmodern discourse is about the recovery of these voices.[2] It concentrates on speakers and groups that have historically lacked access to large audiences, political apparatus, and public media. Its speech is sometimes angry or radical. Often, however, its rage may be disguised by the strategic appropriation of the hegemonic speech of the dominant group. If nothing else, the postmodern critic learns to listen carefully, for one must be aware that the subaltern voice frequently suffers from a "severe speech impediment induced by power relations."[3]

But there is another reason for the shift away from the study of great speakers. Our traditional individualism has worn thin, and today the dominant orator is viewed less as an autonomous moral actor than as the agent of an institution or the embodiment of corporate or cultural interests. Thus, it follows that if the great orator is merely an agent of a matrix of dominant forces, then his or her discourse is not a unitary voice, but a product of group collaboration. From this point of view even the traditional speech loses its character as an individual art object, unique and unrepeatable. Rather a speech may be seen as a fragment of a larger dialogue between contending groups.

A moral relativism also emerges. The inner-directed autonomous moral agent is dismissed, and the individual comes to be viewed as socially constructed. Without an autonomous moral actor, the postmodern will be left without a pantheon of devils to set against a pantheon of heroes. The critic's job is no longer to expose evil people, but to expose only the forms or techniques of power. This creates a tension for many critics who understand the power of fixing blame and who realize that whatever standards academic critics decide to adopt, the dominant culture will go right on assigning praise and blame. Although this removes a powerful weapon from the critical arsenal, it also lends a sort of objectivity to their judgments. As David Bobbitt has pointed out, critics in the past routinely "satanized" whole groups of speakers, thereby impoverishing public debate rather than enriching it.[4]

The postmodern critic is acutely aware of the problem of legitimacy. The old institutional speakers shared in the moral authority of the center. This book deals with speakers and groups that lack access to audiences, may be barred from sites where speaking is being done, do not possess the status to compel others to listen, and typically lack a full understanding of the role and dominion of rhetoric in the modern world. The old orators were emblems of legitimacy, but the spokespersons in this book lack traditional, institutional, or moral authority.

For centuries, rhetorical analysis has been centrist, and rhetorical critics have gravitated toward power. Serious study has been bounded or defined by the state and its institutional apparatus. For the most part, rhetorical critics were latecomers to the study of social movements, entities that lack legitimacy almost by definition. Social movements lack full institutionalization. In Weberian terms, they have not yet routinized whatever mandate their founders have earned. Thus they have an ad hoc quality and a vulnerability that make them less appealing to students with a classical education. On the other hand, the routinization and permanence of great institutions confer a legitimacy on their members that appears unquestioned. Few things are as compelling as the taken-for-grantedness of custom; thus, the day-to-day functioning of the state apparatus is itself a confirmation of legitimacy.

A cursory reading of the studies in this book will show that a primary strategy of the marginal group is to attack the legitimacy of the dominant group. The hegemonic group of a community justifies its pursuit of a partisan agenda through the disguise of universalist appeals (the common good, the will of the majority, or progress), and subordinate groups attempt to unmask and expose the selfish interest hidden by such ap-

peals. Since hegemonic groups and their spokespersons control resources, access to media, speaking sites, and even audiences, a rhetoric
of alternative invention may be said to follow three broad strategies:

1. Performance Argument. This consists of criticizing the dominant group for
   having violated the very norms under which it rules. For example, one may
   accuse the authorities of not keeping their promises.
2. The Generic Argument. This consists of a general criticism of the government
   or of all governments for having violated their own rules.
3. The Revolutionary Argument. This consists of attacking the foundational
   values the government uses to justify its acts. For example, one does not
   merely attack the president, one condemns the institution of the presidency.

These three strategies correspond to Barrington Moore's conception of
the three degrees of radicalism. The first represents an attack upon the
legitimacy of a single person. The second represents an attack upon an
entire governing class. The third is supposedly the most radical of all
and represents an attack on the social order that sustains the government. But as James C. Scott has pointed out, Moore formulated these
tests as political abstractions.[5] In the actual event of an ongoing strategic
war of position between dominant and subordinate groups, the first
strategy may actually be more radical than the third.

This is so for several reasons. Subordinate groups want to be effective,
and they know that by adopting the polite hegemonic criticisms of the
first strategy, they may gain far more than if they employ the more
radical expression of strategies two and three with their wholesale con-
demnations and attacks on fundamental principles. Furthermore, subordinate groups know that dominant groups tend to stay in power for
extended periods of time and will retain the ability to define the meaning
of any challenge. They may dismiss strategies two and three as proof
of the subordinate group's lack of seriousness, of immaturity, or even
of insanity. Finally, as Scott so convincingly argues, a deferential chal-
lenger leaves the ruling group at a serious disadvantage, for the powerful
are often fooled by politeness and may be unable to assess the depth of
disaffection on the part of the subordinate group.[6] As Ian Shapiro has
shown, a curious inversion has taken place that affects the legitimacy
of subordinate groups and their spokespersons.[7] The national state and
the formal institution have been placed at the heart of serious political
analysis. Compared to the massive analysis devoted to these entities,
little attention has been given to the discourse and practice of local
governments—to say nothing of social movements and other inchoate
and open groups.

We are reminded that the Greco-Roman classics dealt with the polis
and later with the civic administration of city-states, or that Jefferson's

conception of authentic governance was emphatically local. Ironically the artificial construction, the nation-state, has become the real polity, and the organic community has become the artificial one. Thus, the town and its hinterland, the ethnic enclave, and the voluntary association are viewed as artificial reality, but the abstract construct (the state) is thought to be as natural as breathing and as fundamental as the law of gravity.

THE TEXT

Those of us who were undergraduates during the New Critical imperium remember the text as a solid thing. It was compared to a rock, a diamond, the motherlode of a silver mine. Its autonomy was our badge of independence from other disciplines. While historians struggled with the ghosts of time or scientists with the vibrations of the ether, we busted our chops on the text. David Thompson of the University of Minnesota was fond of comparing the text to an unpolished gem that required rough handling to bring out its inner light. At Vanderbilt and other Southern New Critical strongholds, students were commanded to "mine the text," "work the text," "interrogate the text," "wrestle the text," and "scrutinize the text." But the text has begun to slip from our grasp. For it is against the traditional text that the postmodern bayonet has been thrust into the very heart of our critical practice. Postmodern critics refuse to countenance the text in the old way; that is, they do not honor it as a discrete object of study. They do not value it as a distillation of a writer's or speaker's richly matured thought. Instead, they view it as a rapidly blurring snapshot or an inchoate series of images rapidly being rewritten, annotated, scribbled over, and revised. In fact, the postmodern view of the text exists in oppositional counterpoint to the modernist. Whereas the text has been viewed as an artistic exemplar, postmodernists define it as a fragment or trace of a larger dialogue. Instead of seeing the text as a product of an individual orator or writer, postmoderns see it as a product of social collaboration. Whereas the text was innocently assumed to speak with a single voice, postmodern critics call attention to the multivoiced or polysemous nature of the text. Traditional scholars noted that certain texts conformed to time orientations (deliberation over the formulation of future action or forensic with the meaning of past actions); postmodernists exposed the illusion of time and noted that the contemporary sensibility produced no dominant tense. Whereas the traditional scholars tended to take institutional sites as given, postmoderns noted that sites played a crucial role in the invention of messages. The place where a speech is given dictates the kinds of things that can be said and the ways they can be said. Whereas the traditional scholar acknowledged a difference between universal and special kinds of arguments and appeals, the postmodern scholar does not honor a distinction between universal and local appeals, but sees all appeals as partisan. In a move that has been denounced as deeply anti-intellectual because it tends to reduce all ideas to their impact upon power arrangements in society, the postmodernists classify all appeals according to their partisan or interest-bearing meanings. Whereas the traditional scholar appraises the strength, range, clarity, and credibility of a message, the postmodernist looks for hidden patterns of dominance, codes of social resistance, and alternative patterns of invention. Increasingly, postmoderns have forced a crisis in intellectual circles by attempting to expose ideas as the real estate of powerful groups.

But most characteristic is the postmodern obsession with narrative. Narrative is given a special status because it arises from local practice. Those who speak of the superior power of narrative are fond of talking about its victory over and displacement of argument in the popular culture. Certainly such a displacement has happened in advertising. Consider the format of turn-of-the-century advertising. In the old print-dominated ads of the late nineteenth and early twentieth centuries, claims were made, evidence was marshaled, conclusions were drawn, and rival claims were refuted. A cursory glance at advertising today reveals that even in the old print bastion of magazine advertising the narrative format is firmly in the saddle. As Kathleen Jamieson has so compellingly demonstrated, the same sort of displacement of argument by narrative has transformed political discourse.[8] Not only does the dominance of narrative provide superior coherence, it also controls the manner of political rejoinder. For example, the power of the "greenhouse effect" lies not in its fragmentary and disputed pieces of evidence but largely in its narrative form. What if the evidence had been put in the non-narrative form? Consider the following: 'We have some evidence that suggests (although this evidence is contradicted by some other evidence) that an uneven pattern of warming is taking place in the temperate zone. It may be related to certain discharges from our industrial installations and from our modes of transportation. This means that there may or may not be some industrial dislocation and that not a few people may have to change jobs.' A much different impact is made by a "scientific" narrative of gradually spreading deserts, an eroding corn belt, oceans turning to steam, an unbreathable atmosphere, Midwestern sterility, colonies under glass domes, space survivors huddled on the cheerless Mercury waiting for the end, and all the fantastic extrapolation and spin-offs eagerly supplied by the listener.

The critic also approaches the text in a radically different manner. Thus, a student of postmodern discourse does not find a text; he or she assembles it. A student studying the discourse about coastal erosion resists the temptation to find the single best speech of a leading environmental spokesperson. Nor does he or she seize upon the definitive utterance of a major coastal scientist or set about assembling a set of debates about coastal erosion. Instead, the student actively constructs the text from popular documentaries, the evening news, snippets of congressional hearings, scare stories of mass circulation magazines, heated public exchanges of warring groups, fisher folk, factory workers, comic books, public documents, leaflets, prime-time entertainment shows, and many other formal and informal sources. The ever-shifting face of the text spans time, space, social class, and perspective. The text has lost its boundaries and is now a social invention rather than the composition of any single individual. One's product is glossed, decontextualized, recontextualized, and put to novel uses.

In the late modern era one still hoped to use language that would construct patterns of action that had permanence. The late afterglow of the Enlightenment with its linear and upward path of progress and its metaphysic of individual power and accountability has faded into night. From the old perspective it made sense to seek out significant mileposts in the upward journey and to mark these with significant texts. These texts "place" each of the acts within the great authorizing story of human progress. The literary world was a world of solid achievement. In the postmodern era we have been thrown on our own resources, and the critic has a new kind of accountability. Without received definitions he or she has become exquisitely aware of the critic's responsibility as a maker of meaning. Whether one can speak meaningfully and at length with this enormous burden is still not clear.

SITES OF DISCOURSE

Because the traditional critics so often elected to study elite speakers with firm institutional anchorage, they tended to take the importance of site for granted. Perhaps the focus on institutional settings blurred rather than heightened the sense of the importance of place. Postmodernism has brought a stronger awareness that the site of speech is also the locus of a network of speech practices sanctioning what can and cannot be said, who may and may not speak, what topics may be introduced and in what order, what constitutes evidence, and which forms of deference are appropriate. Institutional settings are those sites in which the hegemonic group has consolidated its power so that its rules seem an order of nature. We have ignored covert sites of discourse that are outside the observation of the dominant groups or those noninstitutional sites that are places of struggle between groups in order to determine whose rules will become sovereign. We have ignored the folk network that matures and edits its discourse in all those places where the dominant group is not in full control. As James C. Scott has noted, the criticism of elite groups is usually carried on out of earshot. He believes that the "history of discourse has been the history of attempts to control the significant sites of assembly and the spaces of discourse."[9] Contrariwise it has also been the attempt to change the discourse rules of present sites and to find new places in which hitherto muted persons might carry on their own debates.

The marketplace, the tavern, the livery stable, and the deep piney woods are examples of the nonhegemonic sites of discourse where the raw rage of individuals could be framed, edited, and forged into a verbal weapon. One of the great imaginative reconstructions of this hidden process is that of William Styron's literary recreation of the Nat Turner rebellion of 1831.[10] The slaves' retreat, the workers' club, the covered shed at the far end of the school playground are examples of new sites of discourse created for and by subordinate groups.

The interest in sites also alerts us to message features that routinely occur when subordinate spokespersons speak in hegemonic sites. When this happens, subordinate speakers are in the position of Booker T. Washington at the Atlanta Exposition in 1895. They must speak to multiple audiences, employ euphemism, simulate an exquisite politeness, and use codes and other nuanced forms of communication. Avoiding direct reference to the integration of the races, Washington was able to introduce a social and economic bargain with potentially radical consequences for the social order.

A close friend of mine is fond of talking about the "brag speeches" of Saturday night drinkers in the small Dakota towns of his youth and early manhood. After a week of backbreaking work, stoic small farmers found themselves in the tavern, a primary site of antihegemonic discourse. The tavern provided the excuse of alcohol, a willing audience, and an occasion. At times these silent and ordinarily uncomplaining men reached quite poetic flights as they "answered" the bankers, large land owners, water board members, and cooperative officers with what they "should have said" to them in face-to-face confrontation (had they only had their wits about them). Only after an exhaustion of premeditated profanity and poetic invention would these men descend into conventional swearing. These "orations" often provoked critique. Some of the witty sayings and notable images were subsequently taken up by the group and memorable arguments became community property. Other phrases were attacked or revised in order to seem more representative of the group's sentiments. Anyone who doubts the power of this breeding ground of political discourse need only reflect on the vigor with which politicians have attempted to neutralize or silence it. They have sanitized it with surveys, reduced it to polling data, or actively intervened as Huey Long did in 1935 by forbidding free assembly.

Thus, in popular discourse, interest in subordinate groups has moved us beyond the official texts. Dominant groups and their agents produce the official texts, since they control the sites of discourse, the rules of discourse, and even particular message characteristics. Those message characteristics that are most representative of postmodern discourse are discussed in some detail in the final chapter of this work.

THE AUDIENCE

In the age of mass media, one is acutely aware of the problem of multiple audiences. Advertisers that target a particular group must risk being overheard by many others who are bored or offended by their appeals. The spokespersons in this book speak for a particular constituency over and against other constituencies. The message they articulate is a group product. It has been built up out of the daily humiliation, the personal disappointments, the fear, envy, and rage of individual lives. But it has been forged into a group product. The spokespersons of subordinate groups have much practice as code-switchers. They are particularly aware of the fragmentation of the thing we glibly call a national audience. Their message is addressed to those they call "us" as well as to the people called "them" or the dominant elites, rival groups, heretical splinter groups, members of the mass media, and a huge congeries of massively indifferent but potentially dangerous *others*.

The character and composition of the dominant group varies with each subordinate group and its agenda. Duncan's famous formula says that we command our inferiors, we supplicate our superiors, and we argue with our equals. In practice, the mode of address seems dictated by the situation. The attitude toward the dominant group is frequently ambivalent. The powerful are alternately denounced, appealed to, and reasoned with.

In addition to the dominant groups are the attending satellites, the mediating groups that attend upon the holders of power. The press is an important group of mediators. In the contemporary scene, members of the press are to be reckoned with because they possess independent powers of definition. Thus it behooves subordinate leaders to study the hows and whys of the media agenda and to craft their performances accordingly. They must learn to say things that appropriately caption group demonstrations and to perform in ways that have appropriate entertainment (and therefore commercial) value.

Furthermore, because of their crucial role as mediators, members of the mass media may be able to confer legitimacy upon subordinate groups simply by giving them a visible presence and thereby defining their actions as relevant and important. Intellectuals have sometimes exercised this power. One is reminded of Sartre's endorsement of various adventurers as figures of high romance in the third world.

Finally there are those who may simply overhear a message and take action. One is reminded of the white ethnics who "overheard" the civil rights messages during the 1960s that were intended for others. Their mobilization greatly complicated the institutionalization of the movement during the late 1960s and early 1970s.

THE SITUATION

From the perspective of the subordinate group, there is a single situational feature that reigns over all others. Subordinate groups are by their very nature engaged in an unequal dialogue with a more powerful group. They lack resources, legitimacy, and often the self-confidence to mount a critique of the dominant ideology. This generic situation carries opportunities as well as liabilities. The first opportunity is provided by the rhetoric of the dominant group. Dominant groups articulate idealized versions of their conduct and are thus always vulnerable to not living out their own creeds. Frequently the deviations from these articulated justifications are very wide, as when the czar represented himself as the father of the nation at the very same time he also found it necessary to turn his soldiery against the people.

If postmodernism means that no group has full legitimacy, it also provides the opportunity to make use of its master trope: that moral authority has become separated from material power. A conservative rendering of this "truth" is all too familiar: In the information society, ideas and innovation cannot be imposed from the top; hence the utter failure of socialism, command economies, and other top-down schemes. In whatever form it is uttered, this idea of on-site, information-driven social practice provides the logic for another situational opportunity: that quasi-legitimate groups may occupy a discourse space as referees between warring subordinate groups.

Radical intellectuals driven by conspiracy theory have long attempted to sell the idea that knowledge is a function of power. It has become increasingly clear, however, that authority will follow knowledge. Finally—the academy to the contrary—it would appear that the most significant knowledge is local knowledge. The next chapter reviews the events of intellectual history that have brought us to this pass.

NOTES

1. Methodologically, McGee seeks to reconstruct the original rhetorical transaction from its "traces," and Leff sees the "text" as an exemplary product. For a brilliant discussion of these extremes, see Dilip Parameshwar Gaonkar, "Object and Method in Rhetorical Criticism: From Wichelns to Leff and McGee," *Western Journal of Speech Communication* 54 (Summer 1990): 291–92.

2. Jules Chemetzy, *Our Decentralized Literature* (Amherst, Mass.: University of Massachusetts Press, 1986), 4.

3. James C. Scott, *Domination and the Arts of Resistance* (New Haven, Conn., and London: Yale University Press, 1990), 138.

4. I am in debted to David Bobbitt for this concept. His analysis of the discourse of the U.S. civil rights movement accounts for the lack of racial reconciliation in the South twenty-five years after the settlement of various issues.

5. Scott, *Domination and the Arts of Resistance*, 92.

6. Ibid.

7. Ian Shapiro, *Political Community* (Berkeley: University of California Press, 1990), 45.

8. Kathleen Jamieson, *Eloquence in an Electronic Age: The Transformation of Political Speechmaking* (New York: Oxford, 1988), 13.

9. Scott, *Domination and the Arts of Resistance*, 192.

10. William Styron, *The Confessions of Nat Turner* (New York: Random House, 1966).

Chapter Two

Postmodern Forerunners

Andrew King

HISTORY

Can postmodernism be said to have a history? Its dominant style note is ahistorical; that is, it has no privileged tense. In postmodern art the past, the present, and the visionary future are juxtaposed. For post-modernists, the past is not a "legend haunted" repository of moral authority (to use J. D. Plumb's famous phrase) but a huge scrap heap for raiding parties in search of a usable past. Standing upon a vast landscape littered with fragments and traces, time presents a face that is neither whole nor meaningful.

Postmodernism is glibly called the era of the loss of the center. But what do those words mean? Surely the center has been lost before. The Greek Sophists attempted to cut the links between the blessed gods and the earthly polis by dismissing the possibility of knowledge about the former. Other coteries in the Greco-Roman world challenged the uni-versal as the primary locus of meaning independent of human needs or wishes. For many centuries these tiny groups remained on the uttermost margins of power. They were like actors waiting in the wings to be called for a second engagement during the Enlightenment, after the modern West began to commit its great acts of regicide. Postmodernism may be the sunset of Euroman. On the other hand, it may be little more than a severe attack of cultural vertigo.

The loss of the center and the loss of legitimacy are connected. His-torically, power exhibits a characteristic geography. Certain features of the landscape have always been "charged with potency."[1] The Druids had sacred groves, lakes, and rocky eminences that served as collecting places of power. They were the points where the sacred and the profane touched, the contact places with heaven. For example, Geslick sees the doctrine of Karma as elaborating and technologizing a more primal image, the dream of ascent to the center.[2]

The center was the still point around which all else revolved in a syntax of spaces and diminishing grace. At the center was the ruler. The capital city was the site of power. The surrounding provinces were nodes, places of lesser power commanded by nobles of diminishing degrees of merit and status. At the frontier the forces of order ran thin. In the hinterlands there was also power, but it was the chaotic power of old night, dangerous and untamed.

We know only too well about the power of old night, but it is the power of the center that we have come to doubt. In fin de siècle Vienna, doomed artists and intellectuals fought the sense of decay by retiring to the garden where "the crown of perfected humanity . . . once more served the bourgeois as inspiration for an elevated mode of existence."[3] The garden has always served as the matrix where art, nature, technology, and culture are united, the center of the world where earth and sky embrace. One need only recall that moments of enlightenment have always been experienced as a temporary loss of the center followed by a dramatic restoration. Paul on the Damascus road lost and regained the center. Rousseau experienced a profound disorientation before he made his world-ordering discovery. Coleridge felt a sense of dizziness before the sovereign power descended. Even Jean-Paul Sartre experienced his loss of faith as nausea and dizziness in the café in Normandy before he gained his acceptance of a humanly horizoned center.

The loss of center is the loss of universals. As universals fade to a syntactical convention, our discourse is impoverished and we are left with a rhetoric of special topoi. Are we left to suffer a balkanization of discourse—separate domains of experience presided over by elite experts who control the appropriate information and sanction the appropriate procedures? Among the many competing voices, can any claim legitimacy?

Despite its air of sudden crisis, postmodernism has been gathering its forces for centuries. If modernity began with the cutting off of the king's head, postmodernity might be called the final act of regicide. With Copernicus the center was moved. Newton set it in motion hurtling through space; with Louis XVI its corpus was slaughtered so that its principle could be relocated from the sphere of divinity to the sovereign operations of human thought processes. The Romantics made the center plural; Einstein made it disappear; Foucault made it a convention of power, and Derrida assured us that even its memory must disappear.

In its more parochial form, postmodernism appears as a "university-based intervention against the Euro-centered hegemony of literature's classics,"[4] and as such it is occasionally dismissed as an English department quarrel that "conjures up images of the nihilistic, the apolitical, the trivial or worse."[5] It is, we believe, far broader, even in the academy. It has affected every discipline from philosophy to architecture. In a still broader sense it is the name of a process that began with the shattering of the great Christian medieval paradigm.

The two hammer blows of the Reformation and the Renaissance began the fragmentation of Western thought. Since these initial assaults, the multiplication of rival paradigms has been going on at an ever-increasing rate. Authority was relocated from God to the level of the thought processes themselves. Authority became plural, for earlier paradigms were never wholly displaced. After the Christian Chain of Being, no new paradigm—not even Science—achieved full legitimacy. Finally the very idea of Center (Garden, Capitol, Axis, Godhead, Mind, Cosmos) came under attack. And at last we labor under a ferocious epistemological skepticism. It is not merely a case of doubting our traditional beliefs. We now doubt our very ability to know.

The late Jean-Paul Sartre promised us that consciousness raising was liberating; its critical edge would serve as the great solvent of ideology. It was his belief that an understanding of the interest-based foundations of knowledge would soon touch the minds of ordinary people as well as the thoughts of intellectuals. Thus, for Sartre, the ultimate state of Western civilization is a sense of a feeling of ennui and pessimism over the arbitrariness of our values and despair over the class-based character of our higher culture. The vertigo and nausea he experienced in the Normandy Hotel are emblematic of the homelessness of the postmodern spirit.

There were avatars in earlier times, but never such thoroughgoing disenchantment. Aquinas separated the lunar and the sublunar spheres to insulate an arena of wholly secular objects and questions. But he did not shut the pilgrims from their sacred shrines or prevent another Dante from journeying to the axis mundi. The advance guard of postmodernism, Nietzsche and Conrad, arrived by the late nineteenth century as Nietzsche formulated a wholly secular conception of art and Conrad presented to the world a hollow company of mission-haunted European imperials who were no longer able to distinguish between the hearts of darkness and the places of light in a broken world. The sudden sunburst of the old discipline of rhetoric has paralleled the growth of postmodernism. And like postmodernism, this new rhetoric is largely a decentered rhetoric; it has been shorn of any particular institutional commitments. In the second sophistic, rhetoric loosened its anchorage to the Roman state. In this sense one can speak of a new sophistic or third sophistic rhetoric of the postmodern age.

Like its predecessor, the third sophistic rhetoric has several hallmarks:

relativism (it serves no higher interest or credo), virtuoso display, and the elevation of the personal and the immediate over the permanent and the universal. These style notes are the very ones that Wood and Zurcher have employed in their description of the postmodern self. Their study of the transformation of the modern to the postmodern self is a discourse-based computer-assisted analysis coding diaries that spanned more than a century. Wood and Zurcher found a vast sea change in the mental outlook and personality type of the ordinary American during this time. They noted that the moderns had justified their acts in terms of "institutional standards, duty to society and future time," and the postmoderns appealed to "duty to self, gratification and present time." Further, they decried a change from placing a high value on "structure, stability and constancy" to valuing "process, multiplicity and experimentation."[6]

Jacques Derrida, a man of the margin like so many postwar intellectuals, has given postmodernism its pantheon of antiheroes and its sense of mission. Born in Algiers in 1930 of French and German-Swiss stock, he went to France for military service during the turbulent period of the colonial uprisings of the 1950s. He became internationally celebrated because of a happy accident at the age of 36 while visiting Johns Hopkins. His performance at the Conference on Structuralism in Baltimore in 1969 is now described in mythic terms. Invited to explicate structuralism to Americans, he announced that it was already a spent force and introduced his mode of reading (a metaphysical reading over and against a material reading), the "deconstruction" that has become the central pillar in the wider academic movement known as poststructuralism.

Derrida recalls to us the idea of Mircea Eliade that the communal center has always been the imago mundi, the place where body and soul and heaven and earth meet. But Derrida inaugurated poststructuralism by urging that we turn our eyes away from the groups that exercise communal power and toward the invisible modes of thought and ingrained cultural habits that make obedience seem reasonable and necessary. Thus he took at his project the process of intellectual decolonization in affirming that it is the "victims" themselves who transmit the numerous forms of community hegemony and that "the very people it obligates are its active agents, using and extending its webs of power."[7]

The loss of the center forces us back to an infinite regression of texts and resignifications. Derrida has argued that every signified is also in the position of the signifier and so does not work to relate the sign securely to an extra linguistic reality. We cannot, according to Derrida, ever gain access to a pure prelinguistic signified. We can never explicate the final meaning of texts without producing another text, a parallel set of signifiers. This foundational skepticism is the space that is opened for both attackers and defenders. But this carnival of undecidedness is a heavy-footed affair of endless and joyless analysis.

It is tempting to see postmodernism as the sunset of European civilization, and doomsayers have found many ways to link it to the decline of the West. The brilliant rhetorical critic Philip Wander has noted the close parallels between post-1945 French politics and the rise of deconstruction. The larger roots of postmodernism can be found in the rise and fall of Europe's distinctive community, the nation-state. The nation-state did not so much arise from an earlier wave of community formation, such as the dynastic house or free-trade city, as it pulled earlier communities apart and reassembled them. The new community of the nation was born in revolution. It delivered a fresh locus of identity for Europe's detribalized peasants and farmers who thronged by the millions into Frankfurt, Manchester, Glasgow, Milan, Paris, London, and Berlin. Shorn of their religious, familial, and regional identities, these individuals were set in motion and at the same time made dependent upon the new arrangements. The nation-state provided a new focus of loyalty, for it presented itself as more than an expedient structure for popular aspirations. It was a highly abstract and deliberate creation that came to be experienced as a natural community. Names such as Italy and Germany had been cultural expressions or linguistic areas, but in the nineteenth century they became communities of destiny that shaped the careers, aspirations, self-esteem, and outlook of their members as never before.

The new masses had cut their ties with an organic rural culture. Their spiritual homelessness was filled by a new idea, the nation. The new community had been born in revolution and it had enormous potency. Its great power came not from any particular political configuration, but from an ability to provide a new focus of loyalty for millions of people who had experienced a loss of religious belief and whose journey from the European countryside had shorn them of so much of the old culture and rootedness of rural Christendom.

These communities of destiny became the grand success strategies of European consolidation and expansion. So powerful was the new model that it was imitated in areas where far less linguistic and historic unity existed. In the ethnic crazy quilt of the Middle East and in the tribal mosaic of Africa, nations were constructed that did violence to many indigenous groupings.

From the very first, the nation-state promised to be a difficult and demanding master. After World War I it showed a diminution of communal vigor, a kind of hardening of the arteries. It confiscated an increasing share of the individual's wealth and periodically conscripted huge numbers of its youth for the characteristic national war, a butchery that ideally involved the entire citizenry and made the earlier dynastic wars seem like slap parties in a salon. After the terrible bloodletting of World War II in which 47 million people died, a new international entity, the European Common Market, was born. Thus began the gradual loosening of the national fabrics. It seemed apparent that even if nationalism remained an obsession in the "Third World" (that unhappy name coined by Eisenhower-era journalists), it was declining in the old areas of its origin.

By the 1970s even the so-called lucky countries, Canada, the United States, and Australia, were experiencing doubt. Many loyal citizens appeared skeptical of the efficiency of the state. The famous phrase created by Jürgen Habermas, "a crisis of legitimacy," seemed apt as the state could no longer guarantee that it would be able to maximize benefits and minimize risks on behalf of the vast majority of its citizens. During the 1950s and 1960s increasing clientage and social welfare policy had strengthened the social anchorage of the citizenry in the Anglo-Saxon countries. Ironically, the retrenchment of these policies a few years later threatened their belief in the national bargain.

These changes signaled the breakdown of the dream of the old self-confident nation-state. In the vision of the Enlightenment, the nation-state was to have been a way station on the inevitable journey to universal reason and scientific utopia. Following this trajectory, reformers thought to liquidate the culture of the nation in much the same way the nation had liquidated the very folk culture from which it had risen. It is particularly instructive to scrutinize the postwar history of France, a nation that has always walked in the van of postmodern thought. After the horror of two wars, France, the Allied zones of Germany, and the Low Countries became the economic sheet anchor of the New Europe. Decentralization and devolution of the old national states were proclaimed the new order in Western Europe and a deliberate policy within individual nations. In the name of integration, backward regions and uneven development were to be brought up to the level of the most advanced areas. The Paris-based economy was bypassed in favor of the development of new regional centers, and even cultural decolonization was pursued. The capital of Europe found its artistic resources dispersed. By deliberate policy, ethnic and cultural minorities were subsidized and encouraged. There was an almost immediate reawakening of the regional entities that had been officially interred in the French departmental schemes of the 1790s. First, Breton nationalism raised its head. Shortly after, Gasconade, Savoyard, and Burgundian citizens rediscovered the cultural distinctiveness of their provinces.

This is particularly ironic, because the dogma had been that the modernization process itself contained a magic engine of assimilation. After all, it was assumed to possess all the weapons of national cohesion. A shared materialism and the complementarity of money seemed an inducement to national inclusion that even the most exotic and "backward" cultural minority could not withstand. Modernity melted everyone and furthered mass participation in the national enterprise. In many cases, however, national development increased differences between subgroups. Minorities seemed to grow more estranged rather than less so. The French example is particularly poignant. After all the changes in preparation for a European identity that would be both multiethnic and regional, the French have watched their German partners absorbed in a fierce recrudescence of nationhood and ethnic reunification. The strains of nationhood have crippled Ireland, destabilized Britanny and Corsica, and threaten to dismember Yugoslavia. Born out of the demand for unique linguistic and ethnic determinism, nations are now suffering from an extension of the very ideals that gave them birth. Developments intended to stave off disintegration have in fact accelerated it.

In the meantime, the older nation-states have become increasingly heterogeneous. The mobility of international corporations and the disruptive economic migration of millions of individuals have put the economic well-being of the individual and the cultural coherence of the community on a collision course. Even the Japanese worry about what they call "hollowing out." This phrase signals their fears about winning the world economic race at the cost of ceasing to be distinctively Japanese.

Today the nation-state seems to have lost its old capacity to integrate. Mass migrations of Asian, Middle Eastern, and African peoples into Europe and North America have exposed the limits of tolerance in even the most "civil" national states of the West. What is more, attention given to new minorities seems to have awakened the slumbering grievances of old minorities. As the French are so fond of reminding us, we no longer experience assimilation but merely juxtaposition. American and European cities have become vast islands of unfamiliarity to the old core populations. There is a saying among the ninety or more national minorities living in core Los Angeles that only God really knows who lives there.

Yet it might be argued that these conditions are mere symptoms of our quest for a new, more deeply satisfying community. Fewer people these days are willing to make such argument. Whatever the case, postmodernism reflects the spiritual homelessness and skepticism following the collapse of our belief in the dignity and importance of the European mission, and the beginnings of a search among the ruins. In part, the world-weariness of postmodernism is directed against the cultural heritage itself, a heritage grown too vast, unwieldy, and incoherent.

The argot of postmodernism, words and phrases such as "pluralism," "diffusion of power," "loss of legitimacy," and "colonization," is the language of transition, a transition from a house that is on fire to one that has not yet been constructed. Anyone who ponders this strange and highly stylized jargon will note that it savagely denigrates the very idea of nation, but resanctifies the local and personal spheres. A resurgence of ethnicity, of biological, regional, linguistic, and cultural associations, looks like a journey back to less abstract social forms and a rediscovery of the comfortable and the familiar.

If postmodernism can be said to have a political project, it is devolution. In a reversal of hierarchies, received ideas (general topoi) are viewed as invisible agents of domination and local knowledge is privileged. Everywhere—in the reborn nationalisms and culture conflicts of Eastern Europe, in the Roman Catholic church, and within the mature democracies of the West—the drama of the periphery versus the center is being played out. Thus the so-called ideo-topoi have lost their old anchorages in "human nature" and are routinely dismissed as a language of domination employed by hegemonic groups.

The matrix of consensus upon which the old civic discourse rested was a writ that no longer runs on the periphery. Since postmodern discourse envisages a redistribution of power, the very local and regional voices that have been muted during the centuries of urbanization, industrialization, and modernization must be revived.

The heroic stand of Jürgen Habermas against cultural fragmentation is too well-known to be discussed here in detail. But it is worth remembering that he and his cadre do not lament the passing of the authorized topoi of modernity so much as they aim to reconstitute a generic discourse from the ranks of the citizenry upward. They hope that this discourse will prevail in the teeth of cultural fragmentation. But, they caution us, this sort of community building can take place only if discourse is rescued from technocrats, specialists, professional castes, and the academic and artistic custodians of the culture, the latter a mighty congeries that includes advertisers and journalists as well as professors.

Habermas's critique of modernity is derived from Max Weber. According to Weber, the modern era promised a new world in which reasonable citizens would participate in the shaping of ever more enlightened and progressive communities. This prediction was wide of the mark, and Weber's world never materialized. Somewhere along the way the growing complexity of the new world caused the death of genuine public discourse. The amateur spirit of the citizen in the polis did not thrive because knowledge became "splintered into independent specialties" that were given over "to the narrow competence of experts."[8] The domain between the private sensate life of the citizen and formal institutional governance disappeared as an arena of community action.

The space of public discourse was fragmented and taken over by certified experts. Has civil community been lost forever? Not everyone thinks so.

The futurists point to retribalization. They see the struggle for community in romantic terms. The task of the postmodern critic becomes the affirmation of a genuine culture against a syntactic one (i.e., a media culture in which beliefs cannot be validated through day-to-day experience). But others fear that in such a world the best the intellectual can hope for is to be a shamanistic guardian of the local shrines.

However, those who predict the future know only one thing for sure: They will always be wrong. Armed with that stale but comforting bromide, we turn to the case studies.

NOTES

1. Lorraine Geslick, *Centers, Symbols and Hierarchies: Essays on the Classical States of Southeast Asia* (New Haven, Conn.: Yale University Press, 1988), 198.

2. Ibid., 88.

3. Carl E. Schorske, *Fin-de-Siècle Vienna* (New York: Knopf, 1980), 302.

4. Jonathon Arac, *Postmodernism and Politics* (Minneapolis: University of Minnesota Press, 1986), x.

5. William Corlett, *Community Without Unity: A Politics of Derridean Extravagance* (New York: Delta Press, 1989), 3.

6. Michael Wood and Louis Z. Zurcher, *The Development of a Postmodern Self* (New York: Greenwood Press, 1988), 4.

7. Jean François Lyotard, *The Postmodern Condition: A Report on Knowledge* (Minneapolis: University of Minnesota Press, 1988), 72.

8. Jürgen Habermas, *Moral Consciousness and Communicative Action*, trans. Christian Lenhardt and Shierry Weber Nicholsen (Cambridge, Mass.: MIT Press, 1990), 135.

Chapter Three

The Higher Culture as the Site of Struggle

Andrew King

It is necessary to make a brief statement about the cultural warfare being conducted in modern universities. Anyone who looks into a book of literature, rhetorical theory, philosophy, or history will note that a great sea change has taken place. Authority has been shaken. Voices seem to crack under the strain, and a deep skepticism covers every area of human endeavor. The fierce love of learning is out of fashion, and those who speak about the joy of literature are looked upon as the remnants of a vanished innocence. During the 1950s nearly 10 percent of undergraduates studied literature. That number has diminished to a fraction. As television has displaced literature from the center, the voices of the displaced literati have become ever more strident. Now the traditional caretakers of the canon have begun their counterattack with powerful allies outside the university. Whatever the outcome of this struggle, it seems certain to cause even greater fragmentation in the House of Intellect before coherence returns. Despite its early character as an international institution, the European universities of the late Middle Ages struck a difficult bargain with the state. Everyone knows the stories of pitched battles between town and gown, of boycotts at Bologna, of riots at the University of Paris, and the war among student "nations" at Prague. In order to thrive, universities had to make peace with their local hosts and with princes and emperors. The intellectual freedom of the West's universities was purchased at the price of political impotence. The university was able to enjoy at least a theoretical freedom of discussion within its own walls because it ceased to be a political entity. It renounced intervention in local and national issues and agreed to forgo political mobilization of its potentially powerful constituencies.

Centuries later, the bargain still holds. There are protests by university-based individuals, but collective political action has been rare. In fact, the university has often opted to adopt the agenda of some other powerful institution as its own. The renaissance schools gladly produced the new middle-class types for the reviving cities of Europe. These were people schooled in canon law, civil law, and medicine; they were adept in administration. Later, Oxford and Cambridge became training grounds for British governance. German universities of the nineteenth century were the research arms of a vast chemical industry. In the twentieth century, American universities have occasionally seemed eager to function as servomechanisms for American business.

There were peculiar comforts attending the apolitical status of the professoriate in the United States. In North America, the European sense of betrayal and the feeling of lost political opportunities did not exist. There was no history of ignoring dictators or of accommodating fascist leaders. Then too, the euphoria of academic expansion and a belief in the melioristic virtues of mass education allowed American professors to embrace the charismatic quality of intellectual life without cynicism. The beliefs that a life devoted to the mind gave one a special radiance and that ideas contained a unique potency for transforming the world provided a refulgent optimism. It was for this reason that the intellectuals and leaders of our government, the military, and the industrial community gravitated toward one another. Research had a utopian quality.

As always, the characteristically Emersonian union of pragmatism and romanticism had consequences that no one could have envisioned. Beginning in the 1890s and accelerating rapidly after World War II, massive government subsidies changed the shape and priorities of higher education beyond recognition. Two trends that began in the late 1950s are emblematic of these changes: (1) replacing the requirement of two foreign languages for a Ph.D. with a statistical or technical-methods complement, and (2) no longer recruiting university presidents from ranks of classical scholars. Increasingly, they are scientists or businessmen. Although Gerald Graff has warned us that it is "wishful thinking" to imagine the pre–World War I university as a cohesive community, he asserts that the sense of academic anomie has increased alarmingly.[1] Hence, he notes that "the complaint that research and publication have displaced teaching" parallels the more general complaint that "technology or bureaucracy have displaced more human or communal relations."[2]

During the 1950s, the so-called Eisenhower quietism years, an intellectual unrest was apparent on many campuses. The official version of those years is that higher education had urged students everywhere to stultify themselves. Supposedly the humanities had been pacified by a truce between the Old Left and the New Careerists. In literary studies the Nashville Agrarians and the 1930s leftists had abandoned ideology as both embraced the New Criticism, while functionalism in the social sciences expressed a similar arrangement. Richard Weaver and other second-order Agrarians were writing the foundational works of the new conservatism while C. Wright Mills and the Apthekers were rallying a New Left. As late as the early 1960s these groups had reached only small audiences. The middle of the decade gave them a mass audience through the war protests that mobilized one campus after another.

As a young professor just starting out in the 1960s, I was convinced that the institution I was bidding to enter was about to come flying apart. The messages that had circulated among tiny student groups when I was an undergraduate had acquired a mass audience. In the intervening period I had served in the U.S. Army. The nation and the campus to which I returned seemed very different. Aging professors as well as my greenest undergraduate students told me that the great axial moment of history had now arrived. An air of doomsday expectancy was abroad everywhere. It was to be a cultural watershed in human history after which nothing would ever be the same. But the abolition of the draft, disengagement in Asia, gas crises, and the Watergate scandal brought the return of an old-fashioned feeling of business as usual.

As the economy turned downward in the early 1970s, large numbers of engaged students rushed to take their places in commerce and industry. The old radicals still haunted the campus, but their mass base was dispersed, either gone to make money or grown too busy to listen. The message had acquired a nostalgic sound over a matter of long months. With almost the status of Moses in 1967, the campus radical was a quaint survivor as early as 1974. The messages seemed to have lost their salience, except for a coterie of survivors. Former campus radicals paid sentimental return visits to their campuses wearing sincere business clothing. A fraction of a fraction of the old soldiers, as always, could not demobilize. Every war leaves such people in its wake. To experience a sense of community, a common purpose, and a vision of the future at a formative period of one's development is a powerful thing. Small wonder that veterans are gripped with a bittersweet feeling of loss. A portion of these people never left the academy. Having failed to change the larger society, they adopted an enclave strategy. By working in one of the nation's central institutions, the research university, they could continue to fight. This time it would be a war of socialization, a Gramscian struggle for the hearts and minds of American youth. At first their voices were seldom raised. But as they began to move into positions of real power in the early 1980s, the university was transformed into a cultural battleground. The radicals hoped to fight the old family romance of the 1960s, this time with a more conclusive ending.

How have they fared? They command a dominant majority in some

prestigious departments and hold a considerable number of adminis-
trative posts. But it is a hollow triumph. Just what is it that they have
won? Has their victory come from genuine strength? Have they won so
much of the old center because of their strength or because so many of
its traditional guardians have abandoned their posts because of a general
feeling that the American university's moment of grace has passed? The
university is still a central institution, but it is a bit less important than
it was in the 1960s, and its legitimacy is being challenged on every side.
The power of the radicals is very uneven. It is confined almost entirely
to the humanities, an area that is no longer the predominant partner in
major universities. In recapturing the old center, the radicals have almost
certainly accelerated its marginalization. This is not apparent to a great
many who speak and write as if they were in a time warp.

Two things weaken their influence: (1) the adoption of a specialized
postmodern argot, and (2) the endless and joyless proclamation of the
postmodern ethic.

The language of postmodernism is a formidable jargon. Students tell
me that it irritates without informing. It is at once flatulent and strident.
Critics deny the separation of "high" culture and mass culture, but they
have adopted a vocabulary that grates on the ears of the very people
they are trying to persuade. Students tell me they can bear the intellectual
condescension, but the moral condescension infuriates them. Postmodernists embrace this highly ornate mode of discourse but have eschewed
the language of advertising and mass persuasion, leaving this powerful
weapon in the hands of their enemies. From the point of view of practicing rhetoricians and of supposedly astute students of power, this does
not seem a very clever thing for them to do.

Similarly, they have adopted the postmodern episteme, a conception
of knowledge that refuses to acknowledge a privileged point of view.
On the one hand this slashing of the last link between literature and
religion diminishes literature's authority, and on the other hand it abandons the quest for community. Literature is diminished, and any realistic
political agenda is enfeebled. Although utterly parasitic on the organism
called the Western university, they have struck savagely at the cultural
heritage by destroying the authority of the canon of Great Books. Their
conception of knowledge also creates a crisis of coherence in the class-
room. It undertakes to expose our "quasi divinities" (conscience, community, and language) as mere "products of accident and chance."[3]
Truth is no longer seen as corresponding to an external reality. This
radical conception of truth displays a superficial pragmatism. It actually
comes very close to Dewey's "truth" of ordinary language. Truth has
been redefined as social consensus. Similarly, the old Enlightenment
standard of rationality has been redefined in terms of social praxis. The
ramparts of logical consistency have been abandoned for a standard of

civility. Rationality has become a name for politeness in discourse practices.

In brief, human beings become experiments, values are seen as contingent, and there is a refusal to accept any patterns or identities as fixed.[4] This is hardly a doctrine upon which crusades, great revolution, or heroic people's movements are founded. Without a universal standard or a great authorizing narrative, cultural fragmentation is guaranteed. Our moral choices are between better and worse options, a situation compounded by an ever-increasing competition of competing voices. Although non-Western nations are stoutly defended as being entitled to preserve their unique cultures, the ideal for American and Western European nations has become the theme park. Postmodernists argue that intellectual vertigo disappears in practice. They note that we find ourselves with multiple ways of conducting business, solving social problems, or raising children. In a world without the authority of a single cultural horizon, praxis becomes the great test. Accordingly, they imagine that decisions about the best practices will be reached by means of conversational agreement among equals. This sounds suspiciously like the ideal of Jürgen Habermas, which numerous commentators have compared to a very polite graduate seminar and as unlike our overdeveloped sensate world as can be.

What the postmodernists propose, then, is not nihilism but the abandonment of structure. The great Western preoccupation with the location of truth (in God, the mind, or the world) has been simply given up by them. This is the crisis of authority that has gripped the intellectual life of our time, a third sophistic in the twilight of the West. But, as we have just seen, postmodernists tend to argue that the crisis will disappear if only we do not try to live life by the compass of the old Enlightenment metaphysic. More of the very doctrine that has brought us to the morass of ennui and irresolution is recommended, the very hair of the dog. Although we may lack the mettle for great occasions, we are assured that on the day-to-day level of choice, matters can still be arranged and problems negotiated; things are not so serious. We will be guided by the lamps of pragmatism.

The vision of one group after another being thrown upon the authority of its own social practices is one that conjures up images of the fall of Rome rather than the coming of Utopia. But this failure of nerve is not what seems to be in the offing for the near future. True, there are numerous gangs that have replaced General Motors and U.S. Steel as the chief urban employers, and there are many new cultural movements. But the demands of larger global and national order remain. What we must face is more likely to be an increase in coercive legalism rather than a tolerance of new ways of life.

As the final chapter makes clear, the center itself has undergone a hollowing out. Public discourse increasingly shares the same un-grounded and ersatz quality that characterizes subcultural expression. The oppositional quality of much group rhetoric suggests that we still honor an invisible center. It is the specter of the self-confident Euroman that still haunts our dreams and our days. The Euroman does not exist as a real person or even a historical personage; rather it floats like a gaudy fantasy image of colonialist Europe that is not quite past. This is not a Europe that once existed, now exists, or will ever exist in the future. It is a caricature of the bourgeois Western warrior penetrating to all parts of the globe and devouring traditional ways of life, smashing native religious practices, and crushing the cultural self-confidence of non-Western peoples. This stereotype lurks behind the apologetic self-hatred of European and American intellectuals whose postmodern view appropriately humbles their pride and assuages their guilt. Regicide and penance give postmodern criticism its fury and moral authority; unfor-tunately they rob it of a correspondingly powerful positive affirmation.

The cultural warfare of the academy heightens the sense of being overwhelmed by the cultural heritage. Thomas Wolfe tried to drink the ocean, and the young Thomas Mann grew ill in a mistaken quest to acquire all knowledge. But they had a canon of great works to guide them. Postmodernism reaches out to muted voices and continually adds new voices in the name of cultural diversity. The political advantages of this have been described by Gerald Graff's aptly named principle of 'field coverage' (i.e., rather than debate the relative worth of new courses and subjects, we simply add everything). This has resulted in depart-mental growth and in political clout. However, this means of accom-modation has reached its zenith and is starting to decline as we enter an area of shrinking resources. The aftermath of all this has been ladders of courses that lead to nowhere and students who complain that what is taught in one class is ridiculed in another. Those hungry for intellectual coherence become wary cynics patronizing their professors with the correct perspective.

It is rather late in the day for an Einstein, a Newton, or a Maxwell to fuse the fragments of the humanities into a coherent account of the meaning of life. There is a burnt-out-case quality to present intellectual endeavor that is inhospitable to such efforts. But this is not to say that encouraging countertrends are not emerging. A revived and greatly expanded rhetoric has appeared like a rainbow above the humanities. In every discipline rhetoricians have emerged and rhetorical methods have begun to transform them.

The ideal of the essential unity of humane study was first articulated by the greatest rhetorician of antiquity, Marcus Cicero, and it is an idea that is suddenly alive again. It is our hope that the renewal of this foundational discipline will bring a return to the old circle of the humanities with its balance of private cultivation and social responsibility. The utopian, the irresponsible, and the paranoid are three style notes of much current academic discourse. The remedy is to be found in the ancient Ciceronian rhetorical ideal in which learning becomes equipment for achieving the good life and the just community.

NOTES

1. Gerald Graff, *Professing Literature: An Institutional History* (Chicago and London: University of Chicago Press, 1987), 13.

2. Ibid., 5.

3. Ian Shapiro, *Political Community* (Berkeley: University of California Press, 1990), 23.

4. William Corlett. *Community Without Unity: A Politics of Derridean Extravagance* (New York: Delta Press, 1989), 4.

Chapter Four

Marginalization, the Body, and Empowerment: The Rhetoric of the Obese and Little People in America

Kenneth Zagacki

Perhaps no other ideology has exerted as much influence over our culture in the latter half of the twentieth century as "the ideology of health." As Michael Ignatieff points out, it was Friedrich Nietzsche, in *Thus Spake Zarathustra*, who predicted a future generation that would reconceptualize the search for happiness as a pursuit of health. Nietzsche "called these diminished denizens of the future 'the last men,' " and in our own postmodern age they have come to be represented by the millions of Americans who "would convert sex into recreation; the asceticism of religion into the asceticism of athletics; the regimens of introspection into the power of positive thinking; the human good . . . into the glow of physical well-being."[1] Located at the center of this ideology of health is the human body and, specifically, the goal of obtaining particular body forms. Here the popular association of symbols is blatantly clear: Certain body shapes are acceptable, and those that deviate from the norm represent undesirable or anomalous traits.

Certainly, as Michel Foucault and other poststructuralists have noted, the pursuit of health and of control over the body's desires has characterized many cultures in history.[2] This pursuit has typically progressed at the expense of bodily pleasures and excesses. But the contemporary concern for achieving vitality, heightened by a glut of media promotion and medical endorsement, has turned this already powerful hankering into a cultural obsession. The desire for physical well-being and its predicted benefits are deeply ensconced in American popular culture.[3] In this postmodern milieu, the ideals of self-knowledge and self-mastery, once obtained through philosophical and religious inquiry or through political and social involvement, are reduced, as Ignatieff argues, "to a regime of diet and exercise."[4]

Fitness and health appear to be important in postmodern life because, as sociologist Barry Glassner argues, it represents one of the few remaining arenas where an individual can assert control over his or her affairs.[5] And yet, a supreme irony of this postmodern quest to be vital is that the sense of control it fosters is really an illusion. The very drive toward fitness and health forces one into a rigid patriarchal relationship with a cultural system that demands fitness in the first place and then exploits its economic advantages. This pursuit also makes one dependent on a medical community that at once dictates the means (and limits) to physical development while treating (at some expense) the failures and injuries a person inevitably incurs during training.

Of course, in a sense, the drive for control through fitness and health is empowering, if only because it marks and positions those who diet and exercise as combatants in the contest for cultural ideals. In the process of coming to see themselves as altering body form through strict discipline, participants in the fitness crusade can easily point to those who look or act differently and label them as inferior. In its most unsavory form, this process of labeling subsequently leads to tremendous stigmatizing and marginalization. Indeed, for those victims of labeling— those who by choice and/or genetic design cannot or do not attempt to achieve ideal body shapes, yet desire some form of meaningful participation in or alongside of the cultural system—the consequences of failing to obtain cultural standards can be devastating.

The rhetorical struggle of this group to cope with their experience of being marginalized in a culture obsessed with body shape is the subject of this chapter. The particular question asked here is: How do these individuals rearticulate the meaning of the body, of the notion of control, and of their own personal happiness to a culture that has constantly stigmatized and marginalized them because of their physical differences? I am speaking primarily of two groups—the obese and the extremely short-statured—and the respective organizations that represent their interests: the National Association to Aid Fat Americans (NAAFA) and Little People of America (LPA). My intent is not so much to compare them as it is to sort out the rhetorical strategies and tactics they employ to overcome their marginalization. As we look at these groups, we shall discover their discourses to be fraught with many difficulties and ambiguities. These ambiguities, I suggest, thrust NAAFA and LPA into contradictory relationships with the very culture that marginalizes them and illuminate the role of marginal rhetoric in postmodern culture. The first part of this chapter develops a Foucaultian framework for analyzing NAAFA and LPA rhetoric and summarizes the social and psychological plight of both groups. The rhetoric of NAAFA and LPA is then examined.

For the remainder I speculate about the possible effects and uses of the rhetoric of empowerment among the socially ostracized.

FOUCAULT'S CRITIQUE OF CULTURE

Foucault's analysis of the effects of power and discourse on the construction of human subjectivity is a useful way of characterizing the difficult situation of the obese and of little people—most notably dwarfs—in America. A major tenet in Foucault's critique is that crucial human modes of being, such as sexuality and madness, do not represent "natural" realities but rather are the products of systems of discourse and social practices that form part of the increasing monitoring and control of individuals. In Foucault's conception of culture, no fundamental mode of normality exists within human nature. As Mark Philp explains, for Foucault, concepts of "the normal child, the healthy body, the stable mind, the good citizen, the perfect wife and the proper man . . . are reproduced and legitimated through" the practices of teachers, social workers, doctors, judges, policemen, and administrators—all of whom, along with their counterparts in sociology, psychiatry, psychology, and philosophy, form what Foucault calls the human sciences.[6] These representatives define what a society assumes to be normality; "and by establishing this normality as a rule of life for us all, they simultaneously manufacture—for investigation, surveillance and treatment—the vast area of our deviation from this standard."[7] The function of cultural analysis, then, is to provide a critique of the way modern societies control and discipline their populations by establishing the knowledge claims and practices of the human sciences. These sciences have mandated that certain norms are correct, anchored as they are in human nature or natural law. These norms and the knowledge claims underlying them are then recreated and legitimized through the practices of members of a society. For Foucault, one primary result of the intersection between cultural conceptions of normality and individuals is that, as Philp observes, "we have become divided selves, treating sanity, health and conformity to social mores as components of our 'real selves,' and repudiating as foreign to us our diseases, irrationalities and delinquencies."[8]

In Foucault's analysis, individuals are acted upon by a culture and its system of knowledge and truth claims. The culture exercises power over its subjects, not always by forcing or coercing but by subtly persuading them to conform to prevailing social mores and modes of conduct. The culture and its human sciences present us, as Philp argues, with a picture "of society as an organism which legitimately regulates its population and seeks out signs of disease, disturbance and deviation so that they can be treated and returned to normal functioning under the watchful eyes of one or other policing system."[9] In other words, by categorizing them according to preestablished roles and scientifically based assumptions about human behavior, the culture provides individuals with identities from which they can navigate their way within (or toward the margins of) the culture. For Foucault, socialization and inculcation as they exist in the everyday practices of individuals are essentially expressions of social power. And power, as well as molding behaviors and expectations, also structures the subjective experience of the individual, directing responses to both the external and internal world. Indeed, persons failing to obtain cultural norms are made to experience their failure as an intensely individual experience. Therefore, although denigration itself is socially constructed, it is experienced and punished as individual failure. Foucault describes this socializing process as a "form of power" that applies to immediate everyday life; this power classifies the individual, "marks him by his individuality, attaches him to his own identity, imposes a law of truth on him which he must recognize and which others have to recognize in him. . . . .[This form of power] makes individuals subjects."[10]

But what happens to those who refuse cultural definitions of normality? For Foucault, certain groups—homosexuals, the mentally ill, criminals, and, as we shall discover, dwarfs and the obese—are pushed to the margins of the culture until they seek medical or other legitimizing treatments that allow access to mainstream society. In the process of marginalization, their local and differential knowledge—the knowledge that reflects the struggles and experiences of these deviant communities—is suppressed by the modern means of encoding power. Here Foucault invokes his famous genealogical method in order to uncover the problems of marginalized groups, along with their fragmented and oppressed local knowledge. By examining their discourses, Foucault seeks to piece together the ways in which oppressed individuals battle against and live through their social worlds. Moreover, genealogy assaults what Foucault labels "totalizing discourses"—the great encompassing truths and systems constituting a culture that distinguish the power/knowledge configuration of the contemporary order. Genealogy tries to unveil the workings of power in order to illustrate how those who suffer from it can or do resist. Power, in Foucault's view, is a creative force that is both imposed and opposed, in that every act of power evokes a response, whether it be a response of resistance or submission. Foucault's support, as Philp notes, is therefore "lent to those who resist the subjugating effects of power: those who, like some feminists [along with certain dwarfs and members of the obese], refuse to surrender their bodies to the established practices of medicine [or other social forces] . . . and those who resist the identities imposed upon them by others."[11]

With this brief background, we can proceed to examine the ways in which the obese and dwarfs are conceived through various cultural discourses and how they are subsequently pushed to the margins of society.

BODY SHAPE, RATIONALITY, AND LIMINALITY

The Obese

For Foucault, understanding the body and the way it has historically been conceived is extremely important to explicating cultural discourses and their "totalizing" impact. Foucault himself explains that the body is "the inscribed surface of events (traced by language and dissolved by ideas), the locus of a dissociated Self (adopting the illusion of substantial unity), and a volume in disintegration." Genealogical analysis illustrates that the body is "totally imprinted by history and the process of history's destruction of the body."[12] History has imprinted our own cultural conceptions of body with the marks of thinness and obesity. There can be no doubt that thinness is one of the most highly cherished values in contemporary American culture. As mentioned earlier, one need only look at the mass media for examples of the lowly portrayal of obese persons. The medical community has been equally harsh in its appraisal of the obese. Physicians constantly endorse the health problems associated with obesity. Characteristically, doctors are sometimes quick to attribute to the obese a general lack of willpower, self-control, and motivation and to link them with a host of other psychological difficulties.

Consequently, obesity has become a culturally undesirable body form, and the obese have been turned into the victims of alienation and marginalization. As Carole Spitzack describes it, obese persons are frequently "placed beyond the bounds of social participation."[13] Historically, obese individuals have always been the objects of both fascination and scorn. According to Jean Mayer, "there has always been something so fascinating about the mere fact of fatness that men of all nations and many degrees of wisdom or lack of it have formulated opinions of the state, its origins, and its correction."[14] Presently, the obese seem to be mainly the object of scorn: Not only are they the butt of cruel jokes, but they frequently fall victim to social, economic, and political discrimination. The difficulties these people face are real enough to encourage thousands to sacrifice much effort and money on weight-reduction programs.[15]

Symbolically, the most intriguing dimension of obesity is the way it has come to represent deviance and will-lessness. Obese people are deviant because they have failed to meet cultural standards; because, in a culture that equates appetite with weight, they have failed to muster the willpower and discipline necessary to curb the body's powerful de-sires. Associations of deviance can be acutely troubling for the obese person. As Marcia Millman observes, "Once a fat person is perceived as deviant at all, nothing about her is trusted or taken for granted, and the trait that distinguishes her seems to color her entire being in the eyes of others."[16] The deviant, obese body is especially susceptible to cultural bias, for it creates an image, as Spitzack comments, "of disper-sion, i.e., the body exceeds appropriate dimensions, and must be 'pulled together' through mental determination. . . . Excess poundage comes to represent a physical state which negates rational capability."[17]

The struggle to assert the mind's control over the body signifies one of the oldest conflicts in Western thought. This contest between mind and body is well represented in the quest for health and slimness: As a rational mind loses control, catering to the body's every physical whim, the mind, by virtue of its lack of discipline and inability to mold the body, becomes increasingly irrational; hence, obesity comes to signify the triumph of irrationality over rationality, an equation decried in West-ern culture. In fact, the rational person ostensibly is able to maintain strict control over the body through exercise and diet, thus preventing the body from exceeding its culturally determined weight limit and si-multaneously purging the mind of what amounts to its irrational defi-ciencies. In this case, the mind acts in control over a body that it has, through rigorous programming, conquered; meanwhile, the mind de-rives satisfaction and overall benefits from this act of self-control, so that a kind of inner harmony develops, only to be disrupted occasionally by the body's desires (which are again put down by the willful mind). However, from the cultural point of view, for the obese person, lack of rational control and the subsequent change in body form lead to a per-verse reversal of the Western affinity for the triumph of mind over matter. Obese persons experience an inverted mind-body determinism, insofar as the body maintains complete mastery over the mind; the mind and will, as the dominant perspective portrays them, surrender to the material seduction of the body's appetite. This act of surrender, which takes its most obvious form in the way in which obese individuals seem-ingly fail to care for themselves, is what condemns them to the corre-sponding set of cultural deficiencies and marginalization.

Most striking about the obese person's struggle to achieve cultural standards, in Foucault's terms, is that the very application of willful self-control itself masks the presence of the controlling cultural system and its set of totalizing (health-related) discourses. In fact, for those who attempt weight control, the contest between the mind and body is set in motion but rarely consummated (as it supposedly is for the individual achieving thinness). As Spitzack points out, the effort to reduce weight eventually manifests itself in a more tortured form of mind-body dualism. This can be observed when obese people talk of " 'thin' vs. 'bad' foods—the former being coupled with rational behavior, the latter its opposite."[18] In addition, responding to guilt aroused by their failure to lose weight despite attempts at reduction, many obese persons attempt to cope by separating themselves mentally from their bodies. Such distancing tactics appear in the ways in which some obese people play down or conceal the body's importance. The problem here is that such coping mechanisms do not lead to personal contentment; nor do they alter unrealistic cultural standards. Obese people, in short, driven by cultural ideals that constantly point to their failure to conform, are compelled to turn the body into an object of psychological analysis, physical regimen, even surgical or other medical manipulation (what some might consider surgical punishment), which seldom leads to the complete spiritual and physical redemption promised by the ideology of health. In the process, the body is transformed into something that exists out there in the world as a "thing," or an "it."[19] At the same time, the arbitrary standards of attractiveness that lead to the despair of the obese are recreated. As Spitzack explains, from the perspective of the dominant cultural discourses on health, "It is the body, rather than the unrealistic standards for attractiveness, that constrains the individual."[20]

The Short Statured

The problem of social stigma is no better for the extremely short statured, and particularly for dwarfs. As sociologist Joan Ablon explains, "To most people in the United States who share the ethos of 'the bigger the better,' dwarfs represent persons whose abilities and worth will be inferior, or at best different or special. The attribute of shortness is continually denigrated in this society because it no doubt remains symbolically related to a frontier ethos of big, bold, and strong. . . . To most Americans, including dwarfs themselves, who have internalized the values of their culture, large [but not overweight, obese, or giant] body size is a desired physical feature."[21] Shortness has been correlated with a wide variety of negative feelings, whereas relative tallness is related to economic and political success. And though no clear moral indiscretions or perverted mind-body dualism seem to be attributed to short people, dwarfs of proportionate and disproportionate short stature have suffered economic and social discrimination and insult because of their size. As a consequence, dwarfs appear particularly vulnerable to low self-esteem. For dwarfs, body stature and proportion are the central traits that single them out as different. And these traits are characteristics most closely related to the essence of self. Furthermore, Ablon notes that dwarfs, by being extremely small, "share a physical characteristic which is negatively related to the American penchant for abundance of size and quantity as a mark or augur of success."[22]

Ablon employs anthropologist Victor Turner's notion of "liminality" to describe the marginalized situation of dwarfs. Liminality refers to the marginal in-between status of an individual in his or her transitional venture from one stage, age, etc., to another stable point. For Turner, "Liminal entities are neither here nor there; they are betwixt and between the positions assigned and arrayed by law, custom, convention, and ceremonial. As such their ambiguous and indeterminate attributes are expressed by a rich variety of symbols in the many societies that ritualize social and cultural transitions."[23] Dwarfs are clearly marginal, liminal characters. Like the obese, dwarfs appear different, odd even; but they do not seem too different. In their history, dwarfs, too, have been as much the objects of mystical wonderment as they have of ridicule. But because in the popular conception the condition of dwarfs is unrelated to mental will-lessness, they are characterized by a kind of situated ambiguity. As Ablon explains, this ambiguity—the idea that "there's something wrong, not too wrong, but that which is wrong (too small) is of the utmost import—is what makes dwarfs marginal in society and betwixt and between in how they are treated and how they expect to be treated."[24]

Hence, although dwarfs may not be subjected to the same sort of disgust or scorn elicited by obese persons and may, in fact, evoke sympathy, their shortness still makes them objects of perverse attention. They are considered abnormal characters whose ability and value are a matter of serious question. As unwitting or benign as it might sometimes be, this attention directed toward dwarfs nevertheless sentences them to the margins of the culture, where they are likely to find companions in duress and disempowerment like the obese.

THE RHETORIC OF NAAFA AND LPA

National Association to Aid Fat Americans

The primary aim of NAAFA is to promote the happiness and well-being of fat people and to work against oppressive cultural standards of health and body shape. As NAAFA rhetoric illustrates, this organization seems to desire the culture at large to alter its views of obese people and for the latter to be provided the opportunity to exist comfortably within—or at least alongside of—the dominant hierarchy. Toward these ends NAAFA sponsors biweekly meetings and various social events, including fashion shows for the obese, dating and pen pal programs, brochures for teenagers, a discount book service, and annual conventions.[25] NAAFA newsletters point out discrimination against the obese in business, educational services, and other social areas; they discuss means of counseling NAAFA members, admonish against dangerous and faddish dieting techniques, and generally encourage obese persons to work against cultural stigmas.

Rhetorically, the major problem faced by NAAFA is rearticulating the meaning of terms that have been co-opted by the larger culture and, in many cases, infused with socially demeaning value. For NAAFA, this requires regaining control over an entire vocabulary of health used to 'medicalize' and 'moralize,' and thus to objectify the obese and set them apart from the rest of the culture. Gaining control of this vocabulary has to be accomplished in part by redefining the set of signifier-signified relationships associated with the cultural meanings of obesity, thinness, and health. Thus, founder William Fabrey reexamines the connotation of fat, arguing that "Fat is not a four-lettered word." Rather, "Society has taken a simple word and given it a derogatory meaning. NAAFA believes the word fat should be returned to its proper [i.e., more positive] perspective." Neither is the word "overweight" correctly defined, according to Fabrey. Current usages of this term that depend on fluctuations from ideal, thin body weights simply do not "make sense, since NAAFA believes there is no such thing as an ideal weight for everyone; thus the question, 'Over what weight?' " In fact, Fabrey argues that "There is considerable evidence that 'ideal' weight has been poorly and rigidly defined in height-weight tables, and that what is too fat for one person may be normal for another." This tendency of the culture to restrict notions of ideal body size is important because, as Fabrey can attest, it also limits legitimate conceptions of what it means to be healthy. NAAFA asserts that "a fat individual is not necessarily unhealthy." Health depends on much more than the "enormously exaggerated" accounts of health drawn from medical research and popular culture; "it depends on the degree of fatness and the physical characteristics of the person in question."

Furthermore, although many individuals believe that thinness is a natural goal, an absolute good to be realized, Fabrey asserts that thin does not always mean "best"; there simply is no one correct "esthetic standard of beauty." Of course, for NAAFA, more than a mere reexamination is transpiring here. NAAFA at times sees itself engaged in a radical rhetoric, involved in what Fabrey calls a " 'fat revolution' in people's attitudes toward obesity. We in NAAFA are on the front lines of that struggle. . . . Let's make it work!"

Although the culture advocates thinness as a kind of moral and physical absolute, NAAFA views weight as a purely relative matter. As Fabrey declares, "The established cult of slimness is only one point of view. Another held by some NAAFA members, is that fat is beautiful." And the Fat Admirer Program Study Committee, in its publication "Preferences," reports that "People vary in their preferences of beauty. We *all* have our preferences in what we find attractive. . . . Standards of beauty are always changing and vary greatly from place to place [culture to culture]" (emphasis in original). NAAFA members are thus told to reject any absolute standards society might hold regarding physical appearance. Health, beauty, and happiness are important qualities to maintain, but they are not the sole possessions of the thin, nor do they depend on body weight. In other words, emerging from this attempt to redefine cultural terms is a brand of cultural relativism. Such a perspective would seem vitally important for the development of an empowering, postmodern rhetoric; it separates NAAFA members and the obese in general from societal definitions of good and evil by negating and then reasserting a new, more powerful and auspicious meaning of "fat." In effect, this strategy is an effort to force NAAFA members to recreate the parameters of their existence by restructuring linguistically the reality of a bodily form and experience they have been taught to reject. This rhetoric calls its audience to think through and to reconstruct their own relation to social and cultural discourses and to seek a similar change in cultural attitudes toward obesity. For NAAFA, to speak the new language of fatness, and to speak by displaying (not concealing) the fat body, is an assertion that fat is good. So NAAFA members are asked to speak loudly, publicly. Perhaps this is why they are encouraged to display bumper stickers signifying the emboldened NAAFA philosophy: "Fat is beautiful." NAAFA rhetoric, then, is at once a material practice—a direct form of vocal protest that jettisons the obese individual into a position of cultural change—and an idealized site for a group experiment in the recreation of language and meaning and the establishment of a unique community centering around the reinvigorated term "fat."

NAAFA discourse also attempts to associate the causes of other disempowered, minority groups with their own. Writing in a NAAFA newsletter, David Whitess notes how for years minority groups have conformed to societal standards. But recently, he argues, minorities have taken clear and effective action to change their situations: Blacks have "stopped trying to pass for whites"; gays have "come out of the closet"; and women have stopped bending to every "whim and mercurial fancy of their male-dominated environment." Whitess urges fat people too to "look into some of the root causes of their oppression and then try to CHANGE some of these causes" (emphasis his). The message here is two-pronged—first, that only through concerted action and close inspection of their own material and psychological conditions can fat people regain self-confidence and hence alter the oppressive situation in which they find themselves; and second, that fat people, like other minority groups, are sick and tired of hiding themselves from the culture at large. For NAAFA, this message amounts to the credo that it is time for the culture to make room for those who prefer fat to thin. NAAFA must, as the editors of "Preferences" declare, work "to help change a society that has oppressed fat people and fat admirers alike." The appeals to action and introspection are themselves especially significant. In a world that denies the physical and mental capabilities of the obese and other minority groups and negates the legitimacy of their life-styles, claims that reaffirm their capacity to join together establish obese people as reasonable, responsible agents, thereby calling into question the severe judgment about the nature of obesity in American culture. Once again, a critical chord in NAAFA rhetoric is sounded: Obese people, as holistic, fully cognitive, fully functioning beings, and not the culture or some cultural conception of gluttonous bodies gone out of control, determine their own physical and mental well-being, their own mode of (sub)cultural practice.

This notion of holism reveals another rhetorical strategy in NAAFA discourse—an attempt to renegotiate the mind-body tension by calling for a version of mind-body interactionism. Rather than encouraging its members to force the body into physical shape, to ignore or diminish the body's importance, NAAFA rhetoric demonstrates that the obese can, in fact, be very content with their physical stature. Every NAAFA member pictured in its newsletters appears cheerful; rare fashion magazines displaying "gorgeous fat women in attractive youthful fashions" are disseminated to NAAFA members; editorials in these magazines and in NAAFA newsletters openly discuss the pleasures associated with being fat. Even an "increase in fat pornography" is hailed as a sign of the normalization and advancement of fat people's sex—and thus as a symbol of the legitimate nature of their condition and status in the social order. Moreover, against the cultural view that fat people either blame their discontent on excess weight or force themselves to be happy despite their deviant size, NAAFA rhetoric insists that obese individuals can be jovial not in spite of but because of their weight. It therefore invites a "change from the inside out, rather than vice versa." As Fabrey opines, some members of NAAFA "believe that fatness is a desirable trait."

In certain cases, NAAFA rhetoric resists and even attempts to renegotiate the meaning of will-lessness, as this is imposed by the culture as the primary cause of obesity. As Fabrey argues, fatness is often caused by both "environmental" and "hereditary" factors. Obesity comes about as a result of "body type, early childhood influences, metabolism and psychological factors." For Fabrey, the cultural view of will-lessness or mind-body control is dangerously oversimplified and does not account for the complexity of one's body shape: Obesity is not merely the consequence of "overeating. . . . For many people, simple will power is not enough to overcome the presence of several [genetic and environmental] factors at the same time."

So, in the rhetorical world of NAAFA, there is not so much a lack of rational control of mind over body as there is a picture of mind and body living harmoniously and not in competition, one enjoying the pleasures of the other despite cultural judgments to the contrary. In this rhetoric, there can be no distinction between mind and body, for to make such a distinction would be to automatically deny the phenomenal experience of the obese as they learn, in this discourse, to diminish guilt and to focus away from the body as a sign of cultural displeasure. Such a distinction would also enter NAAFA discourse into the realm of culturally decoded rationality, painful discipline, medical intervention, and mind-body control—the very world NAAFA rhetoric is struggling to remake in the image of fatness. This holism advanced in NAAFA rhetoric may represent an extremely revealing postmodern coping strategy. In NAAFA discourse, the mind and body are brought together at long last so that individuals need not, or perhaps because they cannot, experience themselves as "others." In a disconnected, postmodern world, NAAFA rhetoric promotes a marriage between mind and body at least.

Most curious in NAAFA's effort to promote mind-body interactionism is the inclusion of "fat pornography." Seemingly, such descriptions are attempts to normalize the position of the obese in society, in a culture that would label their sexual roles as perverse at worst, celibate at best. For NAAFA, a fat person's sexuality is a quite normal activity revealed in his or her healthy longing for physical love and contact, and even in the desire for pornography. The very fact that the culture openly decries pornography of any type is no doubt seen by NAAFA as strangely liberating, because most NAAFA members themselves probably view pornography as degrading and perverse. Yet this belief in the degrading and perverse nature of pornography, mirroring as it does the negative attitude toward pornography exhibited by the general culture, is what links NAAFA members with the culture that oppresses them. The notion of "fat pornography," in other words, becomes an expression of one important nexus point—a place in the cultural symbology and value network where the obese and the culture may meet.

Including the issue of sexuality is important for another reason: It suggests that most obese persons have chosen to be content with their body size despite having genetic or other limitations forced upon them. This may be why NAAFA rhetoric emphasizes and openly displays the fact that obese persons date and marry their fat companions, not because they have no other alternatives but because they actively choose and fall in love with them. In addition, stories are recounted of handsome young men unabashedly relating to obese women. One slim male interviewed in a NAAFA newsletter happily admitted his attraction to fat women: "Any healthy, red-blooded American man who does not happen to be gay would relish the opportunity to spend so much time around so many women he finds attractive." Obese persons, it would appear, have normal romantic desires and relationships, just like everyone else.

One of the more pressing difficulties faced by NAAFA is the composition of its membership. Although most members desire acceptance of their obese body forms, others clearly wish to reduce their weight, thereby engendering cultural recognition. How, then, does NAAFA rhetorically manage those who perceive obesity as a temporary condition—those who, Fabrey admits, find obesity to be an undesirable trait, one to be corrected through diet, exercise, or medical intervention? After all, these individuals would appear to stand in direct opposition to the organization's agenda, even though Fabrey openly acknowledges that there "is room in NAAFA for many different points of view." NAAFA's discourse employs the strategy of rhetorical ambiguity to cope with this problem. So Fabrey dispels what is for him the myth that being fat is temporary; he asserts that fat people can enjoy their lives as they are, within the experience of obesity itself, without conforming by losing "extra" pounds. He repeats the well-worn but in this case appropriate cliche: "Beauty is in the eyes of the beholder." This cultural demythologization continues as Fabrey points out the arbitrariness that exists in much medical work on obesity, along with the detrimental effects of certain medical prescriptions: "research has shown that weight loss in itself does not automatically solve the dieter's problems. On the contrary, many have found themselves extremely unhappy and uncomfortable with their 'new self,' and unable to deal with any changes that do occur." Although it endorses diets in some cases, as in cases of heart disease, NAAFA again reminds its audience of the arbitrariness involved in medical interventions, that "even here there is no fixed answer for everyone." There is even some attempt to enlist the support of the medical profession for NAAFA's cause, since "Medical opinion has been shifting away from the old-fashioned practice of blaming everything on obesity." Thus, Fabrey works to reverse the process of scientific objectification that occurs with those actively engaging in weight-reduction techniques. For NAAFA, as for Foucault, the struggle to achieve cultural prescriptions through the process of weight reduction engenders an extreme awareness of these unobtainable cultural ideals and the deviant body size possessed by the individual. Fabrey tries to show that the process of weight reduction provokes into full consciousness the very anxiety it allegedly is meant to alleviate. Perhaps more significantly, Fabrey reveals that the "new self" supposedly created by weight reduction is nothing more than a stagnant, unhappy rendering of the homogenized ideal. In the end, rather than blaming individuals or their weight for anxiety, NAAFA rhetoric redirects negative feelings toward the unreasonable cultural expectations and exposes anxiety's harmful consequences. As

Fabrey summarizes, *"constant anxiety about your weight may be more detrimental to your health than the weight itself"* (emphasis his).

Although it obviously demonstrates the hazards and frequent ineffectiveness of dieting, NAAFA rhetoric claims that it "neither condones nor condemns diets." Fabrey himself employs the qualifying term "some" when referring to those who equate beauty with fatness. Other NAAFA members report that decisions to diet are best left "up to personal choice." Hence, by remaining equivocal about dieting, NAAFA rhetoric seems to promote unified diversity between two groups of members whose views are logically incompatible. Although it dilutes the purity of NAAFA's overall appeals, this rhetorical ambiguity serves an important, pragmatic group-maintenance function, attracting and perhaps holding individuals with disparate beliefs and goals. As Fabrey urges, "if you are trying to lose weight, with or without a diet group, by all means, join NAAFA anyway. After all, NAAFA is promoting self-respect and dignity for fat people, whether or not they succeed in losing weight!" NAAFA, in this sense, is constructed out of its rhetoric as a site or place, as a permanent physical and psychological home for some and a temporary sanctuary for others.

Little People of America

Like NAAFA, LPA sponsors various social events for its members and publishes monthly newsletters to keep members abreast of ongoing activities. The major difference between the two groups is the generally low-key approach of LPA. Although its purpose remains nearly identical to NAAFA's—to promote the health and well-being of little people and cultural tolerance for them—LPA tries with less ardor to alter cultural conceptions of smallness or dwarfism. Attempts are made to blame unreasonable cultural expectations for the marginalization of little people, but these efforts are more subdued than in NAAFA rhetoric. The motto here appears to be that rhetorical empowerment is primarily a matter of managing group members and their identities, of redirecting their anger into a reasonable outlet, not changing cultural stereotypes. The functions of LPA within the framework of liminality are aptly summarized by Ablon, who views LPA as a primarily "liminal" vehicle. LPA provides "a *process*, a rite of initiation . . . for *becoming*—from one state to another. . . . It . . . take[s] the individual from a state of disavowal of dwarfism to avowal. As such, it operates as a mechanism for the positive restructuring of the identity to dwarfism, and then a return to productive and comfortable functioning in the average-sized world." Most significantly, LPA works "through a peer ambience of forced viewing and identification . . . affording members opportunities to earn and test social skills in a protected environment of their peers" (emphasis hers).[26]

The major rhetorical problem faced by LPA, then, is inciting short people to take control of their lives. A sense of control is engendered by helping them accept who and what they are and by helping them accept what is in most cases the terminal nature of their body shape. Perhaps this explains the more internal focus of LPA rhetoric when compared to NAAFA's: obese people, with the exception of those suffering from genetic disorders, can choose to change their body shapes; dwarfs have few if any options for bodily change. Therefore, rather than concentrating on rearticulating explicitly the meaning of "smallness," as NAAFA does with "fat," LPA rhetoric expends more effort solidifying the identities of its members. The assumption seems to be that allowing them to accept who and what they are will better enable them to cope with a body that never changes size and with cultural stigmas that are unlikely to alter. As one newsletter writer advises, members must "help each other toward independancy [sic] in order to take control of their own lives, and not to allow what others may think or say to bother or limit them in any way."

Pictorial rhetoric helps exemplify an image of prevailing confidence and high self-esteem among LPA members, and thus projects an image of control. As with NAAFA, LPA newsletters feature photographs of dwarfs and other little people who appear unabashedly jovial. This unabashedness is itself significant insofar as it begins to redefine the identity of members through a literal realization of their physical nature and probably mirrors the process of identity alteration experienced by many first-time participants at LPA conventions. These individuals, as Ablon observes, express initial shock at seeing numerous dwarfs and little people milling about in normal conversation; but this shock precipitates a kind of "cognitive restructuring," so that they come to accept their self-identity and physical identification as dwarfs. In a similar manner, pictures of small people in LPA newsletters undoubtedly shock many first-time readers unaccustomed to viewing large groups of small people. These pictures indicate, in effect, that the world is filled with many different and seemingly aberrant body shapes and sizes—all of them possessed by individuals functioning quite normally and happily in the culture. LPA newsletters convey this sense of shock along with the benefits to which it eventually leads. One individual reveals her transformation of identity in the most dramatic of ways: " 'It blew my mind' to see other little people, as it does for most of us." Despite her initial shock, this little person records how she went on to active and meaningful participation in both LPA and the culture at large.

In essence, then, what is being carried out in LPA discourse is a kind of transference of anger or frustration that underlines the power of control. In the words of James C. Scott, LPA rhetoric moves the discontent felt by many little people from its "raw," individualized state as they experienced it before becoming fully initiated in LPA activities, to a position of being "cooked" within the group matrix in the form of a carefully crafted set of organizational practices. Audiences can see, from the pictures and tales of short people overcoming their disgust and stigmas, persons who have gained control of their lives in order to function normally in the culture. LPA rhetoric displays individual rage transformed into effective, modulated group discourse, not into anger directed toward a culture at large.[27]

LPA rhetoric encourages further normalization by urging members to participate in everyday activities. One newsletter writer reminded readers of the simple importance of becoming involved and working hard in ordinary affairs, regardless of the outcome: "it's more important to play, to participate, to do our best at whatever it is we're doing, than to win." Another LPA member, Ernie Ott, appearing on "Phil Donahue," exhorted fellow little people on to higher goals by citing his and others' achievements as examples of what short people can really do: "I don't want to brag about my accomplishments but I am proud of what I've been able to do in this life. . . . I can point to more stellar examples like Harvard Law School attorneys, Ph.D., MD. . . . You can see all sorts of people with successful careers, school teaching, blue-collar jobs. . . . You can also turn around and see people with families." Other newsletter articles feature the psychological (and physical) rewards attained by "dwarf athletes," who "can compete competitively at the international level in disabled sports." And what better way to illustrate the normal existence of little people than to acknowledge, as one LPA writer does, that God listened to her prayers and helped bring about the recovery of a sick friend. Clearly, for LPA, God recognizes little people and average-sized persons alike.

Equally important to this display of normalization is the sense of expansionism fostered in LPA rhetoric. Like NAAFA, LPA's assumption seems to be that in numbers there is power, although LPA members rarely associate their plight with that of other marginalized groups. Rather LPA rhetoric combs the home front for prospective members and calls for conventions and medical symposiums in cities uninitiated into the practices of this organization. LPA newsletters also document meetings with short persons from other nations, along with the social and economic hardships faced by and the accomplishments of these groups.

In general, the bulk of LPA newsletters and other materials are rather unremarkable in the sense that they simply reveal short people engaging in routine meetings, social events, business ventures, sports activities, and other occasions. Yet this tone of "routineness," this unremarkable flavor to LPA rhetoric, seems to be precisely the impression LPA discourse is designed to create. Images of "ordinariness" defy the liminal, marginal nature of little persons' experiences; these images demonstrate that like their average-sized counterparts, short people are normal and productive members of the culture. In fact, LPA's discussions of little people's accomplishments, together with its inclusion of the geographic locations (i.e., its sense of "expansionism") of other normally functioning little persons, help construct a special site both removed from the surveillance and directly in the midst of the dominant culture. LPA rhetoric, even in its simplest descriptions of conventions and other common social gatherings, proposes that little people can engage in any number of normal activities but not necessarily with the aid of individuals taller than themselves. As Ablon explains, "The very aspect of planning meetings and activities constitutes a rare opportunity for education in social sophistication for many little people. Likewise being the subjects of pictures or of stories that illustrate these activities provides a kind of social recognition often denied little people."[28] LPA rhetoric, then, does more than manipulate the identity of its members. LPA reveals a shift toward a rhetoric of active seekers choosing to create a meaningful life within the culture while still maintaining their own rules and sites of discourse.

LPA rhetoric, like the discourse of NAAFA, is characterized by the development of an ambiguous relationship with medical science. LPA confronts individuals with a wide divergence of opinion about their short stature. Some, like Houshang Garakani, appearing alongside Ott on "Phil Donahue" to discuss the merits of surgical (extended limb implants) and chemical (hormonal injections) intervention, observe that the major problem he has regarding LPA is that it "insists that people should accept themselves, and we have no problem with that. But they have only half of the story. [LPA does not realize that little people] have a choice" to change through medical treatment. Ott's response both exemplifies LPA's ambivalent stance toward medicine and challenges the very assumption promoted by the ideology of health—that the body can be treated as a product or commodity to be constantly designed and improved. He argues that surgical and other medical treatments "introduced huge numbers of complications. Something on the order of one out of five patients had a complication. I have imminent trust in the American doctors, I know they can reduce that. But there is still a huge amount of complications." After citing a list of these horrible complications, Ott concludes, "I'm not going to ban it. I don't want to ban it. What I want to do is have everybody understand that it may reduce the quality of life for each child by having this done." Thus, as Fabrey did earlier, Ott praises medical science with one hand while demythologizing it with the other. He does not wish to deny the ability of physicians to improve their treatments but also worries that such interventions, even in the long term, cause more pain and suffering than they prevent. Of course, both moves entail a serious rhetorical risk: In postmodern cultural politics, all indignities seem to be inflicted "in public." One's group is always being examined as another social problem for the curiosity of quotidian men and women. Ott's admission and denial of the legitimacy of medical science focuses the cultural lens on the needs of little people (i.e., on their dependence on medicine), along with the anomalies (the shortness) and miracles (the ability to get along by themselves) associated with them.

Ironically, despite Ott's equivocal view toward medicine, LPA newsletters are filled with exposés on physicians conducting pioneering work with dwarfs and with announcements about medical consultations at various conventions. The problem for LPA is that although it seeks to undermine extravagant and unproven medical procedures that might cause harm to its members, it must also recognize that many dwarfs are prone (genetically or otherwise) to debilitating illnesses. So the accomplishments of certain physicians who can readily administer to the medical needs of LPA members are frequently featured; the exploits of some are even pictured in near hagiographic terms. "I know of quite a few of these Good Samaritans," one contributor writes, "being called upon in the middle of the night, taking a cab to track down the nearest all night drug store to fill a prescription for a very sick LP." As with NAAFA, then, LPA rhetoric is faced with an unavoidable paradox: To succeed, it must manage a relationship with the very system that objectifies and oppresses it.

THE MEANING OF NAAFA AND LPA RHETORIC

The rhetoric of NAAFA and LPA represents various strategies of resistance against cultural discourses of power and domination over the body. As empowering rhetoric, these discourses attempt to change the perspectives of fat and little people while maintaining the root realities of being obese or small. They work to alter the salience of the social reality of the obese or short individual without changing the physical person, as fitness discourse does. The drive toward becoming more fit (as exemplified in certain body shapes) and its attendant positive traits, from the perspective of the dominant ideology of health, literally changes one's social and physical reality, whereas NAAFA and LPA promote an alteration only in the way in which social reality itself is experienced by their members.

Still, although these organizations attempt to normalize accepted cultural views of obesity and smallness, their rhetorics differ in degree of intensity and focus: NAAFA loudly registers its disapproval of cultural biases, wants to redefine cultural assumptions, and tries to provoke obese people into altering self-images and action. LPA devotes less effort to changing cultural forces of domination (though it does lobby, legally and politically, against discrimination) and more to restructuring the psyche of individual members.

Perhaps the most useful way to characterize these two rhetorics is by conceiving of them in terms of their oppositional nature. NAAFA calls for a version of what Mikhail Bakhtin would call a "Rabelaisian" world, a realm of the "grotesque." According to Bakhtin, in the literature of Rabelais, "grotesque, parodied and clownish" images of the human body "serve to expose the body's structure and its life" and to enrich the idea of the body through a new "world of things, phenomena and ideas that were, in the medieval picture of the world, infinitely far from the body."[29] But this process of grotesque imaging and parody is, for Rabelais, empowering of those possessing such body shapes because it demolishes received views of the body, replacing them with new, heretofore rejected conceptions; it is "aimed at destroying the established hierarchy of values, at bringing down the high and raising up the low, at destroying every nook and cranny of the habitual picture of the world." At the same time, Rabelais "is accomplishing a more positive task, one that gives all these word-linkages and grotesque images a definite direction: to 'embody' the world, to materialize it . . . to measure everything on the scale of the human body, to construct—on that space where the destroyed picture of the world had been—a new picture."[30] Rabelais, argues Bakhtin, was particularly fond of images of eating, of food and drink. These images and the processes they embodied were strangely creative and liberating insofar as they destroyed "archaic and false matrices between objects and phenomena, and create[d] new matrices, fleshed-out ones, that materialize the world." This process of transposition ends in "ideological enlightenment," for out of the culture of eating and drinking arises "a man who is harmonious and whole."[31]

NAAFA rhetoric, in Bakhtin's sense, celebrates the grotesque (i.e., obesity), and in so doing, attempts to infuse the newly inscribed body with material power to tear down preestablished images of acceptable body forms. But his rhetoric, and its repositioning of cultural terms (the creation of "new matrices")—its placing of the term fat with the terms health, happiness, beauty, action, responsibility, social enlivenment, and so on—seeks also to "materialize" the world in the sense that the marginalized obese are shaken free of cultural stigmas (which themselves are attacked and reconstituted) and of oppressive ideologies of health and body and thrust into the world of concerted, meaningful action. In NAAFA rhetoric, a new image is born by casting off old mind-body dualism and establishing a nascent mind-body interactionism; this mind-body relationship in NAAFA rhetoric exemplifies the Rabelaisian drive toward the grotesque in a newly invigorated appearance as the obese individual who is "harmonious and whole."[32]

And yet, though it celebrates the grotesque in its own way, NAAFA rhetoric plays down the Rabelaisian aspect of eating, of food and drink. It does not openly promote dieting (the antithesis of eating), but it does not discourage it either. NAAFA rhetoric tries to construct a new image of obesity, of the obese individual's mind interacting harmoniously with the body, so that pleasure in the form of social relationships, perceptions of goodness and beauty, and productivity can be derived from the new mind-body interactionism. The obese person is encouraged to be content with his or her large form without denying, cloaking, or despising it. Nevertheless, in NAAFA rhetoric the causes of obesity are frequently attributed to heredity and environment, not to exploiting the body's natural desires (what the culture labels will-lessness). Here, obesity seems a condition caused more by genetic shuffling or environmental pressure than by the pure enjoyment of excess as revealed in the Rabelaisian pleasures of consuming great amounts of food and drink. Notably and probably strategically, the rhetoric of excess receives short shrift in NAAFA discourse, even though one surmises that this is just the kind of rhetoric to which many of its members wish to and, quite possibly—within a completely relativized, antirational postmodern framework—should subscribe. Once again, perhaps because it does not wish to simply confirm cultural stereotypes or because it desires to engage borderline members, NAAFA discourse denies that its members are without self-discipline (and therefore tries to overcome cultural stereotypes), but diminishes the idea that they enjoy eating for the sake of eating or for the bodily pleasures inherent in it.[33]

LPA rhetoric seeks social change more covertly. It does not redesign the configuration of cultural discourses on body shape. There are no Rabelaisian worlds inhabited by the grotesquely short statured. The realm of LPA is plain, common, or more to LPA's rhetorical point, a world of normal people doing normal things who just happen to be extraordinarily diminutive. Perhaps because it is a condition that sometimes leads to painful physical suffering and the need for medical intervention, LPA rhetoric does not celebrate shortness as NAAFA celebrates obesity. It calls more for a stoical acceptance of a body shape that cannot be altered. LPA does not revel in difference, in heterogeneity; it does not openly express its anger, but rather uses cool, disciplined codes that employ the hegemonic approval expressions of the dominant culture. Herein lies what might be construed as a fatal rhetorical mistake—LPA fails to sever, possibly even encourages, the damaging drive toward homogeneity. It appears that this discourse contains little of what George Bataille and Foucault would call the rhetoric of transgression, or in Bataille's terms, little transgression through heterogeneity.[34] LPA discourse, seemingly by its own accord, perpetuates the homogeneity of normality, even though "homogeneity orders a social organization which manipulates power to continuously assert its own hegemony . . . [and] insists on the commensurability of elements and spheres of experience, and reduces possible actions to fixed rules culled from well-defined situations."[35] LPA does not want to redefine these situations; it simply desires to be part of the preestablished, prearticulated culture and urges an iota of understanding and tolerance from this culture. Of course, this criticism assumes that using the hegemonic language of hierarchy and difference is less effective than challenging the basis of hegemony itself. Yet a mark of postmodern politics may be that a strategic suturing and a covert transcript of rage and disrespect exist in marginal discourse, as they exist in LPA rhetoric, and are largely concealed from open scrutiny.

We should again remind ourselves that partly out of the necessity for populating and maintaining their ranks and partly for medical reasons, NAAFA and LPA resort to various strategies of rhetorical ambiguity. These strategies would seem to place both organizations in close proximity with the totalizing discourses on cultural body shape and with the deleterious effects of homogeneity cited above. Even NAAFA at moments talks as though its primary aim is to gain entry into the system that denies its importance. (Recall, for instance, NAAFA's concern about pornography, its discussion of the joys of normal sex, along with its occasional denial of excess.) NAAFA and LPA are forced into a rhetorical bind: To keep themselves vital organizations, their rhetorics cannot fully exploit the very culture that brings their rhetoric into existence. To exploit the culture rhetorically might be to risk alienating valuable membership. Perhaps a distinguishing rhetorical mark of socially marginalized groups, then, is that they must concede certain of the culture's appeals, if only to keep their own empowering rhetoric (along with their fragile membership) intact. Such concessions and the contradictions they reveal indicate that this rhetoric is deeply embedded in the postmodern condition, in the sense that it must live with the unresolved paradoxes it raises. Or, perhaps this rhetoric allows for a certain flexibility in a postmodern culture where the bounds of cultural participation and meaning are often in flux, sometimes themselves ambiguous. This discourse moves in and out of the cultural framework, seeking entry at one point when feasible, constructing its own sites of unique social practice at others. Whatever the process, we are left wondering about the rhetoric of empowerment and its effects: Is rhetorical ambiguity a strategy of empowerment through differentiation, division, and diversion, through the exaltation of the unique, the grotesque, or the excessive? Or is it a means of compromise, of accommodation (and co-optation) into the very system it wishes both to be a part of and to change?

CONCLUSION

Doubtlessly NAAFA and LPA serve important functions for their constituents. NAAFA and LPA members alike record the overall benefits
associated with membership within each organization. Furthermore, in
view of the fact that both organizations have undertaken media promotion in recent years—and that the media provide a few more compelling examples of obese and small people succeeding in the culture—
the prospects for empowerment and some acceptance look promising
for these groups. Nevertheless, with the great clamoring of media, sport,
and health discourses pronouncing the continued benefits of exercise,
dieting, and thinness—of health—it is difficult to imagine that either
NAAFA or LPA rhetoric will have much effect in changing cultural
perceptions of obese and little people.[36] Perhaps the truly empowering
function of marginal discourse is that it supplies deviant individuals
with a variety of sites, whether they be the actual physical locations for
social meetings or the mere act of discoursing itself. Whatever the site,
the marginal discourse examined here allows individuals to practice their
life-styles and not feel odd or liminal about them; its constructs a place
to cultivate new qualities, new personal goals and social arrangements;
and it sets forth a systematic public defense of their individual dignity.[37]
The power of marginal rhetoric is the power to make it, to carve out a
definition for one's group in relation to the status quo. In other terms,
the rhetoric of NAAFA and LPA functions similar to Richard Gregg's
notion of protest discourse—it galvanizes and reinforces in-group feelings rather than altering cultural conventions or developing new con-
verts from the world of "normal" people.[38] In a culture obsessed with
beauty and health, yet one fragmented into many marginalized, subcultural groups of various bodily dimensions and states, the power to
make rhetoric is better than no power at all.

NOTES

1. Michael Ignatieff, "Modern Dying," *The New Republic* 28 (26 December
1978):28.

2. See Michel Foucault, *The Use of Pleasure*, vol. 2 of *The History of Sexuality*,
trans. Robert Hurley (New York: Pantheon Books, 1985); *The History of Sexuality
Vol. 1: An Introduction*, trans. Robert Hurley (New York: Vintage Books, 1980);
and Bryan S. Turner, *The Body and Society: Explorations in Social Theory* (Oxford:
Basil Blackwell, 1984).

3. Consider the vision of the perfect physically and mentally fit man in Joe
Weider's *Muscle Power* series; *Self* magazine's open proclamation that an individual's job, relational, and emotional satisfaction are predicated on working
the body into shape; and Jane Fonda's assertion that physical fitness is the route
to the empowerment of women. Other popular magazines and their advertise-

ments cater to the slim, attractive young "model's" figure, which according to these sources can be achieved only through the careful combination of exercise, diet, beauty enhancers, and other vital products and medical procedures. Though some exceptions exist, television and its commercials differ little from the print media in their promotion of the slim body shape. From the thin and beautiful stars of soaps to the plethora of exercise, weight-loss, and other health-related programming, television and television advertising portray and in some cases vividly dramatize the detriments and assets linked to various body types. For descriptions and analyses of health and fitness in popular culture, see Wendy Chapkis, *Beauty Secrets* (Boston: South End Press, 1986); and Barry Glassner, *Bodies: Why We Look the Way We Do and How We Feel About It* (New York: G. P. Putnam's Sons, 1988).

4. Ignatieff, "Modern Dying," 28.

5. See his "Fit for Postmodern Culture," in *Symbolic Interaction and Cultural Practice*, eds. Howard S. Becker and Michael M. McCall (Chicago and London: University of Chicago Press, 1990), 210–35. Criticisms of the ideology of health have come from many circles, including the neo-Marxists. As Glassner demonstrates, these theorists have viewed the images of idealized bodies found every day in popular culture as "dominant symbols" of commodification. These symbols, "thanks to their pivotal position in structures of social exchange . . . channel capital and serve as a common resource for judging the adequacy of the self and others." However, as Glassner argues, the problem with this neo-Marxist critique is that it overlooks a critical point about the meaning of the fitness movement within our postmodern culture: The fitness craze is "an encompassing attempt to disengage the negative effects of life in modern culture. . . . Fitness programs promise direct control over the effects of nature, as well as freedom from medical professionals, and the achievement of personal morality" (p. 215).

6. Mark Philp, "Michel Foucault," in *The Return of Grand Theory in the Human Sciences*, ed. Quentin Skinner (Cambridge: Cambridge University Press, 1985), 67.

7. Ibid.

8. Ibid.

9. Ibid., 75–76.

10. Michel Foucault, "The Subject and Power," appendix to Hubert Dreyfus and Paul Rabinow, *Michel Foucault: Beyond Structuralism and Hermeneutics* (Chicago: University of Chicago Press, 1982), 212.

11. Philp, "Michel Foucault," 76.

12. Michel Foucault, "Nietzsche, Genealogy, History," in *Language, Counter-Memory, Practice: Selected Essays and Interviews*, ed. Donald Bouchard (Ithaca, N.Y.: Cornell University Press, 1977), 148.

13. Carole Spitzack, "The Obese Person as a Subject in American Culture" (Paper presented at the annual meeting of the Speech Communication Association, Washington, D.C., November 1983). For a more complete analysis of the plight of overweight women in American culture, see her *Confessing Excess: Women and the Politics of Body Reduction* (Albany, N.Y.: State University of New York Press, 1990).

14. Jean Mayer, *Overweight: Causes, Costs, and Control* (Englewood Cliffs, N.J.: Prentice-Hall, 1974), 84.

15. The problems of obesity seem especially acute for women. Of the annual 5,000 or so individuals undergoing the surgical removal of intestines in order to bring about weight reduction, 80 percent are women. Perhaps the most poignant reminder of the obsession with weight is the condition of anorexia nervosa; 90 percent of those affected are women. See Kim Chernin, *The Obsession: Reflections on the Tyranny of Slenderness* (New York: Harper Colophon Books, 1981), 62; see also Edwin Bayrd, *The Thin Game* (New York: Avon Books, 1978).

16. Marcia Millman, *Such a Pretty Face: Being Fat in America* (New York: Berkley Books, 1981), 36.

17. Spitzack, "The Obese Person," 8.

18. Ibid., 10.

19. Ibid.

20. Spitzack, *Confessing Excess*, 78. Following Foucault, Spitzack demonstrates the quest to achieve cultural ideals represented in weight reduction (like all quests toward perfection) only uncovers the impossibility of obtaining these ideals in the first place. Such a paradoxical realization further frustrates the obese person's attempt to cope with deviant body size.

21. Joan Ablon, *Little People in America: The Social Dimensions of Dwarfism* (New York: Praeger Publishers, 1984), 25.

22. Ibid., 28.

23. Victor Turner, *The Ritual Process: Structure and Anti-Structure* (Chicago: Aldine, 1969), 95.

24. Ablon, *Little People*, 29.

25. The quotes that follow on pages 38 through 48 are drawn from the author's personal collection of NAAFA and LPA newsletters and fliers. Most of this material consists of unpaginated single sheets. Those requesting specific sources or further information may contact Dr. Kenneth Zagacki, 1975 Stanford Drive, Baton Rouge, Louisiana.

26. Ablon, *Little People*, 170.

27. See James C. Scott, *Domination and the Arts of Resistance* (New Haven, Conn., and London: Yale University Press, 1990), 119.

28. Ablon, *Little People*, 167.

29. Mikhail Bakhtin, *The Dialogic Imagination: Four Essays*, ed. Michael Holquist, trans. Caryl Emerson and Michael Holquist (Austin, Tex.: University of Texas Press, 1981), 176.

30. Ibid., 177.

31. Ibid., 187.

32. There is, of course, a darker side here. Bakhtin's carnival can also be read by the dominant class as chaos and wildness. So they can respond: "See how dreadful, hideous, drunken, and chaotic life would be if this reversal were permanent." This is the world turned upside down, as viewed by an audience of an unsympathetic, perhaps even hostile or frightened dominant group.

33. In this way, it could be argued that NAAFA rhetoric does not fall into the rhetorical trap of celebrating countervirtues to the extent of François Rabelais (1494–1553), who lived at the time of Europe's great paradigm challenges.

34. See especially Georges Bataille, *Visions of Excess: Selected Writings, 1927–*

1939, Allan Stoekl, trans. Allen Stoekl with Carl R. Lovitt and Donald M. Leslie, Jr. (Minneapolis: University of Minnesota Press, 1988); see also Peter Stallybrass and Allon White, *The Politics of Transgression* (Ithaca, N.Y.: Cornell University Press, 1986).

35. Andrew Haase, "Body Shops: The Death of Georges Bataille," in *Body Invaders: Panic Sex in America*, ed. Arthur Kroker and Marilouise Kroker (New York: St. Martin's Press, 1987), 122–3.

36. Ironically, even the rhetoric of health associated with AIDS—where one might expect gradual shifts away from images of health and thinness being equated with frequent and varied sexual relationships—will unlikely improve the lot of obese and little people. This is so because the fear of contracting deadly diseases will give rise to the belief that a well-groomed, well-exercised, and moderately fed body will be better able to fend off these viral-based illnesses.

37. We must take note that whatever the official intention of such rhetoric, individual audience members might have all sorts of personal satisfactions as a result of processing this discourse.

38. See Richard B. Gregg, "The Ego Function of Protest Rhetoric," *Philosophy and Rhetoric* 4 (1971): 71–91.

Chapter Five

The Reciprocal Power of Group Identities and Social Styles: A Note on a Specimen Deviant Youth Group

Calvin Morrill and William Bailey

How is one to understand the power of "spectacular" youth subcultures[1]—the punks, skinheads, rastas, rappers, hippies, mods, and beats—to command so much of Western society's attention during the past three decades? Are they a threat to value systems and "ways of being" in the dominant society?[2] If so, how are these threats manifested? Do they simply represent age-old expressions of youthful rebellion against parental authority?[3] Are they simply attempting to reclaim some "sense of place" in a society that has been leveled by mass media and other postwar losses of collective identity?[4]

In this chapter we present a conceptualization of power that centers around the notions of *social identity* and *social style*. To do so, we draw on recent sociological and journalistic descriptions of a single specimen of youth subculture: the skinheads. By youth subculture, we mean any social group that primarily the younger population participates in and is drawn toward and that contains what Raymond Williams terms "a particular way of life which expresses certain meanings and values in . . . ordinary behavior."[5] We intend our analysis to cast light on the specific case of youth culture and the general nature of power, social identity, and social style.

THE RECIPROCAL PRINCIPLE OF POWER AND IDENTITY

We conceive of power as the likelihood of achieving one's will within social relationships in the face of resistance by coacting others.[6] Because power is embedded in social relationships, it may be understood as a continuum of social coactions that range from treating all others as objects to being treated as an object by everyone. Thus, pure power is pure freedom; pure powerlessness is "social death."[7]

Although no individual or group is ever purely powerful, those who exercise power with idiosyncratic discretion are more powerful (have more freedom to act relative to others with whom they are in action) than individuals or groups who cannot do so. To the extent that the powerful can treat another person as an object, the powerful determine the identity of the less powerful, as Janeway makes clear. Power and social identity are therefore two closely related concepts.[8]

Within this perspective, we conceive of social identity as a set of attributions associated with a name or other signification. Even when slaves rebel or escape, they still carry the social identity of slave as defined by their former masters. Until they find themselves in completely different social relations, they will never regain the power (the social life) to renounce their imposed social identities.

The reciprocal principle of power can be stated simply as an equation in which one person's or group's enfranchisement to act disenfranchises another's in precisely the same actions. Thus, claims to power involve complementary claims to positions in social space. If one person or group has power to act in a certain way, others must necessarily be restricted from coacting in that same way within the same social space. For a member of a group, the more power the group has over the person, the less autonomy the person has. This is the same as saying that a person has no social identity except that which the group allows; the person is totally the group's object. Conversely, the more discretionary influence a person has in a group, the more power the person has. The reciprocal principle of power and identity thus means that a group may be reduced to virtually an ego-extension of a charismatic, tyrannical leader. The greater a person's or group's power within the same social space, therefore, the more complementary the behavioral relationship must become: masters-slaves, employers-employees, parents-children, and so forth.

The same analysis may be applied to groups seeking to control the production of social identities in larger social space.[9] Here again, the ultimate group power is to treat all other groups and their members as objects. Such an exercise of power enables the members of a group to be maximally free in their behaviors toward all other groups. Only their own group contains maximally competent humanity, and thus they need to exercise care only around their own group members. Even a benevolent group must ultimately seek to have its brand of benevolence prevail over any competing benevolence and over ignorance or recalcitrance.

THE PROCESSES AND LOCATIONS OF POWER

Thus far we have focused on the nature and outcomes of power—the reciprocal principle of defining social identities of powerful and powerless making them stick—but not on the processes or the social locations of power. Here we draw attention to the processes of power as continual struggles between actors over the production and living of social identities. The production and living of social identities are never completely static. Even in the most asymmetric power relation the powerless still have some degrees of freedom in exercising upward discretionary influence over the powerful, in one sense reversing, if only temporarily, their regular complementary roles. The slave, for instance, can withhold labor power or covertly sabotage agricultural production.[10] Power relations and the identities within them are by nature a function of process.

Because we are talking about social relationships, struggles over social identities must occur in social space. To borrow Goffman's useful phrase, such struggles occur somewhere between the almost totally public front stage and the far more private back stage.[11] The minimal social distance in which struggles over social identities occur is the interpersonal dyad. The maximal social distance involved in social power struggles, through mass mediation, might involve an entire society or world.

COMMUNICATION AND THE SUPERNATURAL MYSTIQUE OF POWER: THE CONSECRATION AND DESECRATION OF SYMBOLS

Communication has a multifaceted role in the function of power. In the present context we are interested in the role of symbols in the mystique of power. In this role, symbols acquire an almost magical dimension. In this section we attempt to anchor that dimension to its experiential basis and look at the social use of symbols to diminish or increase power.

The sources of power are many, as traditional typologies of power bases make clear.[12] Janeway argues that power exudes mystique; mystique may even be said to constitute the ultimate basis of power. She sees mystique as an intersection between power and magic that is a primitive residue in modern secular society.[13] Folger and Poole describe power similarly.[14] As an example, Janeway notes that individuals who achieve the office of president, even if unlikely material, are made more glamorous by the office. They take on an "aura" that transcends mundane, individual political morality. They have duties and obligations to more fundamental categories conditioned by culture. The great mythological themes of good and evil manifestly operate in the mystique of power.[15]

Those who wield power in our approved social institutions (e.g., the presidents) benefit from an aura of positive power. Their identities and images intimately fuse with the use of sacred symbols and seals. Their names, in effect, become sacred symbols on paper to empower laws and regulations that must be obeyed under penalty of prison or even death. In one sense, they become "heroes" in our cultural mythology.

Conversely, those who degrade or attack our institutions and their symbols acquire auras of power from the evil or "dark side." We are not all that far from the days—if, in fact, we have left them—when even troublesome children were identified as "limbs of Satan." Negative power was everywhere to vex the good operation of our society. God, indeed, was on our side—if not our children's—and Satan ruled the enemy.[16]

Janeway points out that myth incorporates the notion of legitimate boundaries in the exercise of power. Here she refers to the classical myth of *moira* (sometimes capitalized and represented as a goddess), the inhabiting principle of the universe that establishes the proper place and power of all things, including the gods. A violation of the boundaries represents an act of *hubris* as much for the gods as for humans.[17] Heraclitus comments that should the sun (Apollo) overstep its boundaries, it would be punished by the Furies.[18] The misuse of official power for personal ends is a violation of boundaries. Thus, the misuse of presidential power, as in Nixon's case, made the presidential aura dark. As Janeway puts it, Nixon acquired a "sinister glamor."[19]

Two sets of mythological dimensions are consequently involved in the mystique of power: good and evil and the sacred and the profane.

Janeway's conception of magic as a residue from primitive beginnings, noted above, is problematic. What makes older or traditional societies primitive? Does this not place our society at some endpoint in a Eurocentric perspective of social evolution evocative of Spencer, Tyler, or Durkheim? What is the location of the residue? Does each of us carry a genetically encoded and transmitted chunk of information that makes us responsive to magic? Is the magic located in the persistence of primitive magical rituals in society? Or are psychological and sociological residues mutually enabling?

Also, "magic" is an awkward, probably misleading, conception for this aspect of power. No machinations, incantations, or spells are involved in the exercise of presidential power. It seems preferable to think of power as involving some elements and rituals of the supernatural rather than magical incantations and spells. What is the basis of the magic-like aspect of power?

Our experience of supernatural aspects of power is probably not much different from that of our ancestors, but we shy away from intellectually scrutinizing intrinsically magical behaviors and are much too secular to attribute our experiences to the supernatural. Nevertheless, we persist in the commonly noted superstitions such as knocking on wood after boasting of health or carrying a lucky piece. We also engage in animistic behaviors, such as patting the hoods of faithful automobiles and slamming the doors of the faithless, and feeling faithless when we sell "Old Faithful." We observe many silent taboos, such as keeping a clutter of unwanted photographs of loved ones because we cannot bring ourselves to destroy them. We generally recognize words as merely agitations of air particles. Although most of us do not profess to believe in verbal taboos, few are able to comfortably say aloud, "I hope my mother (or any loved person) dies a terrible death next week." In sum, and in spite of secular beliefs, humans inhabit a world in which there are consecrated objects and events. These objects are consecrated because we experience our own affective responses as if they were intrinsic attributes of the objects and events. The way we feel toward a picture of mother prevents our burning it.

We devise secular "covers" to talk about the experience of mythological power. For example, burning a picture of your mother is avoided not because it endangers your mother, but because it shows a lack of respect or feelings. One does not do some things or act in some ways out of deference to social norms. However, the connection between the material act and the reason for its avoidance is no clearer than if the burning were thought to be a voodoo ritual.

The supernatural is not inherently a part of the symbolic process. As already noted, the emotional charging of objects and events through animistic behavior may not involve any element of the supernatural. The supernatural enters as we invest such objects with properties and powers beyond their material possibility. Again, as noted above, burning a picture of a parent can produce emotional responses inappropriate to the actual material significance of the act. Symbolic elements involving moral values or religion usually involve the same sort of emotional charging but rest upon more overt assumptions of supernatural powers.

Desecrations blatantly involving the supernatural may be assumed to involve major power dimensions. The assumption is that it takes a powerful person to commit a desecration of major proportion. That is, only a major devil would challenge a major benevolent being. Thus, a person who desecrates a flag has more perverse, or negative, power than one who merely advocates its burning. A person who desecrates the Bible has more negative power than a mild heretic. At the supernatural extreme, the desecrator is seen to be possessed by or to be a willing agent of Satan.

The recent flag desecration debate is instructive because it is about whether a cloth of a certain design has supernatural properties that are sacred. Proponents of constitutional amendments or laws making flag desecration a crime do not acknowledge that they are assigning the flag magical properties. They argue that the flag is the special symbol of the country (civil society and the state fused together) and/or that desecration dishonors those heroes who have died for the flag. One just does not do those things. But why not? A picture is only a picture, and a flag is only a piece of colored cloth and a stick. Desecratory acts violate fundamental social boundaries through representations of the socially consecrated as profane, or worse. The desecration of the flag is a violation that nature or goodness (or moira, in the Greek tradition) recoils against and punishes—or presumably ought to.

The flag as symbol functions to represent the identities of the powerful who exert influence under its aegis. If that aegis is violated, those under it lose power. It is obviously in the interests of the socially powerful to make us see the violation of the flag as a crime against nature, as a violation of the natural order of things.

Following the reciprocal principle of power, the more the natural order is violated, the more it becomes unnatural, arbitrary. The more routinely one sees the flag treated profanely, the more difficult it becomes to feel strong emotional responses toward its profanation. The more the sacred objects and symbols representing the sacred are routinely desecrated, the more they become experienced as profane and, by symbolic extension, the powerful become less powerful. Symbolic desecration, in brief, is a means of diminishing the power of the powerful.

STYLE, SYMBOLIC DESECRATION, AND POWER

Style is certainly one of the most dominant elements of social life. Style communicates values and attitudes: It is a concrete, symbolic, and ritualistic enactment of values in society. A counterculture and a counterstyle are therefore synonymous. Through style, the counterculture can explore the full boundaries of freedom of speech and thought espoused by Western cultures and encroach upon legally safe but less tolerated behavior. Style invites participation rather than intellectual debate and is therefore more "subversive" to establishment values than the overt expression of counterculture ideology. The counterculture ideology expressed in logical discourse may be rendered ridiculous or hopelessly inoperable in the face of practicality. But the only refutation of style is another style.

· Clarke compares fashion to discourse, specifically to the mythic discourse Levi-Strauss described as "bricolage."[20] In overly simplified terms, *bricolage* refers to a piece of work by a handyman, put together out of odds and ends, that has both function and artistic merit. The youth subculture creates its style with bricolage of existing objects or "gear." Within the context of the whole, the individual odds and ends undergo "transformation" and "resignification." Obviously, the subculture does not want to use the objects conventionally; quite the contrary, the subculture especially strives to create meanings that run counter to the dominant culture.[21] Thus, a primary effect of the styles of youth subculture is the desecration of symbols of the parental society.

Symbolic desecration occurs when a style includes elements or behavior deprecating objects or events charged with emotional significance. For present purposes, we may define "symbolic" as characterizing the use of an object, event, or behavior as a sign of something else to elicit emotional responses appropriate to what is signified.

In Clarke's conception, we may think of the style process as the use of a system of signs—again as a discourse.[22] One contrary "essay" written by the counterculture style is a desecration of the beauty standards of the society. Youths make themselves ugly but wear the ugliness as if it were beauty. The shaved head selected by the skinheads is not usually a feature of advertised beauty; it is more associated with violent types, such as wrestlers, or Nazis sporting dueling scars. Other counterculture groups violate the norms against males wearing makeup, a violation popularized by the "mascara rock banks." Desecrations of sexual and religious mores of the parent culture are special targets of countercultures. Both males and females may affect excessively provocative dress and makeup styles in relation to dominant culture standards. Satanic or other "evil" insignia may be worn. The makeup and clothing may take on the qualities of "costume," and boundaries between stage makeup and dress and everyday styles may disappear.

Artifacts offer considerable iconographic possibilities for adornment. For example, the swastika and "Iron Cross" are frequent insignia of counterculture groups. The tough, brutal image seems to be in vogue among some counterculture groups. A safety pin through the cheek, nose, or ear heightens that effect and offends the squeamish. Although some of these symbols have special significance for some groups (e.g., for neo-Nazi skinheads) within the counterculture generally, they have little more ideological meaning than the death's-head or other eschatological symbols on biker jackets. The symbols simply "fit" or complete the bricolage: the safety pin, swastika, or Iron Cross completes the ensemble of leather and spikes rather than endorses masochism or a particular political group.

Social style is also a process of using physical appearance and adornment, artifacts, and behavior to identify one's social group. There is some point in this process at which variance from the central norm becomes recognized (labeled) as deviant. The subculture presumably prefers that its variations of style not be mistaken as elegant variations of the dominant culture—that is, as merely *avant garde*. For that reason, counterculture style may run to the garish or blatant or, from all perspectives outside the subculture displaying it, be unintelligible but identifiable.

It is, of course, difficult for the older parent society to divorce the symbols from the negative emotions engendered. Youth subculture flaunts its rebellion in the face of the parent culture principally through style. Thus it advertises to youth generally that the parent culture is impotent to exercise control. The counterculture is the "bad child" that Mother Society does not want playing with her child but that eludes control.

The power of the youth counterculture derives principally from its capacity to shock or horrify the establishment with style that captivates the rebellious young. Without that power, it could hardly be taken seriously as a counterculture. Who the group is (its identity) and its efficacy depend on that power. Consequently, the youth counterculture is inevitably involved in the desecration of the establishment's symbols through the creation of a counterstyle. With these ideas in mind, we turn to an illustrative analysis of the "threat" posed by a single youth group in society: the skinheads.

THE ORIGINS OF THE SKINHEADS

Evidence in the mass media of the skinheads' appearance in contemporary American culture is abundant. In *USA Today* headlines blare: "Skinheads: A New Generation of Hate-Mongers";[23] in *Macleans*, skinheads are called "a growing menace [that] are raising urban fears";[24] and *Time* magazine declares "from L.A. to Boston, the skinheads are on the march."[25] Whence did this "threat" spring?

The origins of the skinheads can be traced back to the "mod" movement among white youths that swept England during the second wave of rock and roll. The first wave originated in the United States with the crossover of fast-paced backbeat rhythms from so-called black music to mainstream pop by such artists as Elvis Presley, Chuck Berry, and Jerry Lee Lewis; the second originated in England with such musical groups as the Beatles and the Rolling Stones. By the late 1960s the mods had split into two polarized groups: the "extravagant mods," those more attuned to the hippies and emergent acid rock, and the "hard mods," those "who [wore] heavy boots, jeans with braces, [and] short hair" and championed music from the Caribbean, particularly reggae.[26]

The skinheads evolved from this latter group. In the early 1970s the skinheads drew their members from the youth of England's working class. Early on they affected a "kind of caricature of the model worker'" with their heavy work boots, shaved heads, stay-pressed trousers or traditional denim jeans, and plain button-down shirts.[27]

During this period, skinhead style took several cues from the great numbers of black Jamaican workers who immigrated to England in the hopes of escaping the poverty of a newly independent Caribbean. The skinheads shared not only their neighborhoods with these immigrants, but their bars, dances, dress styles, and mannerisms.

These initial manifestations of skinhead culture certainly express attempts by proletarian youths to recover a loss of "working class identity" in the wake of England's postwar decline.[28] Yet, at a more general level, they evidence the reciprocal principle of power (and identity) among social groups. In their style of dress, skinheads mixed their eccentric working-class ensembles with elements from very different sources, the strongest of which originated in Jamaica. Thus, they used bits of styles from traditional working-class clothes and hairstyles (their parent culture; in one sense, the natural, mythological good) and also borrowed various cultural forms from West Indian immigrants (the "other"), producing an unnatural style that desecrated the dominant (parent) cultural symbols of the working-class community (i.e., they danced to reggae in ordinary work boots or wore knitted tams from Jamaica with their button-down shirts). The mystique of this mixture was such that the skinheads began to commandeer a location in social space: a cultural island in which they began to have discretion and freedom.

In so doing, the skinheads and their West Indian foils defined themselves in opposition to other ethnic and youth groups, most notably Pakistanis, but also Asians, mainstream youth of other social classes, and hippies. By the late 1960s, the hippies had successfully carved out a social niche proclaiming their power in a new harmony of peace, love, and drugs. Skinheads, then, initially witnessed an uneasy truce between themselves and blacks. As the mid-1970s approached, the truce was broken as English blacks began to define, through the songs of reggae, their own location in social space, assert their own identity, and seek social power. And they did so with idioms that were strangely similar to those of the hippies. In so doing, they drew the lines of power between blacks and whites, the powerless and the powerful:

The skinheads turned away in disbelief as they heard the Rastas sing of the "havenots seeking harmony" and the scatting dee-jays exhorting their black brothers to be "good in (their) neighborhood." The wheel had come full circle and the skinhead, who had sought refuge from the posturing beatitudes of the pot-smoking hippie, was confronted with what appeared to be the very attitudes that had originally dictated his withdrawal. It must have seemed, as the rudies [blacks] closed their ranks that they had also changed their sides and the doors were doubly locked against the bewildered skinhead.... Reggae had come of age and the skinheads were sentenced to perpetual adolescence.[29]

The split produced ever more energetic attempts by the skinheads to control their social space, to be powerful on their own terms, to control their own culture. The exercise of this control intensified violent skinhead "bashing"[30] against youth groups coacting in the same social space much as the skinheads bashed physical places such as bars and football stadiums; skinheads came to treat coacting groups as objects. In the aftermath of this split and in the context of their feverish struggles to be powerful in the face of challenges by blacks, other ethnic groups, other youth groups, and other classes, the skinheads made their way across the Atlantic to North America in the form, once again, of music and the bands that played it.

SKINHEAD POWER IN THE UNITED STATES

The English skin bands that first appeared in this country in the mid–1970s arrived stripped of their heterogeneous origins. All that remained was the seemingly monolithic, hard-working class nihilism that mixed well with the nascent working-class "punk" culture just beginning to live in a few "alternative" bars. The skins, still predominantly working class or "lumpen" (to use Marx's term for those out-of-work proletarians who slept under the bridges of Victorian England), expressed the same style in their dress that their English brethren favored. They then rode the increasing popularity of punk among white youth into the 1980s and began to intermingle with older white supremacists of somewhat similar articulated political ideologies and aims.

The print and electronic media sounded an alarm of the skinhead threat to the United States in the mid-1980s. Since that time, several instances of violence by skinheads against nonwhite, homosexual, and politically liberal individuals have been reported. And the skinheads have increasingly become the front lines for white supremacist organizations catering to youth, using live music concerts and comic books to appeal directly to working-class skinheads alienated from competition with other working-class ethnicities for jobs in an economically "declining" America.[31] Although the skinheads have received a great deal of press attention, the numbers involved remain small. Various estimates of committed skinheads, those whose entire activities revolve around the skinhead style,[32] range from 1,000 to 2,000 in twenty-one states.[33]

The violence of the skinheads against other groups and individuals (some of it argued to be organized by white supremacist political groups such as the Aryan Youth Movement, the American Nazi Movement, or the Order), while repugnant in and of itself, does not appear to be different on a case-by-case basis from similar incidents involving ethnic and youth groups (including blacks and Hispanics striking out against whites). On these grounds alone, the characterization of the skinheads as a distinctive or unique threat seems unwarranted. Yet their actions have induced deep reactions in the mainstream society. Calls demanding that "adults become aware of the politics of their community's children" abound.[34] The National Council of Churches concluded in 1988 that: "Bigoted violence [with skinheads implied to be willing perpetrators] has become the critical criminal-justice issue of the late 1980s."[35] Deep reactions are also readily present in many who see skinheads on the street or even in pictures.

POWER AND YOUTH SUBCULTURE

What then is the "threat" embodied in the skinheads, and do they raise any greater social threats than previous spectacular youth cultures that have swept the United States (the beats, bikers, or hippies, for example)?

The skinhead threat differs little from the youth subcultural threats that preceded it. The skinhead threat can be understood using the reciprocal principle of power and its close alliance with the concept of social identity. We also draw upon the idea of referent power, which deals with the desire to be like, to act like, and to be accepted or liked by some other person or group.

Against the backdrop of the reciprocal principle of power, the more one identifies with one social group, the less one can identify with other different or antithetic groups. The more one identifies with a deviant group, such as the skinheads, the less one can identify with the mainstream culture. The principal threat to society is the loss of the primary group for whom identification with deviant groups is most possible—the youth group. In other words, the referent power of the deviant group is "Pied Piper" power: Social harm is inflicted through the loss of children, or possibly through the acts of children.

From this perspective, the skinheads do not pose a direct and general social threat by means of the violence they inflict on others. Such criminal acts have the same social significance as other criminal acts of violence. The political rallies organized by white supremacists and attended by skinheads are also too minor to constitute a direct and general social threat. The principal threat is indirect: It is the parent culture's loss of the social power to define children as powerless; it is children commandeering their own social space, expressing their own freedom, being able to define their own identities as powerful. Like the beats and hippies before them, the greatest skinhead threat emanates from their power to commandeer, transpose, and display for their own artifacts that are charged with emotional symbolism.

Although we have hung some rather heavy theoretical baggage on a flimsy set of data, we can suggest some answers (already implicitly or explicitly apparent in our arguments above) to the questions with which we began this chapter. We can understand youth subcultures as power struggles between youth groups and their parent cultures and youth groups and other youth groups. Such struggles are more fundamental than those played out in the realms of commodities or politics, for they are framed within the basic mythological categories of the sacred and the profane, of good and evil, of the natural and the unnatural.

The spectacular youth cultures, such as the skinheads, are spectacular because they transpose sacred elements from their parent (dominant) cultures into the profane through *front stage* desecration. Such desecration allows them to be powerful, to have discretion in their lives, to fend off the application of identities from other sources, and to reclaim a "sense of place" in social space. Their place, however, displaces others, especially dominant groups that would claim the capacity to define youth's social identity. It is this latter outcome that threatens society.

A poignant example drawn from the spectacular youth cultures of 1960s America underscores the irony of our arguments. Some young protesters' signs declared, "Don't shoot we're your children" while other protesters hurled rocks and expletives at the Establishment. Youthful protesters averred roles that their actions rejected; by claiming themselves powerless, they disclaimed accountability for their behavior. In defining *their own* powerlessness, youths themselves become empowered to act as they wish. Should the skinheads ever realize this last implication of the reciprocal principle of power, they will truly pose a threat to society.

NOTES

1. Dick Hebdidge, *Subculture: The Meaning of Style* (London: Methuen, 1989), 136.

2. Stuart Hall and Thomas Jefferson, *Resistance Through Rituals: Youth Subcultures in Post-War Britain* (London: Huchinson & Co., 1976), 13.

3. Erik Erikson, *Childhood and Society* (New York: Norton, 1950), 5.

4. Joshua Meyrowitz, *No Sense of Place: The Impact of Electronic Media on Social Behavior* (New York: Oxford University Press, 1985), 7.

5. Raymond Williams, *The Long Revolution* (London: Chatto and Windus, 1961), 41.

6. This general notion appears in a variety of classic and contemporary works across the social sciences: Max Weber, "Class, Status, Party," in *From Max Weber: Essays in Sociology* eds. Hans Gerth and C. Wright Mills (New York: Oxford University Press, 1946), 180; Kurt Lewin, *Field Theory in Social Science* (New York: Harper and Row, 1951), 3; Ronald Lippitt Norman, "The Dynamics of Power," *Human Relations* 5 (1952): 37–64; Robert Emerson, "Deviation and Rejection: An Experimental Replication," *American Sociological Review* 19 (1954): 688–93; John R. P. French, Jr., and Bertram Raven, "The Bases of Social Power," in *Group Dynamics: Research and Theory*, ed. Dorwin Cartwright (Ann Arbor: Michigan Institute for Social Research, 1959), 607; and Jeffrey Pfeffer, *Power in Organizations* (Boston: Pitman, 1981), 2.

7. Orlando Patterson, *Slavery and Social Death: A Comparative Study* (Cambridge, Mass.: Harvard University Press, 1982), 38.

8. Elizabeth Janeway, *Powers of the Weak* (New York: Morrow Quill Paperbacks, 1982), 18. It is possible that the conception of power advanced here could be interpreted as a tautology. Admitting to the possibility of dialectic, however, removes such a possibility.

9. We conceive of social space following the somewhat complementary conceptions in Donald Black, "A Strategy of Pure Sociology," in *Theoretical Perspectives in Sociology*, ed. Scott G. McNall (New York: St. Martin's Press, 1979), 149; and Pierre Bourdieu, "Social Space and Symbolic Power," *Sociological Theory* 7 (1989): 14–25. In these writings, social space is conceived as observable social interaction along several dimensions, including the economic, relational, cultural, organizational, and normative.

10. M. P. Baumgartner, "Social Control from Below," in *Toward a General Theory of Social Control*, vol. 1, ed. Donald Black (Orlando, Fla.: Academic Press, 1984), 305.

11. Erving Goffman, *The Presentation of the Self in Everyday Life* (Garden City, N.Y.: Doubleday, 1959), 107.

12. French and Raven, *Bases of Social Power*, 607; Andrew King, *Power and Communication* (Prospect Heights, Ill.: Waveland Press, 1987), 4.

13. Janeway, *Powers of the Weak*, 188.

14. Joseph P. Folger and Marshall Scott Poole, *Working Through Conflict* (Glenview, Ill.: Scott, Foresman and Co., 1984).

15. Janeway, *Powers of the Weak*, 188.

16. Kai T. Erikson, *Wayward Puritans: A Study in the Sociology of Deviance* (New York: Wiley, 1964).

17. Janeway, *Powers of the Weak*, 155.

18. E. R. Dodds, *The Greeks and the Irrational* (Berkeley and Los Angeles: University of California Press, 1968), 7–8; see also F. M. Cornford, *From Religion to Philosophy: A Study in the Origins of Western Speculation* (New York: Harper and Row, 1957).

19. Janeway, *Powers of the Weak*, 66.

20. John Clarke, "Style," in *Resistance Through Rituals: Youth Subcultures in Post-War Britain*, eds. Stuart Hall and Thomas Jefferson (London: Huchinson & Co., 1976), 177.

21. Ibid., 177–8.

22. Ibid., 182.

23. Eva Sears, "Skinheads: A New Generation of Hate-Mongers," *USA Today*, May 1989, p. 24.

24. Barry Came, "A Growing Menace," *Maclean's*, 23 January 1989, pp. 43–44.

25. John Leo, "A Chilling Wave of Racism," *Time*, 25 January 1988, p. 57.

26. Stanley Cohen, *Folk Devils and Moral Panics* (London: Macgibbon and Kee, 1972).

27. Hebdidge, *Subculture*, 55.

28. John Clarke, "The Skinheads and the Magical Recovery of Community," in *Resistance Through Rituals: Youth Subcultures in Post-War Britain*, eds. Stuart Hall and Thomas Jefferson (London: Huchinson & Co., 1976).

29. Dick Hebdige, "Reggae, Rasta, and Rudies," in *Resistance Through Rituals: Youth Subcultures in Post-War Britain*, eds. Stuart Hall and Thomas Jefferson (London: Huchinson & Co., 1976), 152.

30. Clarke, "Skinheads," 101–2.

31. Sears, "Skinheads," 25.

32. Kathryn Joan Fox, "Real Punks and Pretenders," *Journal of Contemporary Ethnography* 3 (1986): 344–70.

33. Came, "A Growing Menace," 43.

34. Sears, "Skinheads," 26.

35. Leo, "A Chilling Wave," 57.

Chapter Six

Sanctuary Confronts the Court: An Unrepentant Prophet

Jeanne E. Clark

THE SANCTUARY CHALLENGE

On March 24, 1982, Southside Presbyterian Church in Tucson, Arizona, and five churches in Berkeley, California, proclaimed their status as sanctuaries for Central American refugees. In so doing, the churches publicly acknowledged their violation of Immigration and Naturalization Service regulations. From a governmental perspective, the churches stood outside the law as they protected undocumented Central Americans.

The public voice of the Sanctuary movement had already been heard critiquing mainstream society. Two months earlier, Jim Corbett, the Quaker "coyote"[1] considered a founder of the movement, had challenged the National Council of Churches' consultation on immigration:

Much more than the fate of the undocumented refugees depends on the religious community's participation and leadership in helping them avoid capture. If the right to aid fugitives from government-sponsored terror is not upheld in action by the churches—regardless of the cost in terms of imprisoned clergy, punitive fines, and exclusion from government-financed programs—the loss of many other basic rights of conscience will surely follow.[2]

Corbett's statement was clear, uncompromising, and spoken from the periphery of society. Corbett and the churches working with him assumed the role of prophets confronting the religious and social order.

The prophet is one of the classic figures in radical discourse. From Amos to Martin Luther King, people have taken the prophetic mantle to empower their critique of dominant society, but the authority-wielding role is a rhetorical "mixed blessing." The prophet, endowed with tremendous authority by a "call" to speak, is nonetheless dependent on audience acceptance of that authority. The would-be prophet may be rejected as theologically illegitimate by members of the dominant religious order. The message, framed with moral-religious justification, may be considered socially irrelevant or inappropriate by the mainstream social order. The prophet challenging the prevailing social order must bridge the gap between a sacred ethical-moral message and a secular society; failure to do so means that the message and its fringe-group adherents will lack the power to enact their vision.

As Sanctuary grew, the movement sought to address that challenge. A January 1985 Inter-American Symposium on Sanctuary, the first national gathering of the movement, drew some 1,300 people to Temple Emanu-El in Tucson. At that time the movement included representatives from many mainstream religious bodies: Catholic, Friends, Unitarian, Presbyterian, United Church of Christ, Lutheran, Methodist, Mennonite, Baptist, Episcopal, Disciples of Christ, and Reform Jew. By April 1985, 214 churches, schools, and communities from La Jolla to Boston, from Baton Rouge to Minneapolis, had joined the Sanctuary movement. With endorsements from organizations as diverse as the American Friends Service Committee, the Rabbinical Assembly, the Maryknoll Fathers, and the Association of Evangelical Lutheran Churches,[3] and with the declaration of the entire state of New Mexico as a sanctuary,[4] the movement was clearly seeking to gain a central authority and thus to enhance rhetorical credibility and potential social power. Nevertheless, the government still viewed participants in the movement as a group of radicals on the fringe, a group of law violators and misguided foreign-policy protestors in need of government investigation and indictment. When Sanctuary activists were charged with criminal conspiracy, the "mixed blessing" of the prophetic voice was clear.

To be effective public theologians and critics whose concerns affect public policy and opinion, the leaders of the Sanctuary movement needed to overcome what could be an inherently polarizing rhetoric of moral assertion. A rhetoric of transcendent values was inadequate if the moral authority of the speaker to espouse those values was not recognized. A rhetoric of the social periphery had to extend its mantle of moral authority.

Attaining the power and authority to redefine the social condition for the majority without compromising the purity of the ethical critique is the dual challenge faced by any rhetor who would employ a prophetic style or stance. After examining the theoretical implications of this problem—achieving a balance of social power and ethical message purity—this chapter analyzes the attempt of one Sanctuary prophetic rhetor,

Sister Darlene Nicgorski, to overcome that problem and bridge the religious moral fringe with central legal authority through careful manipulations of role and narrative.

THE PROPHETIC PROBLEM

Abraham Heschel strikes at the heart of the prophetic problem when he expresses "surprise . . . that prophets of Israel were tolerated at all by their people. To the patriots, they seemed pernicious; to the pious multitude, blasphemous; to the men in authority, seditious."[5] Now as then, prophets bring an unpopular message, typically outside the expectation of mainstream secular or religious society. One Benedictine, recognizing the difficulty of jarring people out of a comfortable existence into recognition of the need for potentially uncomfortable change, dubs the prophetic role a function of a peripheral, or fringe, minority within the church: "The Church by and large is people by and large, and people by and large do not uncover reality nor locate the latent injustice in their society as long as the goods are being delivered."[6] The larger body of faith may not see the need. Speaking in the time of a generally unrecognized crisis—political threat, social injustice, or moral-religious failure—the task of the prophet "is to nurture, nourish, and evoke a consciousness and perception alternative to the consciousness and perception of the dominant culture around us."[7] The prophetic rhetor transforms our perception of reality, clarifying the exigencies of the age.

The discourse is motivated by perception of "the tragic discrepancy between the faulty creatures we are and the destiny to which we are repeatedly called,"[8] a Burkean awareness of our lapse from perfection. Crisis produces critique,[9] and the renaming of the condition in that critique as a lapse from the covenant, a drawing back from earlier ethical and spiritual concerns, seems an incongruous redefinition to those caught up in the sociopolitical realm who must to some degree accept the new perspective if it is to be empowered.

In *Rules for Radicals*, Saul Alinsky denigrates the moral-ethical justification employed in prophetic social criticism, thus providing a distinction between secular radical discourse and prophetic discourse:

I've been asked . . . why I never talk to a Catholic priest or a Protestant minister or a rabbi in terms of the Judaeo-Christian ethics or the Ten Commandments or the Sermon on the Mount. I never talk in those terms. Instead I approach them on the basis of their own self-interest, the welfare of their Church, even its physical property.

If I approached them in a moralistic way, it would be outside their experience, because Christianity and Judaeo-Christianity are outside the experience of organized religion.[10]

The moral-religious argument base provides the authoritative foundation for a prophetic critique: To abandon that base is to lose prophetic message purity. But Alinsky rejects that base as hopelessly ineffective, lacking the capacity to stir a sedate central power or even a mainstream religious power. Alinsky suggests a prophetic dilemma: Maintain message purity and lose the potential for social power, or abandon that purity in the quest for power. Taking the latter option means renouncing the prophetic role. A legitimate claim to a prophetic role is rooted in the quality of the fit between the current prophetic message and the moral-religious tradition; to ignore or contradict that tradition is to abandon the authority assumed in the prophetic role.[11] The prophet is thus left with the problem of finding a rhetoric that can motivate a central power to move without abandoning the moral-religious power base that justifies and requires that move. Society may indeed be more self-interested than religiously or ethically motivated, but the reform rhetor who is also a prophet does not have the option of simply taking Alinsky's advice. The prophet reformer may argue from audience self-interest, but he or she must also argue from religious ethical norms in order to retain prophetic authority. The prophet seeks a renewed understanding and application of those norms.

Burke terms this quest for understanding, enactment, and empowerment of the disconcerting critique an "evangelizing tendency" that "is interwoven with the whole process of socialization, the tendency to justify one's change by obtaining the corroboration of others."[12] Such evangelization for "a new way of seeing" puts the prophetic rhetor at risk. The incongruous vision, too distinct from central society's construction of reality, may prove seriously unpopular. In the past a prophet might die for a false message or an unacceptable legitimate message; this "obverse" aspect of social "guilt," "divergency from his group," leads the prophetic critic "not merely to endure persecution, but to court it."[13] The leaders of the Sanctuary movement were no exception.

By achieving recognition and support from major religious organizations, Sanctuary leaders had achieved legitimacy and power in the religious community, but the governmental authorities of secular society did not accept religious argument. Sanctuary leaders were put on trial before they gained more social power.

THE PROPHET ON TRIAL

In January 1985, Sanctuary workers were arraigned for trial in Tucson. At the time they stated, "the inter-congregational provision of sanctuary for Central American refugees is simply the practice of our faith as a covenant people. . . . We have signed our release agreements under the conviction that our faith *is* consistent with the laws of our country."[14]

The trial itself, running from October 1985 to May 1986, was "uncommonly contentious,"[15] but not the setting for pure prophetic discourse. When eight of the eleven indictees were convicted, government officials said, "To us it's been an alien smuggling case."[16] Sanctuary workers objected to the judge's decision to exclude any defense based on religious or humanitarian motive. Darlene Nicgorski, a Franciscan nun convicted for her work in the Phoenix Sanctuary community, said it "was not a trial about truth. . . . Judge Earl Carroll was not concerned about justice. The jury was denied the facts."[17] A convicted Presbyterian minister expressed no regret about the decision to have none of the defendants testify: "The Bible says when there is no opportunity to speak for the truth . . . then stand silent."[18] Sanctuary leaders were still proclaiming a radical redefinition of terms that found no place in the law court: "If I am guilty of anything, I am guilty of living the gospel. . . . The government has called this a criminal conspiracy. We call it a conspiracy of love."[19]

The sentencing statements following the Tucson trial were the first opportunity for the Sanctuary workers to tell the court the motivation for their action. A variety of responses was made: nationalistic, legalistic, patriotic, and prophetic. Typically the stances were merged in some way to broaden the potential appeal. Perhaps the most deft statement, most consistent with a prophetic base but carefully interweaving secular authority and shared value appeals, came from Nicgorski. Her fourteen-page single-spaced statement was the longest of those given by the convicted Sanctuary workers in Tucson. In contrast to others focusing on a legal justification for Sanctuary action, Nicgorski spoke as a prophet, employing a rhetoric of transcendent value, stressing a distinction between that which is legal and that which is just. She employed secular authority to extend her credible base of appeal, but her primary authority was religious. Most of her examples came from religious worker witnesses. She offered the biblical prophets as the model for her behavior. Her central thesis was a choice forced by religious belief. More explicitly than any of her fellow workers, Nicgorski depicted the persecuted, prophetic community, inviting others to join.

NARRATIVE: A PROPHETIC MODE

Part of the strength of Sister Darlene Nicgorski's statement lay in her capacity to secure heightened emotion without going to the polarizing language extremes of early Sanctuary discourse. A rich use of emotional imagery is typical of prophetic discourse; eighth-century prophets of the Old Testament employed a heightened style between poetry and plain exposition that biblical critics consider distinctive.[20] Edwin Black mistakenly denounces such exhortative discourse:

"Prophetic utterance avoids the tortuous justifications that moral arguments usually require. Thus the didactic function of the prophetic tone is to simplify discourse."[21] Nicgorski's sentencing statement helps us understand Black's error in judgment. Her use of prophetic discourse is not a simple reliance on assumed authority in order to avoid logical proof, but a careful employment of narrative argument to secure identification and more aptly justify her moral concerns. The narrative paradigm is a ready tool for Nicgorski: Over half of her statement consists of stories.

Her own experience in Central America and her direct, detailed narratives of refugee conditions add credible emotional impact to her argument. She opens "eager to address" the "why" behind her actions. That "why" takes her to personal narrative, which begins with a climax of immediacy and emotional impact:

Five years ago today, July 1, 1981, in Campos Nuevo, Izabel, Guatemala, our pastor Father Tulio Marruzzo was shot twice in the head while returning to his home. . . . At his funeral, Bishop Luis Maria Estrada of Izabel said: "Why was he killed, if he was not involved in anything? Many people have asked me. I would say, yes, he was involved, and he was involved very deeply . . . the gospel of Jesus is bothersome to those who do not wish to see the light."[22]

Between the murder and the funeral, Nicgorski recounts her pastor's service to the poor, his pacifist stance, and the increasing threats against his life. After follows the "planned attack against the church" and Nicgorski's experience "in my own flesh [of] a little bit of what it means to be a refugee. . . . the challenge of LIFE which is the daily experience of Central Americans."[23] In a quick, gripping narrative, Nicgorski establishes her eyewitness credibility and her active religious authority base. Her faith and the observed conditions required her to act: "Our faith would not allow us to abandon the Guatemalan people."[24]

This opening story of Nicgorski's martyred pastor, her own experience as a refugee, and her forced choice serves as a "call" narrative. From a religious prophetic perspective, such narratives, recounting the "call" or commissioning of the prophetic messenger, are used to establish prophetic credibility.[25] From a central secular society perspective, these narratives partake of the descriptive base for narrative rationality, which "offers an account, an understanding, of any instance of human choice and action."[26] In either case the narrative takes her beyond assumed authority into a demonstration of her right to act and speak as acknowledged authority. In the context of the sentencing statement, the narrative allows Nicgorski to present herself as someone who knows and understands the home conditions of the people she stands convicted of assisting. Hence she is a reliable source by secular authority standards.

The narrative also clarifies her role as someone answerable to and directed by a different authority, the "God" she has "proclaimed from childhood."[27] Thus, the first function of narrative within the statement is to establish credibility—following the traditional proof form for prophetic authority and extending that form to provide the story "why" for the secular audience.

Narrative also functions to help Nicgorski's central secular audience comprehend the moral-ethical justification for her participation in the Sanctuary critique. Addressing Judge Carroll and the public, she engages in public moral argument: "oriented toward what ought to be," "founded on ultimate questions—of life and death, of how persons should be defined and treated," aimed at a broad audience untrained in theology and inconsistently trained in the judicial process.[28] Her story provides reasonable and emotional proof for her action and its undergirding morality.

She relates her work in the refugee camps in Mexico, mentioning "the tragic tales" she heard that were "central to the *why* of my response to Guatemalan refugees here. I had every reason to believe the Marias and Joses I later met here in Arizona. They told the same tragic stories." Nicgorski affirms the "fidelity" of the narratives motivating her action: They are "faithful to related accounts we already know and believe."[29] The local stories defining people as refugees gain narrative fidelity from the earlier stories, providing reasons for her action and audience belief. Further credibility is sought for the stories through reference to their recording in "the Diocesan Office of Refugees" and "various human rights organizations";[30] the implication is that what concerned authorities have accepted as reliable the audience should accept. Entwined with religious motivation is a seemingly conscious adaptation to the authority needs of a broader audience.

She furthers the sense of need, discussing the attacks on the refugee camps in Mexico and citing specific cases of attacks on religious workers with a rich narrative detail: "armed men, dressed in civilian clothes and with faces painted, entered the mission. . . . They physically attacked the Brothers. . . . Neither refugees nor those who assist them are safe in Mexico."[31] Nicgorski carefully builds a sense of the inevitability of her work, the critical necessity, as she depicts the horror of the conditions and the pervasive demands of her faith; but although her accounts are emotionally gripping, she carefully casts the narrative as eyewitness testimony and interweaves it expertly with statistics regarding the need. She builds an argument on a prophetic thesis, rooted in religious motivation, with an eye to the logical and emotional needs of a broader audience.

Her stories are aids to identification with the audience, enabling her to bridge the protest gap "by telling stories that do not negate the self-conceptions that people hold of themselves."[32] Nicgorski involves the auditors in her narrative; they are not to remain passive spectators. She details a refugee report of war conditions in El Salvador: "On January 10, 1986, a nightmare began for our people. . . . Some people were captured, others were killed. . . . Our houses were burned, our clothes were burned. . . . The army should fight the guerillas, not unarmed campesinos like us."[33] Nicgorski then turns to stories of conditions facing the refugees in the detention camps in the United States:

During the summer temperatures at the camp reach 110–120 degrees. Detainees are forced to remain outside in the summer heat from 6 A.M. to 6 P.M. even though the barracks have air conditioning. . . . One man in El Centro who had fallen while on kitchen duty could not bend his right elbow and was obviously in great pain. The guards refused to treat him or even give him a pain reliever. . . . A doctor [later] . . . confirmed that the man's arm had been broken.[34]

The enemy is cruel and faceless, clearly not sharing the basic human values of members of central society, even though we have been explicitly told that both aspects of the enemy are supported by the bureaucracy of central society. Story detail echoes newscast images of other wars and other inhumane jails. The builds a sense of narrative fidelity and leads the auditor to share Nicgorski's horror at the conditions she once lived in and now hears of regularly. Nicgorski then asks questions designed to force a supportive response from an audience already confronted with her uncomfortable narrative truths: "What should I have done, knowing about the persecution and random violence in Central America? What else should I have done in the face of INS treatment of Central Americans? . . . What should I have done with all I knew to follow my call as a SSSF to 'defend life'?"[35]

Nicgorski uses story to give a sense of inevitability and appropriateness to the actions for which she stands condemned. To accept her stories is to acknowledge a need, to recognize the prophetic redefinition of the social condition. Through careful application of the narrative paradigm, Nicgorski maintains the purity of her prophetic message, establishes her own role as a credible prophet, and encourages her audience to identify with the value actions required by her message. Use of the narrative paradigm establishes credibility for the prophet and secular social accessibility for prophetic justification. Her story has fidelity with other stories, so the Sanctuary story apparently must be taken seriously.

THE PROPHETIC ROLE AND A TRANSCENDENT MESSAGE

Nicgorski uses narrative to win a hearing and soften the audience for a harsher indictment that is presented as an argument of transcendence.

With a transitional quotation from Justice Oliver Wendell Holmes ("This is a court of law . . . , not a court of justice."[36]), Nicgorski moves us from the attempted forced acknowledgment of the necessity of her action to her thesis: the necessity of justice, a higher order value, and its distinction from mere legality. She offers a forced choice couched in uncompromising language and transcendent values: "The blood is now on the hands of the American people who have a chance to make a difference. . . . When the question is one of life or death there is no room for equivocation or reasonable doubt. We must always side with protection of life."[37] The choice is then explicitly directed to Judge Carroll, who is told he can "make a difference. . . . 'Justice' is in your hands and yours alone. . . . The American people are taught to be obedient to the 'law.' To get beyond the narrow concept of law and to respond to the issues of justice is very difficult."[38]

With this thesis the indictment of governmental bureaucracy, of central social power, is made unavoidably explicit. Nicgorski has earned prophetic credibility with narrative; now she details a prophetic denunciation:

God is justice and asks us to act justly. . . . The situation to which the Hebrew prophets expressed their strongest words was not to so-called "non-believers" but to idolators. . . . The three most potent idols are money, power, and the law. . . . I realize I am treading on delicate ground as I address this court of law, with many officers of the court who hold much power and make their money by debating the law.

My point is that law and governments can lose their God-given authority when they become idols unto themselves. When justice is no longer served corruption has occurred. . . . God usually sends new prophets to call us back to right relations. . . . In practice the prophets, as voices of dissent, are often labeled as unpatriotic.[39]

Her indictment is harshly clear; this is a pure prophetic message. Nicgorski critiques the nature and state of justice in a court of law and so becomes a Burkean prophet critiquing the central social order with its own self-contained "germs" of "dissolution":[40] Law and power have broken covenant with the service of justice, the legal system as a court of justice has dissolved, and the prophet has named its state of corruption. This denunciation of the existing power structure might well be rejected out of hand, but Nicgorski is a canny rhetor with an acute awareness of the prophetic difficulty in maintaining purity and securing power. Having prepared the audience with narratives fostering identification, she now manipulates her role during the ironic interaction of theme and setting.

Burke describes apparently antagonistic roles within a social order: the priest—anything from advertising copywriter to college professor—

who supports the orientation of the class morality; and the prophet, who critiques that decaying orientation.[41] Nicgorski has already defined and justified herself as prophet, and Judge Carroll seems appropriately cast as the priest upholding the orientation of central society by enforcing the law. Nicgorski, however, strengthens her prophetic critique by taking on the priestly role and so seeking to usurp the power preserved in that role.

She begins her usurpation within the context of legality—condemning the "bold dismissal" of "international and humanitarian law in the refoulement or returning by deportation of those fleeing war-torn countries."[42] She compares those who ignore this law to Kurt Waldheim, then "being pursued for war crimes," and asks, "Is it possible then that some in this country who hide behind a righteous interpretation of the law might someday be branded by the world community as public criminals?"[43] Nicgorski treats this "righteous interpretation" as an outdated "piety" for a misguided "orientation";[44] she tells us that those people who believe that the bureaucracy upholds legality are actually ignoring the laws within the social order by which they will one day be judged. She becomes the priest, protecting the social order from criminal action.

As she develops the ironic distinction between justice and legality, Nicgorski raises the value-laden subissue of the suppression of dissent, but focuses on the inadequacy of law and the importance of religion in matters of justice: "laws are not the totality of the life of a religious or morally upright person. . . . Oftentimes the legal system lags behind 'the sense of right and justice' as expressed by the community."[45] Nicgorski's analysis of evolving societal pieties recalls Burke's designation of law as "hardly more than a codification of custom," probably formed "because the customs are ceasing to possess unquestioned authority among the group as a whole."[46] Nicgorski employs the priestly concern for central society orientation, that "expressed by the community," and a similarly priestly role of upholding the Constitution, to support a prophetic focus on justice and social dissent.[47]

Further, Nicgorski depicts her sentencing statement as the enactment of a priestly piety. Judge Carroll is implicitly an inadequate priest in his own temple of "law," for his "restrictions on defenses and . . . narrow instructions to the jury made it impossible to present to the jurors the issues of motivation and justice that I thought were so important to 'the law.' "[48] Nicgorski redresses that lack by telling "why" in her statement; thus she preserves the apparently pious concern for justice that we are told the judge has ignored. She nears the close of her appeal with another labeling of herself as the true priest of the law: "I am not acknowledging wrongdoing but rather the travesty of justice that this court has allowed and fostered."[49]

Through a careful manipulation of roles and interpretation of societal pieties, Nicgorski has attempted to claim the power of the priestly per-spective for her prophetic message. With a thesis based on a transcend-ent value—justice—that is crucial to the setting of her discourse, she furthers her claimed role as a true protector of central society. She cri-tiques as the prophet but attempts to empower that critique by em-ploying priestly pieties.

THE CLOSING INVITATION

The prophet ends with an invitation to her sentencer. She has been called by her "faith . . . to take all steps, not to count the cost." Now he is called:

You and only you, Judge Carroll, can still make a difference. You have the authority and power. Many have prayed for your conversion, hoping you would see the light of truth and life. You by your sentence can add your YES to the God of Justice and Life and therefore your NO to the Caesar who wants to use his money, power, and law to silence the witnesses of its policies in Central America. I do not ask for myself but ask because it will be a symbol of the change of your heart and herald of hope to Central America.[50]

Having clarified her own forced-by-faith choice, having indicted the government for its lapse from justice into corruption, the prophet invites an expression of repentance from a representative of that lapsed central authority. The prophet alludes to narratives of credibility: prophetic supporters who "have prayed" and the "God of Justice" who now, as in the New Testament, opposes the Caesar of law when Caesar falls into idolatry.[51] The prophet calls the priest to an acceptance of prophetic pieties, to a clarified perception of the new, prophetic way of seeing.

The prophetic problem is clear: how to empower a radical message in a mainstream secular society while maintaining a commitment to the moral-ethical purity of the message. Alinsky denied the efficacy of the moral-ethical argument base. Black denounced that moral-ethical base as lacking real argument, being an irrational reliance on emotional im-agery and assumed authority. An application of a narrative paradigm suggests that both of these critics are wrong. The moral constructs of story offer a reasonable base for public moral argument with lay and expert audiences. Story can establish prophetic credibility and aid iden-tification with the values and radical redefinitions within the prophetic vision. A manipulation of the Burkean roles of priest and prophet, using the germs of dissolution within the priestly orientation, can increase the power of the prophetic social infection. The prophet is not trapped by a rhetorical dilemma. The radically redefining prophetic message can have the purity of transcendent moral-ethical values and the power of earned and usurped authority.

NOTES

1. In the slang of the Southwest, a "coyote" is someone who smuggles undocumented people across the border.

2. Paul Burks, "This Is Sanctuary: A Reformation in Our Time," *Sequoia: The Church at Work*, February 1985, p. C.

3. Paul Burks, "This Is Sanctuary: A Reformation in Our Time; Denominational Breakdown of Sanctuaries—4/85," Sanctuary Media Office.

4. "New Mexico Is Proclaimed a Sanctuary for Refugees," *New York Times*, 30 March 1986, national edition, p. A17.

5. Abraham J. Heschel, *The Prophets*, vol. 1 (1962; reprint, New York: Harper and Row, 1969), 19.

6. Thomas Cullinan O.S.B., "The Church as an Agent of Social Change—From the Edge," *Agenda for Prophets: Toward a Political Theology for Britain*, eds. Rex Ambler and David Haslam (London: Bowerdean Press, 1980), 136–7.

7. Walter Brueggemann, *The Prophetic Imagination* (1978; reprint, Philadelphia: Fortress Press, 1982), 13.

8. Philip Wheelwright, *The Burning Fountain: A Study in the Language of Symbolism* (Bloomington, Ind.: Indiana University Press, 1954), 14–15.

9. Robert Carroll, *When Prophecy Failed* (London: SCM Press Ltd., 1979), 9.

10. Saul Alinsky, *Rules for Radicals: A Practical Primer for Realistic Radicals* (New York: Random House, 1971), 88.

11. Deut. 13: 1–3b; W. Sibley Towner, "On Calling People 'Prophets' in 1970," *Interpretation* 24 (October 1970): 497.

12. Kenneth Burke, *Permanence and Change: An Anatomy of Purpose*, 3d ed. (Berkeley: University of California Press, 1984), 154.

13. Ibid.

14. Jim Corbett, *Borders and Crossings*, vol. 1, *Some Sanctuary Papers, 1981–1986*, June 1986 ed. (Tucson: Tucson Refugee Support Group, 1986), 140.

15. Daniel R. Browning, "8 Sanctuary Defendants Found Guilty; 3 Acquitted," *Arizona Daily Star*, 2 May 1986, final edition, p. A2.

16. Richard Charnock, "U.S. Officials Laud Sanctuary Verdicts as 'Good Result,' " *The Arizona Republic*, 2 May 1986, p. A4.

17. Gene Varn, "8 Convicted in Sanctuary Trial," *The Arizona Republic*, 2 May 1986, pp. A1, 4.

18. Carmen Duarte and Jane Erickson, "Defendants Vow to Resume Work with Movement," *The Arizona Daily Star*, 2 May 1986, final edition, p. A7.

19. Browning, "8 Sanctuary Defendants Found Guilty," p. A2, quoting Darlene Nicgorski.

20. Chaim Rabin, "Discourse Analysis and the Dating of Deuteronomy," *Interpreting the Hebrew Bible: Essays in Honour of E.I.J. Rosenthal*, eds. John A. Emerton and Stefan C. Reid (New York: Cambridge University Press, 1982), 176–7; Francis I. Anderson and David Noel Freedman, *Hosea: A New Translation with Introduction and Commentary*, vol. 24 of *The Anchor Bible*, eds. William Foxwell Albright and David Noel Freedman (Garden City, N.Y.: Doubleday, 1980), 62, 132.

21. Edwin Black, *Rhetorical Criticism: A Study in Method* (Madison: University of Wisconsin Press, 1965), 144.

22. The text of Darlene Nicgorski's sentencing statement was obtained in photocopied typescript from the office of the Tucson Ecumenical Council Task Force on Central America. Darlene Nicgorski SSSF, Statement before sentencing to the court and public, Federal Court, Tucson, Arizona, July 1, 1986, before Judge Earl H. Carroll, p. 1.

23. Nicgorski, Statement before sentencing, 1–2.

24. Ibid., 2.

25. Hans Walter Wolff, "Prophecy from the Eighth through the Fifth Century," *Interpretation* 32 (January 1978): 20–21.

26. Walter R. Fisher, *Human Communication as Narration: Toward a Philosophy of Reason, Value, and Action* (Columbia, S.C.: University of South Carolina Press, 1987), 66.

27. Nicgorski, Statement before sentencing, 2.

28. Fisher, *Human Communication as Narration*, 71–72.

29. Ibid., 194.

30. Nicgorski, Statement before sentencing, 3.

31. Ibid., 3–4.

32. Fisher, *Human Communication as Narration*, 75.

33. Nicgorski, Statement before sentencing, 5.

34. Ibid., 7–8.

35. Ibid., 8–9.

36. Ibid., 9.

37. Ibid., 10.

38. Ibid.

39. Ibid., 10–11.

40. Burke, *Permanence and Change*, 169.

41. Ibid., 179.

42. Nicgorski, Statement before sentencing, p. 9.

43. Ibid.

44. Burke, *Permanence and Change*, 76.

45. Nicgorski, Statement before sentencing, 10.

46. Burke, *Permanence and Change*, 186.

47. Nicgorski, Statement before sentencing, 11.

48. Ibid., 10.

49. Ibid., 14.

50. Ibid.

51. Ibid., 11; Matt. 22: 15–22, Mark 12: 13–17, Luke 20: 20–26.

Chapter Seven

Chicano Utopianism in the Southwest

Richard J. Jensen and John C. Hammerback

To some, a utopia is an idealized location with perfect social, political, and economic systems—a place where people exist in nearly perfect surroundings. Individuals who believe in utopia may be able to imagine a world in which society is constantly being improved.

This idealized image is difficult, if not impossible, for many members of American society to imagine. Those individuals subsist in less than perfect surroundings. To them, a utopia may simply be the achievement of the normal life-style already achieved by most Americans.

In the 1960s leaders of minority groups in the United States set out to improve the social, political, and economic systems in their communities. In many respects, their goals were utopian because they called for a dramatic alteration in society, a change that would raise the poor and downtrodden to a status equal to that of the rest of society. In order to improve the living conditions of people in their communities, these leaders needed the power necessary to convince society to accept their proposed changes.

In his book, *Power and Communication*, Andrew King argues that, "since power is enacted, it is a relationship that is both activated and sustained by human communication. Power is a communication act. It begins with a strategic message which is formulated by a person (or group) and is addressed to an audience. The impact of the message upon the behavior of the audience has consequences that can be judged effective or ineffective, good or evil, artistic or clumsy."[1]

If King is correct in saying that power can be created by communication, then rhetorical scholars should attempt to understand all forms of communication in order to learn how power might be achieved through a variety of forms of communication. Unfortunately, there are types of discourse that have not yet been studied by rhetorical scholars. For example, in the past scholars of social movements have focused on speeches and nonverbal tactics such as clothing, gestures, dress, esoteric symbols, marches, rallies, and sit-ins, but have focused little attention on the use of written messages such as plans, proclamations, and manifestos. These documents are issued by groups as a means of achieving internal unity and attracting members. They are, therefore, vehicles for building power.

These written documents help create a sense of identity and pride in the movement. As Conrad states, "as a movement develops, its rhetors consolidate and express the beliefs, feelings, and frustrations of its members. Public expressions of the resulting ideology both unify the movement and separate it from other parts of a society."[2] King argues that a sense of power can come through such a positive identity: "Group identity is made up of common prejudices and shared images of the world and of the group's role in it. In addition, they may share a common language or argot, and distinctive rituals and procedures. . . . The degree of group power depends upon the homogeneity of common images and the intensity of attachment to consensual beliefs."[3]

Those beliefs are often expressed by groups in the form of a plan, manifesto, proclamation, or declaration. In issuing such papers, a group of like-minded individuals gathers to produce a document expressing the essence of their movement's beliefs and goals. That paper sets forth the movement's ideology, an "elaboration of rationalizations and stereotypes into a consistent pattern." The document, according to Stewart, Smith, and Denton, "serves three important functions: (1) to identify the problem, (2) to identify the devils, scapegoats, and faulty principles that have caused and maintained the problem, and (3) to prescribe the solution, and the gods, principles, and procedures that will bring it about."[4]

Such writings may articulate what members of the movement think or believe. By putting words on paper, those thoughts or beliefs are legitimized. The writings also are an attempt to awaken individuals who might be open to the message as well as to perhaps convince individuals outside the group to listen.[5]

Support can be created outside the movement if the ideology seems logical and "consistent with verifiable evidence." These statements "must provide definition of that which is ambiguous in the social situation, give structure to anxiety and a tangible target for hostility, foster in-group feelings, and articulate wish-fulfillment beliefs about the power to succeed."[6] Ultimately, such ideological statements are important "in forging a political identity."[7]

Although the ideology may serve as a means to achieve specific goals,

"In movements as in politics generally, principles must be adjusted to pragmatic exigencies. Thus formal statements of ideology—such as those contained in manifestos, declarations, bills of rights, and constitutions—are often made sufficiently vague, ambiguous, and mysterious to allow for a variety of interpretations." These "statements of ideologies are used to mold and reinforce the views of constituents, to influence outsiders, and to protect the movement against attack." The messages serve rhetorical functions by "providing rationales for movements' goals and tactics; by offering 'correct' and understandable interpretations of past, present, and future; by delegitimizing competing ideologies; by offering defenses against counterarguments; and by providing 'immunizing' rationales for potentially embarrassing situations."[8] Robert Heath agrees when he declares that such documents "reflect the ultimate motives of the people and establish these motives as norms. These documents provide the basis for enforcing these norms."[9]

Although plans, manifestos, and declarations may seem to be vague, the process of writing them may actually provide clarity to ideas. The document may become "clearer on certain fundamental issues than its own authors were."[10]

Simons, Mechling, and Schreier outline how some "statements of ideology are highly elaborated . . . others are simplified for mass consumption . . . some are reduced to catchwords in leaflets, posters, chants, and songs. . . . Full blown ideological statements imply an epistemology, an ethic, and a theory of human nature." Furthermore, they contain "a revisionist history, a morally toned interpretation of present conditions, and an account of the future in which the movement is said to play an important role."[11]

King points out that "a movement gives its constituents a language in which its new experiences may be expressed. This is the so-called party line, the cluster of cliches that distress outsiders who may partly agree with the beliefs of the movement but are repelled by the threadbare slogans and tired shibboleths in which these beliefs are couched." According to King, the language in these written documents have several functions: "1. They provide ready answers for outsiders and members of the established order who may oppose the movement; 2. They provide a cognitive structure in which further change may take place; 3. They provide a codification for beliefs and experiences that were hitherto inaccessible or ineffable; 4. They give the individual a sense of personal power and control over his or her own world (despite the deep fatalism in which many movements speak)."[12] Often the power of the language is based on the ability to control definitions. The written documents help build group power through possession of "the power to define."[13]

Many recent movements, particularly minority movements, have issued such plans, proclamations, and manifestos as an integral part of their rhetoric. One particular group that used such documents extensively was the Chicano movement of the 1960s and early 1970s. As one leader, Rodolfo "Corky" Gonzales, states, "Plans and manifestos provide the ideology, philosophy, and direction for the forward march of the Chicano Movement."[14]

Perhaps a reason for the use of such documents by Chicanos in the United States is the tradition of issuing such plans before any major movement in Mexico. For example, the Plan of Delano, which explains why California farm workers made a pilgrimage to the state capital in Sacramento, was "inspired by [Emiliano] Zapata's Plan de Ayala."[15]

The person who is responsible for producing the written ideology "may be seen as the most knowledgeable authority on the doctrine, or may be seen as nearest in spirit to the doctrine. . . . The leader with the gift of prophecy elaborates, justifies, and explains the movement's values, myths, and beliefs. The prophet knows the 'truth' and sets a moral tone for the movement."[16]

This chapter illustrates the power of such plans in the Chicano movement by focusing on two plans inspired by two different prophets, Rodolfo "Corky" Gonzales and Cesar Chavez.

GONZALES AS PROPHET

Gonzales was born in Denver on June 18, 1928. As the son of migrant workers, he labored in the fields in the summer then returned to Denver in the winter, so he was able to appreciate both rural and urban life. Because of his itinerant life, he received little formal education, but his teachers taught him "how to forget Spanish, to forget my heritage, to forget who I was."[17]

As a teenager he became a boxer as a vehicle to improve his life. He became a national amateur champion and a successful professional. After retiring in 1955, he was able to use his fame to become successful in politics and business. By the early 1960s he had risen to a prominent position in the Democratic party. He resigned from the party in the mid-1960s because he felt the party was using him and was not helping improve the lives of Mexican-Americans.

In 1965 Gonzales founded an organization called the Crusade for Justice in order to help meet the educational, legal, medical, and financial needs of Chicanos in the Denver barrio. The Crusade proposed reforming the legal system, better housing for Chicanos, relevant education, and better employment opportunities.[18]

Gonzales became a powerful spokesman for his people. His rhetoric attempted to raise the awareness of people by showing how they were oppressed, outlining how the Anglo power structure used Chicanos by forcing them into the military, detailing how Chicanos were forced into second-class citizenship by the educational system and the legal system, outlining how the Catholic church attempted to needlessly dominate their lives, and showing how they were negatively stereotyped by the media and Anglo history. He believed that in order to overcome these problems, Chicanos had to unite to oppose Anglos.

By 1968 Gonzales had attracted significant support in the Chicano community. In that year at the Poor People's March on Washington, D.C., he issued his "plan of the Barrio," which called for awareness of Chicano culture, improved education, and Chicano businesses. That proclamation showed his faith in the power of such statements. Similar proclamations became a standard part of his rhetoric.[19]

El Plan de Aztlan

In 1969 Gonzales hosted the first national Chicano Youth Conference. He explained the reason for the gathering: "I thought about all the young people who are confused and who don't want to identify with these old politicos, those old figureheads. They don't want to identify with the same old answers. They want to get into something. I talked to a lot of these young people, and they decided they needed a conference. They wanted to come to Denver. So we decided to hold it here." The conference resulted in the publication of "El Plan de Aztlan," a document "which would serve as a plan or ideology to unite other Mexican Americans at various conferences in years to come" and which clearly demonstrated "the growing concept of ethnic nationalism and a self-determination among Chicanos in the entire Southwest."[20] Gonzales tied his fortunes to the young because he saw the Chicano movement as "the biggest, strongest and most powerful movement in the nation."[21] The young people in the movement needed "guidance and guidelines."[22]

These plans, such as El Plan de Aztlan, provide a "plan of survival, a plan of life, a plan of freedom."[23] The Plan of Aztlan has been called "a virtual Declaration of Independence of the brown people of America."[24] The plan attempted to resurrect the name of Aztlan, "the ancient nation of the Aztecs." The young people who gathered in Denver in 1969 to write the document attempted "to revive the spirit of that defeated nation."[25] The plan's basic goals were "to build Chicano strength and unity and to win CHICANO CONTROL OF COMMUNITIES."[26] In order for it to achieve its goals, the plan "is not meant to be a rigid blueprint with every line drawn in. It is alive, growing, and changing all the time."[27]

The plan is composed of three sections: a justification for writing such a document, a program, and a final appeal for action. The opening section provides a justification for the writing of the document:

In the spirit of a new people that is conscious not only of its proud historical heritage but also of the brutal Gringo invasion of our territories, WE, the Chicano inhabitants and civilizers of the northern land of Aztlan from whence came our forefathers, reclaiming the land of their birth and consecrating the determination of our people of the sun, DECLARE that the call of our blood is our power, our responsibility, and our inevitable destiny.[28]

That opening paragraph illustrates how such documents can use god and devil terms in order to polarize young Mexican-Americans against the Anglo establishment. The devil terms label the Anglo as an oppressor "who exploits our riches and destroys our culture." The labeling of Anglos as "brutal gringos" and "Gabacho" gives young Chicanos reason to reject Anglo values and actions. Such language effectively polarizes the community in opposition to Anglos.[29]

On the other hand, authors of the plan try to emphasize positive aspects of the Chicano culture, such as its proud history, its ties to the land, its sense of community, and its culture. God terms include "Aztlan," the Chicano homeland, "bronze," a reference to pride in color and race, "Chicano," "brotherhood," and "mestizo." Such terms help create pride and unity among young Chicanos.

The most prominent word is "Aztlan," the term for a Chicano homeland. Although Aztlan is never clearly defined by Chicanos, it is an expression with a variety of possible meanings. Some historians say that Aztlan may be the land from which Aztecs began the long wandering the finally led to Mexico City. Others say that Aztlan is physically located in northern Mexico, and still others say that it is the American Southwest. At any rate, "Aztlan may be a myth or it may be a real place, but it always stands for the idea of homeland, of freedom from that which we are not, or reclaiming what we are." To Gonzales, "Aztlan is a spiritual call for self-determination. It has become a program to inspire and to commit all Chicanos to start to develop their own leadership, make their own decisions, take over their own communities and liberate the institutions which direct and control our lives."[30]

Once Aztlan is created, there will be a sense of nationalism among Chicanos. The plan calls for the creation of an independent nation. This concept of nationalism is difficult to describe. Gonzales proclaims that nationalism is the key idea to raising a consciousness among Chicanos: "Nationalism comes first out of the family, then into tribalism, and then into alliances that are necessary to lift the burden of all suppressed humanity." Nationalism becomes a tool to organize and a vehicle whereby people can "analyze and recognize themselves."[31]

Once the reasons for the plan are outlined, a specific program is offered. That program is based on nationalism "as the key or common denominator for mass mobilization and organization." By adopting the idea of nationalism, Chicanos can declare their independence from the oppression, exploitation, and racism practiced by Anglos. After independence, the people can struggle to control their own lands, economy, culture, and political life. According to the plan, "Nationalism as the key to organization transcends all religious, political, class, and economic factions or boundaries. Nationalism is the common denominator that all members of La Raza [the race] can agree upon."[32] The plan then outlines seven organizational goals: unity, economy, education, institutions, self-defense, cultural values, and political liberation.

In his rhetoric, Gonzales often spoke of how Anglos had successfully divided Chicanos by forcing them to become a part of the Anglo establishment. He believed that Chicanos could become successful in an Anglo world only by rejecting other Chicanos and their way of life. He called for unity to oppress this clever tactic used by Anglos. The plan reflects this view when it calls for "the poor, the middle class, the professional" to all be committed to the liberation of Chicanos.[33]

Gonzales believed that Anglos had forced Chicanos to accept their definitions of success, thus forcing young Chicanos to become carbon copies of Anglos. He believed that one way to counter this trend was for Chicanos to begin making their own choices: "we will start making our own decisions. We will make our own mistakes. And if they're wrong, we'll suffer from them."[34] This Anglo control could be broken, according to the plan, by Chicanos assuming "economic control of our lives and our communities . . . by driving the exploiter out of our communities, our pueblos, and our lands by controlling and developing our own talents, sweat, and resources." People must reject the materialism of the dominant culture and cooperate in building a stronger, fairer Chicano community.

Another way Anglos had destroyed Chicano self-identity and pride was through an educational system that forced young Chicanos to reject their language and culture. To counter this problem, Gonzales and the young Chicanos who wrote the plan, called for education that is relevant to the people, an education that teaches Chicano history, culture, and contributions to American society as well as community control over the schools.[35]

Gonzales believed that other institutions beyond the schools served Chicanos badly. Too often the institutions that ministered to the Chicano community were Anglo-dominated, so they imposed Anglo values on Chicanos. Gonzales believed that organizations like the Crusade for Justice could provide the assistance Chicanos needed as well as unify Chicanos, train leaders, and control mass actions in the community. Reflecting this belief, the plan called for institutions that "belong to the people."[36]

Once Chicanos gained control over the educational system and other institutions, they could move to create a better life for the community. In the plan, the young activists called for self-defense in the community based "on the combined strength of the people." Once the community learned to run its own businesses and institutions, as well as defend itself, the community would be liberated from the power of the Gringo.[37]

Once the people were united, their cultural values would "serve as a powerful weapon to defeat the Gringo dollar value system and encourage the process of love and brotherhood." One way to encourage these values was to make sure that Chicano "writers, poets, musicians, and artists produce literature and art that is appealing to our people and relates to our revolutionary culture." Gonzales typified this call. He produced the most influential poem of the Chicano movement, "Yo Soy Joaquin" (I Am Joaquin). That poem is a powerful call for action by his people. Rodolfo Acuna calls it "the most inspiring piece of movement literature written in the 1960s. Its impact was immeasurable."[38]

One further sign of rejection of the Anglo establishment was the call for political liberation through independent action. In comparing the two-party system as one "animal with two heads that [feeds] from the same trough," the young activists called for united Chicano political action outside the two-party system. Several years earlier, Gonzales had used the same image when he resigned from the Democratic party. Within a few years he and other Chicano leaders would organize an independent Chicano party, La Raza Unida (The United Race) in an attempt to achieve power in the community.[39]

The program outlined by Gonzales in his rhetoric and by his young followers in El Plan de Aztlan was an ambitious one. The final section of the plan called for specific actions to implement the program. They called for the "awareness and distribution" of the plan at "every meeting, demonstration, confrontation, courthouse, institution, administration, church, school, tree, building, car, and every place of human existence." Therefore, the plan provided a concrete point of departure for discussions among Chicanos in future years.[40]

In order to gain control of their communities, they called for "a national walkout of all Chicanos of all colleges and schools" each year on September 16, the birth date of Mexican independence. These walkouts would eventually force the schools to serve the needs of the community. Furthermore, they called for "self-defense against the occupying forces of the oppressors" (Anglos), "community nationalization and organization of all Chicanos," an economic program that drives the "exploiter out of our community," "a welding together of our people's combined resources to control their own production through cooperative effort," and "creation of an independent local, regional, land national political party."[41]

The plan concludes with a call for the creation of the Nation of Aztlan: "A nation autonomous and free—culturally, socially, economically, and politically—will make its own decisions on the usage of our lands, the

taxation of our goods, the utilization of our bodies for war, the determination of justice (reward and punishment), and the profit of our sweat.
El Plan de Aztlan is the plan of liberation!"[42]

The document provides a powerful tool for the building of pride based
on race, culture, family, and a rich heritage. It defines the community's
enemies, outlines the problems in the community, and provides solu-
tions to problems. The document provides individuals a symbol around
which they can unite. It also provides a world view for young Chicanos
in their quest for power.

John R. Chavez in his book *The Lost Land* described the Plan of Aztlan
as "a document that declared the spiritual independence of the Chicano
Southwest from the United States." To Chavez it was paradoxical that
"this sentiment was expressed in a city [Denver] never legally within
the confines of Mexico. . . . This declaration from Denver signified the
desire of a minority group for independence from the colonialism that
had subjected its native land and that continued to affect the individuals
of the minority no matter where they resided in the United States."[43]

Plan of Delano

Like the Plan of Aztlan, the Plan of Delano is a reflection of the ideas
of a Chicano prophet, Cesar Chavez. Chavez was born in 1927. For the
first ten years of his life he lived on the family farm near Yuma, Arizona.
Unfortunately, the family lost the farm during the Depression of the
1930s and they were forced to become migrant workers. Like Gonzales,
Chavez received little formal education because of his family's life-style.

In the 1950s he became active in the Community Services Organization
(CSO) in San Jose. Chavez's work with the CSO taught him valuable
skills as an organizer. After ten years with the CSO he realized that
there needed to be more focus on improving the lives of Mexican-
Americans, so he resigned from the CSO and moved to Delano, California, to organize a labor union for farm workers, the United Farm
Workers (UFW).

In order to build the union, Chavez had to spread the message to
farm workers and to potential supporters. He adopted a variety of rhetorical tactics including speaking tours, public letters, articles, and television appearances in addition to face-to-face meetings with workers in
their homes and in the fields.

Chavez was a devout Catholic. His religion served as a model for his
life and ideas. He believed that it was his mission to organize workers
into a powerful organization that would improve their lives. His rhetoric
reflected the moral nature of his protest: "we have seized upon every
tactic and strategy consistent with the morality of our cause to expose
. . . injustice and thus to heighten the sensitivity of the American con-

science.''[44] His Plan of Delano, like all his rhetoric, focuses on this moral view of the world.

The Plan of Delano has been described as a "Mexican-style proclamation stating the discontent of farm workers and the aim of Chavez and his movement.''[45] In March of 1966, Chavez issued the plan during a 250-mile pilgrimage from Delano to the state capitol in Sacramento as his blueprint "for the liberation of farm workers in the United States of North America, affiliated with the unique and true union of farm workers . . . seeking social justice in farm labor with those reforms they believe necessary for their well-being as workers." Because farm workers must be granted their "basic God-given rights as human beings," Chavez asked for support from all groups, particularly the Catholic church. He announced that all farm workers "across the country—the Mexicans, Filipinos, blacks and poor whites; the Puerto Ricans, the Japanese, the Indians, the Portuguese and the Arabs" would unite in a nonviolent movement to improve the lives of farm workers.[46]

The plan, like the Plan of Aztlan, begins with a description of the reasons for the pilgrimage being undertaken:

We, the undersigned, gathered in Pilgrimage to the capital of the State in Sacramento, in penance for all the failings of Farm Workers as free and sovereign men, do solemnly declare before the civilized world which judges our actions, and before the nation to which we belong, the propositions we have formulated to end the injustice that oppresses us.[47]

The pilgrimage is symbolically important because it passes through all the towns where Mexican-Americans had worked and suffered for generations: "Our sweat and our blood have fallen on this land to make other men rich." The pilgrimage also symbolized the long "historical road we have travelled in this valley alone, and the long road we have yet to travel . . . in order to bring about the Revolution we need.''[48]

The introduction focuses on the suffering of the farm workers and how that suffering has only benefited others. It is a call for justice in a region that has given little justice to workers in the past.

Once the reasons for the march were detailed, its six propositions were outlined. The first proposition outlines how the pilgrimage is the beginning of a social movement to "seek our basic, God-given rights as human beings." The movement is not afraid to suffer in order to survive and fight for justice.[49] Even though the workers had suffered they refused to use violence to fight their oppressors.

The second proposition calls for support from all political groups and protection from the government. The plan outlines how Mexican-Americans "have been treated like the lowest of the low. Our wages and working conditions have been determined from above." The farm workers no longer wanted words from politicians but actions in support of promises. In the past farm workers had remained silent, but now they were uniting and creating leaders to improve their lives. The action can come only from power. "WE SHALL BE HEARD."[50]

As a practicing Catholic, Chavez desired support from the church. The United Farm Workers used symbols of the church such as the Virgin of Guadalupe and crosses. They called upon the church to live up to its own ideals in protecting workers from exploitation. They used the words of Pope Leo XII for inspiration: "Everyone's first duty is to protect the workers from the greed of speculators who use human beings as instruments to provide themselves with money. It is neither just nor human to oppress men with excessive work to the point where their minds become enfeebled and their bodies worn out." They concluded that "GOD SHALL NOT ABANDON US."[51]

Because they were already suffering, the workers were not afraid to suffer more in order to win. They suffered on the job, endured the injustices of the system, and were used by greedy people: "They have imposed hungers on us, and now we hunger for justice. We draw our strength from the very despair in which we have been forced to live. WE SHALL ENDURE."[52]

In order to overcome the suffering, the workers vowed to unite: "The strength of the poor is in union." They were aware that the ranchers wanted to keep them divided and weak, but they realized the need for unity and organization. Power can come through organization and the right to bargain collectively: "We must use the only strength we have, the force of our numbers. The ranchers are few; we are many. UNITED WE SHALL STAND."[53]

Once united the workers planned to use the strike as a weapon to achieve their goals. As "sons of the Mexican Revolution," they sought a nonviolent revolution to overcome their treatment on "those ranches where we are not treated with the respect we deserve as working men, where our rights as free and sovereign men are not recognized." Like other workers, they wanted "a just wage, better working conditions, a decent future for our children." In order to achieve their goals they would work until they won. "WE SHALL OVERCOME."[54]

The plan expressed the hope that the poor would be treated with respect. "To those who oppose us, be they ranchers, police, politicians, or speculators, we say that we are going to continue fighting until we die or we win."[55]

Finally, the plan is a call to action:

Wherever there are Mexican people, wherever there are farm workers, our movement is spreading like flames across a dry plain. Our Pilgrimage is the match that will light our cause for all farm workers to see what is happening here so that they may do as we have done.

The time has come for the liberation of the poor farm worker. History is on our side. May the strike go on! Viva la causa![56]

The Plan of Delano, like the Plan of Aztlan, presents a powerful call for unity among Mexican-Americans. The poor of the nation could easily recognize their own plight in the problems of farm workers. Chavez defines the problems of the poor, their reasons for forming an organization, and the goals of the organization. He provides a powerful argument for change.

CONCLUSION

The use of plans by Chicano activists is significant in several respects:

1. The issuing of plans by activists in the United States is a fascinating adaptation and continuation of a similar practice in Mexico. Since the Mexican War, when the United States conquered the inhabitants of the American Southwest, activists in the Mexican-American community have issued such plans. The long-term use of such documents illustrates how the use of such plans has become an accepted form of spreading messages in the Chicano community.

2. The focus and tone of a plan are reflections of the person most closely linked to its issuing. The Plan of Aztlan reflects the fiery beliefs and attitudes of the person who inspired its publication, Rodolfo "Corky" Gonzales; the Plan of Delano mirrors the nonviolent, moderate stance of Cesar Chavez. Plans, therefore, tell rhetorical scholars a great deal about the beliefs and feelings of the individuals who inspire significant movements.

3. These documents detail why the movement began, the concerns of its members, and specific proposals to solve these problems. A scholar of social movements, therefore, can gain an overview of a movement in a brief, coherent form.

4. Like most pieces of rhetoric, some of the documents are more interesting and artistic than others. By comparing the numerous plans available, a critic could reach conclusions about the effectiveness of documents as well as their artistic value.

5. The documents' goals are to build power in the movement through the creation of unity in the Chicano community. The movement has a document that outlines commonalities around which the movement can organize. As King points out, such unity leads to power.

The documents also outline the means a particular movement will use to gain power, whether those means be violent or nonviolent, militant or moderate, within our outside the system.

The study of such documents will tell rhetorical scholars a great deal about how groups attempt to gain power in our society as well as fill a gap in rhetorical scholarship. Such studies are one more means of broadening and refining studies of the rhetoric of social movements.

NOTES

1. Andrew King, *Power and Communication* (Prospect Heights, Ill.: Waveland Press, 1987), 4.

2. Charles Conrad, "The Transformation of the 'Old Feminist' Movement," *Quarterly Journal of Speech* 67 (1981): 285.

3. King, *Power and Communication*, 49.

4. Charles J. Stewart, Craig Allen Smith, and Robert E. Denton, Jr., *Persuasion and Social Movements*, 2d ed. (Prospect Heights, Ill.: Waveland Press, 1989), 24.

5. Milton Viorst, *Fire in the Streets* (New York: Simon and Schuster, 1979), 195; Tom Hayden, *Reunion* (New York: Random House, 1988), 74.

6. Herbert W. Simons, "Requirements, Problems, and Strategies: A Theory of Persuasion for Social Movements," *Quarterly Journal of Speech* 56 (1970): 5–6.

7. Maurice Isserman, *If I Had a Hammer?* (New York: Simon and Schuster, 1987), 43.

8. Herbert W. Simons, Elizabeth W. Mechling, and Howard N. Schreier, "The Functions of Human Communication in Mobilizing Action from the Bottom Up: The Rhetoric of Social Movement," in *Handbook of Rhetorical and Communication Theory*, eds. Carroll C. Arnold and John Waite Bowers (Boston: Allyn and Bacon, 1984), 797.

9. Robert L. Heath, "Dialectical Confrontation: A Strategy of Black Radicalism," *Central States Speech Journal* 24 (Fall 1973): 173.

10. Paul Berman, "Don't Follow Leaders," *The New Republic*, 10 and 17 August 1978, 34.

11. Simons et al., *Functions of Human Communication*, 797.

12. King, *Power and Communication*, 23–24.

13. Ibid., 68.

14. Rodolfo Gonzales, *I Am Jaoquin* (New York: Bantam Books, 1972), 118.

15. Elizabeth Sutherland Martinez and Enriqueta Longeaux y Vasquez, *Viva La Raza!* (Garden City, N.Y.: Doubleday, 1974), 196–7.

16. Stewart et al., *Persuasion*, 41.

17. Christine Marin, *A Spokesman of the Mexican-American Movement: Rodolfo "Corky" Gonzales and the Fight for Chicano Liberation. 1966–1972* (San Francisco: R and E Research Associates, 1977), 2.

18. Richard J. Jensen and John C. Hammerback, "No Revolutions Without Poets: The Rhetoric of Rodolfo "Corky" Gonzales," *Western Journal of Speech Communication* 46 (Winter 1982): 75.

19. Ibid.

20. Marin, *Spokesman of Mexican American Movement*, 12, 15.

21. Gonzales, quoted in Carlos Larralde, *Mexican-American Movements and Leaders* (Los Alamitos, Calif.: Hwong Publishing Company, 1976), 201.

22. "Colo. Raza Unida spokesman: The People are starting to move collectively," *The Militant*, 4 December 1970, 10.

23. Martinez and Vasquez, *Viva la Raza!*, 258.

24. Jay Schulman, Aubrey Shatter, and Rosalie Ehrlich, eds., *Pride and Protest: Ethnic Roots in America* (New York: Dell Publishing Co., 1977), 138.

25. Stan Steiner, *La Raza: The Mexican Americans* (New York: Harper and Row, 1969), 391.

26. Martinez and Vasquez, *Viva La Raza!*, 252–53.

27. Martinez and Vasquez, *Viva La Raza!*, 256.

28. Marin, *Spokesman of Mexican American Movement*, 35.

29. El Plan de Aztlan, in Marin, *Spokesman of Mexican American Movement*, 36.

30. Jensen and Hammerback, *No Revolutions*, 85–86.

31. Ibid., 85.

32. El Plan de Aztlan, in Marin *Spokesman of Mexican American Movement*, 36.

33. Ibid.

34. Robert Tice, quoted in Jensen and Hammerback, *No Revolutions*, 75.

35. El Plan de Aztlan, in Marin, *Spokesman of Mexican American Movement*, 36.

36. Ibid.

37. Ibid.

38. Ibid.; Rodolfo Acuna, quoted in Jensen and Hammerback, *No Revolutions*, 76.

39. El Plan de Aztlan, in Marin, *Spokesman of Mexican American, Movement*, 37.

40. Ibid.

41. Ibid.

42. Marin, *Spokesman of Mexican American Movement*, 37.

43. John R. Chavez, *The Lost Land* (Albuquerque: University of New Mexico Press, 1984), 136.

44. John C. Hammerback and Richard J. Jensen, "A Revolution of Heart and Mind: Cesar Chavez's Rhetorical Crusade," *Journal of the West* 27 (April 1988): 71.

45. Chavez, *Lost Land*, 142–3.

46. Cesar Chavez, quoted in John C. Hammerback and Richard J. Jensen, "Cesar Estrada Chavez, Labor Leader and Minority Activist," in *American Orators of the Twentieth Century*, eds. Bernard K. Duffy and Halford R. Ryan (Westport, Conn.: Greenwood Press, 1987), 56–57.

47. "The Plan de Delano," in *Aztlan*, ed. Luis Valdez and Stan Steiner (New York: Vintage Books, 1972), 197.

48. The Plan de Delano, 198.

49. Ibid.

50. Ibid.

51. Ibid., 199.

52. Ibid., 199–200.

55. Ibid., 200.

54. Ibid., 200–201.

55. Ibid., 201.

56. Ibid.

Chapter Eight

The Goddess of Democracy as Icon in the Chinese Student Revolt

Kenneth C. Petress

For several days in May and June 1989, a crude, but majestic handcrafted statue, vaguely resembling New York Harbor's Statue of Liberty, stood prominently in Tiananmen Square. Chinese student demonstrators named it the "Goddess of Democracy." This statue was an icon symbolizing the student demonstrators' idealism, courage, frustration, and yearning in search of basic freedoms. It was also an icon representing "counterrevolutionary thought," anarchy, foreign intervention invitations, and a growing national disrespect by the younger generation in China's rulers' eyes. Officials also saw the statue as symbolically threatening to their position and authority. The American people, through the vivid interpretations of media personalities, were presented with still another view: that Chinese demonstrators yearned to see China become more like the United States. Such was not the case in most demonstrators' minds, but that image seemed to persist in the U.S. media (extensive TV coverage by ABC, CBS, and CNN).

This chapter argues that the Goddess of Democracy (GD) held three audiences, with three divergent interpretations, captive with its presence and symbolism. These three audiences were (1) student demonstrators and their on-site sympathizers; (2) Chinese government leaders; and (3) the international media (predominantly U.S.). The statue was a rhetorical symbol that took on divergent interpretations and that, some have argued, precipitated the bloody confrontation commonly known as the Tiananmen Square massacre. For analysis, Lloyd Bitzer's rhetorical situation method has been chosen.[1] Bitzer's framework focuses upon rhetoric being a fitting response to an exigence, aimed at a given audience, and operating under certain constraints. The GD was such a rhetorical act; it was a statement made by student demonstrators in response to negative reactions by government officials to their demands and to reactions by international media personalities. In creating the statue, students took full advantage of certain sociopolitical opportunities and overcame other political obstacles. A counterresponse was launched by China's rulers (the massacre), which also capitalized on other opportunities and overcame its own barriers.

In the logic of postmodernism, Tiananmen Square became a new site of discourse, a place where the dominant discursive practices could be challenged. Within this new political and social space, students could articulate a language of protest. Formerly, this language had to be covert or uttered only in concealed sites. By going public, the students seized the opportunity to take raw and inchoate forms of protest and create an elaborate consensual discourse of dignity and justice.

THE BUILDUP TO THE 1989 DEMONSTRATION

Historically, Chinese university students have been a rebellious group. They were active during the 1860s Taiping Rebellion, the 1900 Boxer Rebellion, Sun Yat-sen's long work for a Chinese Republic, the 1940s fight for Communist "liberation," the Cultural Revolution in 1966–76, in protests after Zhou Enlai's 1976 death, and most recently in the 1987 student demonstrations for basic freedoms. Chinese rulers have long kept a wary eye on university students. The 1987 uprising showed students' ability to garner increasing urban popular support. A few prominent government officials had supported student demands and rights. This support exemplifies Burke's concept of "disassociation," a concept with explanatory power.[2] The identity of the Chinese government was associated with a group that would never negotiate with adversaries or sympathize with opponents' causes. The rare official who chose to negotiate and to empathize with others began to be seen by China's rulers as dangerous, but these same daring leaders became heroes to students and many other common citizens. There was a break in the mold when some government support was tendered. This support was only symbolic. But even this gesture appeared to legitimate the belief that subordinate assertions and criticisms might be safely spoken under some circumstances. The most publicized student support came from Hu Yaobang, the man who, up to that time, had been assumed to be Deng Xiaoping's successor. Hu's reputation was ravaged, and he was stripped of all authority and position after he lent students his support. Hu did not lose everything, however; he became a student hero.

It was Hu Yaobang's sudden death on April 15, 1989, that spawned the newest student demonstration. Hu's passing invited a student outpouring of grief. Government leaders, cognizant of his hero status in student eyes, planned to jam Tiananmen Square with loyal communists during Hu's funeral ceremony, thus pushing students aside and eliminating any embarrassing posters, slogans, or statements. However, students discovered this plan through government leaks and swarmed into the square hours before the army planned to barricade the area. Students took advantage of their position and used the opportunity to voice grievances and to plead with government leaders for change. Students appealed for greater freedoms of speech, press, and assembly. Officials tried to ignore the students, but their numbers steadily grew and their protests got louder. These demonstrations were orderly and peaceful. Few personal injuries or acts of vandalism were reported to have occurred at this time.

When government officials concluded that the demonstrations would not end quickly and that repeated and angry student claims of government corruption were not going to stop, leaders resorted to intimidation and character assassination. Deng Xiaoping ordered that an editorial be printed in the *People's Daily*.[3] The editorial excoriated the students, labeling them as "counterrevolutionaries," a term not unlike "treasonous." The newspaper piece ridiculed student demands as silly, denied as unfounded student accusations of government corruption, and demanded that the demonstrators return immediately to their homes, jobs, or universities. As one student leader commented: "Deng believed his editorial would scare us into ending our rally; we were determined that the People . . . know our positions and understood how terrible corruption had become."[4]

The demonstration got larger and seemingly more vocal.[5] Student leaders formally requested a meeting with government officials to negotiate their grievances and demands. Chen June,[6] Shiang Shiaoji,[7] and Wuer Kaishi[8] were among student leaders who requested a dialogue with high-ranking officials. Initial requests for face-to-face exchanges were ignored; however, demonstration persistence and unfavorable press coverage likely convinced officials to relent. Li Peng, a high-ranking government leader, consented to student requests that the two parties meet. Li agreed to meet student leaders in the Great Hall of the People, seat of China's national government. Most surprising was that this meeting was to be televised *live* on national Chinese TV.

During this unprecedented meeting, Li Peng tried, without success, to dominate and control the dialogue. Li was told in direct language that it was the students who were in charge and that officials were the guests. Wuer Kaishi's public rebuke of Li—an official, an elder, and a "guest"—was not in keeping with traditional Chinese decorum. It was feared by some demonstrators who listened to the meeting over loudspeakers in the square that such insolence might lose the movement some of its cherished support. Gauging by subsequent public opinion reported by many diverse press sources, such was not the case. It appears that many Chinese citizens who viewed or heard the meeting (it must be noted here that the live audience was very small, as the meeting occurred in midmorning on a workday) or who heard about it interpreted Wuer's rebuke as fitting for Li's authoritarian tirades. Nothing substantial was accomplished at this meeting; however, student causes and solidarity were highly publicized and were lent legitimacy by the meeting. Also, government leaders were shown to be evasive, recalcitrant, and arrogant.

Here, Chinese leaders assumed that time-honored sequences—(1) age leads to high position, position leads to power, and power leads to obedience; and (2) age begets respect, and respect begets deference—would dominate the meeting. These traditionally unchallenged sequences were now being shadowed by their dialectical antithesis: what Kenneth Burke beguilingly calls "disassociative pairs."[9] Now, respect and deference were being tied to tangible acts. Obedience was linked with legitimacy rather than age or position. The long-honored Confucian edict of "honor your superiors and elders"[10] most certainly was being directly challenged. Condition and state pairs that automatically led to anticipated ends were now replaced, at least temporarily, by new and dissonant ones.

The fact that this meeting between government and demonstrator leaders continued to be televised and that the insolent students were not quickly punished opened the way for divergent interpretations of the meeting and its results. First, it could be argued that government leaders saw student actions as so incongruous with Chinese norms that these acts and their actors would certainly be dismissed or condemned at once by all who witnessed them or heard of them. Second, it may have been interpreted by government officials that the demonstrators had at least some degree of sympathy from the masses and that for the government to terminate the meeting or to act punitively might make their situation even worse.

My personal relationships with young and elder Chinese tell me that this traditional break came as a welcome move to many of those who witnessed it on TV at home and abroad.[11] Many Chinese citizens have expressed to me their anger and resentment over their leaders' arrogance, corruption, and authoritarian activities. Would the students have been more or less effective had they elected to use the hegemonic language of hierarchy and deference? One might argue that this appearance of loyalty, by demonstrators, might have prevented attacks upon them. As grudging recruits to the official language, they might have continued building a network through which the "missing" parts of their speech could be filled in and interpreted.

THE DEMONSTRATION TAKES ON A NEW DIMENSION

Students then decided to take greater advantage of focused foreign press coverage; they began a hunger strike. This ploy gained student protestors widespread popular support as the demonstration grew even bigger. Student protests spread to other major Chinese cities (Shanghai, Chengdu, Wuhan, Xian, and Nanjing). The demonstration had now become a national urban nightmare for government leaders.

Then, students gained the greatest advantage yet: It was announced that Soviet president Mikhail Gorbachev would visit Beijing in a few weeks. This was an advantage for the demonstrators in that it guaranteed increased foreign press coverage and it provided student leaders with a quid pro quo offer: government admissions of and reductions in official corruption and concessions on freedom demands in exchange for a termination of the massive protest. Such an offer was tendered by student leaders.[12] Detailed offers were not answered by government rulers.

Vocal rallies, long-term square occupation, hunger strikes, demonstration eruptions in other cities, and overt tangible and symbolic support from tens of thousands of Beijing residents, it seems, made little impression on rigid, hard-line government leaders. Zhao Ziyang, the latest assumed heir to Deng Xiaoping's position of authority, publicly announced personal support for student causes and rights to demonstrate. This open break with hard-line leaders was reminiscent of Hu Yaobang's support two years earlier. Zhao met with the same fate: He was stripped of all positions and power and became an instant student hero—history had repeated itself again. Zhao's support, although a small act, was a stinging blow to China's rulers.

Government control and authority was waning in other ways as well. Chinese astrophysicist and dissident Fang Lizhi and his wife fled to the U.S. embassy in Beijing and were granted asylum. In order for them to gain admittance to the embassy, Chinese guard cooperation or negligence had to occur. Local hospital workers treated hunger strikers without charge and without reporting instances to authorities. Food and water were freely supplied to demonstrators against official edict. Citizens talked freely with foreign press reporters, which was also illegal. Respect for government rules was lessening. Chinese leaders were so insulated from the public that they did not realize the extent to which their authority had deteriorated.

Student numbers, stamina, energy, and support could not be sustained forever. There was an urgent need for a *symbol* to (1) rhetorically unite Beijing demonstrators with comrades in other cities, (2) focus added international attention on their causes, and (3) substitute for sometimes confusing and disjointed student appeals (e.g., speech,

press, and assembly freedoms; the release of famous democratic movement leader Wei Jingsheng; the end of official corruption; and greater
economic and political reforms). *One* symbol was sought to accomplish
all this; the task was a Herculean one. The Gorbachev visit created a
national and international media glut in Beijing, and in order to take
full advantage of this, a unifying icon was needed—one that was visually
striking and strategically chosen for TV coverage. Such a symbol, in
order to unify Chinese movement participants and followers with foreign
reporters and witnesses, needed to have universal appeal. This icon
needed to be found quickly, as the student movement was slowly
stagnating.

Beijing art students created a three-story-high statue that had a strategic similarity to the Statue of Liberty. The demonstrators christened
this papier-mâché and plaster lady holding a torch with two hands the
"Goddess of Democracy." This statue was a highly visual, universally
understood symbol of freedom. It was the fitting response students felt
they needed to invigorate their protest movement.

BITZER'S RHETORICAL SITUATION

Bitzer most certainly recognized that certain rhetorical events invite a
"fitting" response, and that such responses seem to be most effective
if struck at just the right moment.[13] The Goddess of Democracy was a
planned rhetorical response by demonstrators to the Chinese government's denials of wrongdoing, foot-dragging in relation to student negotiation requests and demands, and threats made to demonstrators
and movement sympathizers. The GD transcended verbal arguments,
chorused appeals, and media reporters' interpretations of student intentions and demands. The statue empowered those who witnessed it
or heard of it with the right to internalize its meaning in a way that
greatly moved each individual. Stokely Carmichael most astutely made
the point: "It [definition] is very, very important because I believe that
people who can define are masters."[14] Each witness to the goddess was
self-enfranchised to define its meaning. As Haig Bosmajian constantly
tells us: "Self-determination must include self-definition."[15]

HOW THE STATUE ACQUIRED MEANING

In many ways, the Goddess of Democracy became a metaphor, an
icon for freedom, change, democracy (loosely defined), ties with the
West, revolutionary thought, frustration, and an unsettling sign to
Chinese leaders that the heretofore acquiescent urban population was
unhappy with their rule. Its failure to flow in a purely ritual channel
was due to its multivocal and polysemous function within its setting.

Each faction in the June 1989 Beijing turmoil saw the statue in a some-what different light; the prism of opinion relevant to student protestors ranged from playful student pranks with Western symbols to highly loaded protests wielding symbols of the enemy to outright antisocialist treason. The spectrum of reaction by sympathizers and observers in-cluded characterizations such as heroic, majestic, prophetic, alarming, disgusting, and dangerous. No single connotation subsumed the others, thus overtaking public opinion and granting a consensus identity to the statue in Tiananmen Square.

After it was erected, however, the goddess statue caught the attention of many Chinese citizens, both within and outside Beijing, who had, up to that point, seemed to be isolated from or disinterested in the student-citizen uprising. The goddess had a galvanizing capacity in what was inexorably becoming a slowly waning movement. Although little collective protest was evoked following the statue's placement in the square, Chinese leaders must have been uneasy. Would this Western-style statue with its revolution-inspiring imagery supported by vocal international reporter enthusiasm coalesce unified demonstrator fervor? Might it not focus undue attention on the ruling elite? Might such at-tention inevitably raise and spotlight the issues of official corruption and of reluctance to grant basic freedoms?

Some metaphors were merely expressive (e.g., "the lady in the square," "the 'mother' of the rally"); others were calls to action (e.g., "the torch of freedom," "the light to expose our leaders' crimes"); while still others became alive (e.g., "our cherished Comrade," "the eyes that never fall asleep"). These organic metaphors were so intense, so vivid, and were seen as so central, to causes that they compelled concomitant action, action that was congruent with the metaphor. The April 17 *People's Daily*[16] editorial had begun the official labeling of demonstrators as subversives, hooligans, and traitors. Both Deng Xiaoping and Li Peng had publicly relabeled the demonstrators in like fashion, and failed attempts to use the army to quell the demonstration gave reason to believe that the gov-ernment intended to act consistently with its rhetoric, violently.

Demonstrators, too, invested intense, loaded, and repeated rhetoric on the statue's representation of their aspirations and intentions. Inter-national press accounts began pointing to revolution. The press, al-though technically an inactive background player in the demonstration scenario, took on a very active role. With the Chinese press blacked out to a great extent and with the few active press outlets being heavily censored, the international press, with its expanded access to infor-mation and uninhibited reporting, acquired an equal or greater voice in the student protest than many active demonstrators.

The Goddess of Democracy metaphors, it seemed, became the con-tending forces in the battle for the minds and hearts of the Chinese people. For these metaphors to "stay alive," they needed to be enacted. Demonstrators' causes were mediated by foreign reporters' idealism, hopes, and fantasies independent of demonstrator needs and motives. The images and emotions created by the demonstrators and the international press threatened the hegemony of the government's reactionary images of revolution, government overthrow, anarchy, and cultural downfall.

Eventual government violence against the students was likely a coldly planned event. China's leaders knew that their weapons, including media coverage blackouts, propaganda, its inherent and deep foreign intervention suspicion, and its taking advantage of an inbred peasant suspicion of urban movements, had a long history of success in silencing subordinate groups. These factors helped isolate demonstrators and their sympathizers from the rest of the nation, thus reducing chances of mass rallying to their cause.

There were gross distortions of the statue's appearance, such as newspaper cartoonists depicting it as a Western beggar lady threatening to torch the city in an insane excitement.[17] Newspaper editorials distorted its symbolic use by suggesting that the statue was a veiled invitation for foreign domination of China. Some Chinese students and innocent common citizens were later prosecuted and punished as a direct result of scurrilous editing of select videotaped statements. Fear-generating versions of real and claimed events accomplished by editing and superimposing diverse nonconnected videotape and still photography were aimed at a naive and uninformed public, intimidating many who may have been inclined to join the protestors into withdrawing present and potential support.

Once it was metaphors that were vying for control and not substantive accusations, evidence of wrongdoing by government officials, rebuttals against government attacks and denials, and excuses, it became easier for the government to justify its military slaughter. The government carefully wove a rebuttal image of a righteous government under siege valiantly fending off zealous, unswerving enemies. Students became foes; pleas for freedoms and less corruption became threats of overthrow and anarchy; the foreign press was portrayed as yet another example of foreign attempts to dominate China's affairs. This is just how the authorities have used carnival: You see what chaos occurs when the lower orders are let loose.[18]

The war of symbols, it appears, played into the hands of government leaders. The government had vastly superior symbol-generating capability and greater symbol access and denial methods. The government also enjoyed greater credibility for its statements, interpretations, and images with the masses. When metaphors replaced issues as the weapons of conflict, the battle lines shifted dramatically.

The name "Goddess of Democracy" held great symbolic weight in

China. In ancient Chinese mythologies and religions, the term "goddess" connotes attributes of the divine, mysterious, powerful, and good. "Democracy," as used by student demonstrators, evoked antiestablishment, foreign intervention, and individualistic rather than traditional collective Chinese visions.

A great proportion of time referents employed by student demonstrators was focused on the past and future. Historical traditions and comparisons were frequently evoked, and visions of a better future received great attention. Apocalyptic statements by government officials and its propaganda machine vied with more optimistic images driven by student demands.

The past and future symbolic references were interpreted by many in the indirect image-conscious Chinese public as (1) a metaphoric vise by which government leaders were being pincered, or (2) a rhetorical strategy depicting the comparatively finite present-day regime as insignificant compared to the lengthy and world-acknowledged glorious past and the infinite and hopeful future. The interweaving of this fabric of chronometric meaning likely did not go unnoticed by China's rulers or by China's growing intellectual class.

Although these subtleties may have sufficed for the intellectual class and for China's government leaders, a more visual cross-cultural meaning had to emerge for foreign consumption. The Goddess of Democracy, with its ties to old values and visions of a brighter future, met these needs. Such an image needed to be attractive to the international media, which would then translate, promote, and broadcast its likeness throughout the world. Demonstration leaders were also conscious of the fact that large-scale foreign media coverage would be viewed by Chinese citizens living abroad and by Chinese leaders who regularly monitored foreign press coverage. Many Beijing citizens were in daily contact with foreign reporters and would thus become opinion leaders laden with foreign interpreted reports.

Thus, the form of the goddess took on an all-purpose form: The likeness between the goddess and the Statue of Liberty was strikingly evident, but still sufficiently abstract to retain its own Chinese characteristics. These native attributes saved the icon from instant rejection by government propagandists who likely feared a backlash should their outcries over the symbolic uses of the demonstrators' statue be viewed as criticisms of the movement's inherent Chinese attributes such as indirect symbolism, nonviolence, invocation of transcendent powers, and prominence in Tiananmen Square. Government propagandists seemed to be caught in a double bind. The demonstrators had creatively intertwined their symbols with icons of Chinese mythology and long-standing political forces. The government risked destroying cherished myths by wantonly demolishing demonstrator icons.

When the student protest came to be seen through the goddess's image, Chinese officials deemed it necessary to crush the movement. It is argued that the statue was a rhetorical response to government inaction and student frustrations, and that the government's brutal response was a rhetorical countermove. Because of the complex ties between events, they may be viewed as a composite rhetorical situation. Bitzer defines a rhetorical situation thus:

a complex of persons, events, objects, and relations presenting an actual or potential exigence which can be completely or partially removed if discourse . . . can so constrain human decision or action as to bring about the significant modification of the exigence.[19]

Demonstrators, active sympathizers, the international press and most of its global audience, and many of China's young people were pitted against Chinese government leaders, their loyal followers (which were decreasing daily), and Chinese citizens who were influenced or intimidated by the official pronouncements. A statue, heavily vested with many individual and collective interpretations, now vied seriously for hegemony with government propaganda, loyalty to China's leaders and their corrupt system, and tradition. The statue, with its homemade but foreign roots, clashed harshly with government control, and it seemed jarring in its placement in China's secular holy place, Tiananmen Square. The square, perimetered by (1) Mao Zedong's mausoleum; (2) the Great Hall of the People, the seat of China's government; (3) the Forbidden City, the icon of dynastic rule; and (4) the Revolutionary Museum, housing revered trappings of Socialist revolutions, represented, through its expansiveness, China's endurance and strength. Here, China's leaders formed a nation and ruled with ironclad authority. This square was now the resting place of the Goddess of Democracy, a symbol anathema to Chinese officials' identity, ideals, and visions. Demonstrators represented openness, less restricted ties with the West, freedom, and change. Government visions symbolized secrecy, xenophobia, dominance, and rigidity. These variables constituted the complex that Bitzer claims is requisite for a rhetorical situation.

THE EXIGENCES

Student demonstrators saw their government, the nation's economy, and their own futures as endangered. Relative isolation still plagued China. Leaders seemed oblivious of public protest about oppression, corruption, inflation, and rampant general dissatisfaction. Nepotism, favoritism, and cronyism threatened China's brightest youth; the brightest and most talented young people were not assured of an education, good jobs, or even recognition for their talents. This was the exigence that most demonstrators were reacting to.

An exigence is "an imperfection marked by urgency: it is a defect, an obstacle, something waiting to be done; a thing which is other than it should be."[20] An exigence is rhetorical only if it can be modified by discourse. The "controlling exigences" for the students were the government's denial of problems and its reluctance to negotiate grievances.[21] The controlling exigences for the government were fear of anarchy, loss of face, and diminished personal power.

Both disputing sides perceived their brand of "discourse" to be capable of modifying the exigences (their own exigences, not necessarily the opponents'). Demonstrators seemed convinced that vocal repetition of their concerns, condemnation of media exposure, heightened embarrassment of the government as an institution, embarrassment of specific officials, and growing support from Chinese citizens would induce negotiations or concessions to take place. Government leaders, on the other hand, appeared convinced that authority, coercion, name-calling, and military threat would be adequate to assure students' eventual recanting of their accusations and lessening of their demands. Neither side gave evidence of much interest in the other camp's issues, needs, or concerns. It was a classic standoff with little chance of discourse-centered exigence modification. The local press, which may have had mediating potential, was muzzled by the government; the foreign press, which had an outside chance of mediating the crisis, seemed content with sensationalizing and capitalizing on the lack of resolution between the opposing parties.

RHETORICAL AUDIENCES

A rhetorical audience consists of "those persons who are capable of being influenced by discourse and being mediators of change" in a community.[22] These persons are distinguished from a collection of mere hearers. A rhetorical audience is essential because "only by means of its mediating influence can the exigence be modified."[23]

Student demonstrators identified several audiences that they conceived of as potential mediators, including (1) the general Chinese public, (2) the Chinese national press, (3) the international press, (4) the United Nations (UN), (5) various international money-lending organizations (e.g., the World Bank, the International Monetary Fund, Assistance Fund for Southern and Eastern Asian National Development, or ASEAN), and (6) the international diplomatic community.

Demonstrators did secure an impressive urban citizen following, but that support was short-lived, devoid of tangible power, and it represented only a minority of the total urban population. Students had no ground swell of rural sympathy, understanding, or support. The few rural citizens who learned of the movement dismissed it as unimportant to them and thus unworthy of action on their part. Since farmers were uninformed and uninvolved (farmers constitute 80% of China's total population), they posed no threat to government officials and gave no aid to the protestors.

The Chinese press remained under government control. When a few instances of "accurate reporting" surfaced, these reports were censored and blacked out in regions beyond Beijing. All Chinese TV reports were subjected to postreport interpretation by other government spokesmen. The international press was not under direct Chinese government control. It was, however, subject to jamming and eventual total blackout; reporters were forced to depart the country. The international press played a role in forming world opinion about current disputes and had influence on local Beijing views, but the global audience was unable to exert any influence on local Chinese affairs. The greatest single influence that the press did have was to convince foreign governments to begin evacuation of foreign nationals as the situation worsened.

The UN had no authority to act on a member's internal affairs; students had a naive notion that the UN could and would somehow get involved. The most the UN could do was to propose a nonbinding resolution condemning the Chinese government's acts, and that resolution was vetoed by China's delegation.

International money-granting agencies temporarily slowed down their lending, but only after the massacre. Their very purpose of lending money to troubled governments fairly precluded them from mollifying China's ongoing problems.

The world's diplomatic corps issued resounding pleas for harmony and negotiation, but little action against China's government was taken or even suggested. Even postmassacre actions taken in symbolic response to the crackdown's brutality have subsided and have been replaced with a "situation as normal" mentality.

Student demonstrators identified several potential audiences that could have modified their identified exigences; however, these audiences seemed unable or unwilling to be active parties to solving the dispute.

Government rulers appear to have addressed messages to three audience segments. Citizens outside of Beijing were alternately ignored, propagandized, or intimidated into ignoring, belittling, or disputing student claims and the movement itself. The Chinese press was effectively suppressed; almost no news relevant to the demonstrators, their demands and claims, or the demonstration was being aired outside Beijing. The government initiated a campaign that created a "foreign inspired plot to seduce a small cadre of naive Chinese college students; a plot hatched by Western nations using the foreign press to overthrow the government and subject China to a new round of foreign domination."[24] This fabricated story played well to the countryside's vast illiterate masses.

Rumors spread via travelers and tourists, and *some* real news did get to outlying areas; however, the news stream was small and rebuttable. Student demonstrators received the ultimate attention from the government when all other attempts to disgrace them, ignore them, and frighten them seemed to fail.

The government's self-isolation and authoritarian control assured that the demonstrators' audiences were impotent. Due to government isolation and inattentiveness, these audiences also were incapable of modifying government-identified exigences.

Student naivete, government isolation, an inner contempt by officials toward students, and government control of resources such as the domestic media (and eventually by default the foreign press), the propaganda machine, civilian jobs, the military, and public loyalty gave little hope that officials would be swayed.

The saddest facet to the affair is that both parties convinced themselves that they were addressing a common audience as well as each other and that the common audience was empowered to mediate and alter unfolding events. Such was not the case. Both sides, in fact, shouted past each other. Each group acted, in its own way, as if Bitzer's audience were in place; but in reality, the lack of a common influential audience doomed both parties' efforts until Chinese authorities invoked the ultimate convincer: armed aggression.

MAJOR CONSTRAINTS

Bitzer sees constraints as opportunities taken advantage of or obstacles overcome in appealing to an audience to mediate exigences in a creative manner.[25] Each side had rhetorical opportunities. Students capitalized on policy leaks and learned about government plans to finesse them out of Tiananmen Square for Hu Yaobang's funeral, thus getting to the square ahead of troops. Students took great advantage of Gorbachev's visit, marring Deng's political showcase. Demonstrators used press coverage to a remarkable extent. Students played to public sympathies with their hunger strikes. They created a novel Goddess of Democracy, which now boasts of replicas in Paris, Los Angeles, and Hong Kong, perpetuating memories of student activism and government brutality. Students, until the brutal end, overcame vicious name-calling, intimidation, and being ignored by their antagonists.

Government officials invoked Nixonesque isolation, claims of sovereignty, propaganda, appeals to blind loyalty, and needs for calm and stability. Chinese leaders overcame an international media blitz, a large and vocal public protest at the seat of government, growing urban support for the opposition, accusations of corruption, and calls from students for officials to resign.

It seems that the last straw for China's leaders was the Goddess of Democracy—not the object, but its values and placement. The statue was seen by officials as a veiled invitation to (1) Western-styled individualism, (2) Western influence in government decisions, (3) foreign control of China's economy, (4) a blunting of leaders' power and authority, and (5) possible anarchy. Officials obviously had exaggerated many unlikely problems to catastrophic proportions for their own benefit, and a mass groupthink seemed to pervade China's inner circle. The hard-line military bloodshed that ended the student movement lends credence to the view that the goddess's image and its concomitant values frightened China's rulers. Deng Xiaoping is reported to have said that he believed the student-erected statue desecrated the square that they hold as sacred.

CONCLUSIONS

Symbolic representations of causes and aspirations play potent roles in movements. They can unite disparate, weakened, splintered, or dissimilar groups. Details that seem difficult to coalesce can be transcended and replaced by one or a few simpler symbols. Press coverage and hype is enhanced by playing into the media's desire for a sound (and sight) bite.

There are limiting factors about icons as well. They must be "enacted," and the enactment frequently obscures the less dramatic processes of negotiation, mediation, and compromise. They tend to evade detailed issues. Success often becomes an all or nothing venture, since issues become transformed into monolithic symbols. When highly symbolized, complex movements enter negotiations on select issues, the overriding symbol is often too rigid to accommodate subtle or partial change. Symbols seek universal interpretation; adversaries often see common symbols in diverse ways.

The Goddess of Democracy was aimed most effectively at foreign audiences. The statue succeeded in mesmerizing a global audience. Unfortunately, that audience had no potential to mediate the dispute. The statue's symbolic impact, by being placed in Tiananmen Square, actually widened the gap between government leaders and demonstrators.

Bitzer showed great astuteness when he observed that there needs to be an audience that is capable of mediating an exigence, and that effective performance is not merely doing things in public. The lack of a common audience in Tiananmen Square was the precursor to bloodshed. The press really did not perform its long-standing, traditional duty: to inform the public (both Chinese and global), to critically analyze vital issues rather than to sensationalize and capitalize on them, and to make available alternative interpretations of events, claims, possible outcomes, and personality images to the public. A vigilant *reporting* press may have alerted both sides that they were, in fact, not addressing each other's concerns and needs. This reality may have saved China from its bloodiest act.

NOTES

1. Lloyd F. Bitzer, "The Rhetorical Situation," *Philosophy and Rhetoric* 1 (1968):1–14.

2. Kenneth Burke, *A Rhetoric of Motives* (New York: Prentice Hall, 1950), 150, 305.

3. "Students Should Go Home," *People's Daily*, 17 April 1989, 1.

4. Michael Calvin McGee, "In Search of the People: A Rhetorical Alternative," *Quarterly Journal of Speech* 61 (October 1975):235–49.

5. Chen June, symposium on Tiananmen Square demonstrations, University of Maine, Presque Isle, Me., 20 April 1990.

6. Ibid.

7. Shiang Shiaoji, symposium on Tiananmen Square demonstrations, University of Maine, Presque Isle, Me., 20 April 1990.

8. *People's Daily*, 1.

9. Burke, *Rhetoric of Motives*, 305.

10. Arthur Waley, *The Analects of Confucius* (New York: Random House, 1938), 71.

11. Kenneth C. Petress, personal correspondence with participants and witnesses to student demonstrations May and June 1989; personal visit to the People's Republic of China, June–August 1990.

12. Ding Tzu and Liu Sicheng, symposium on Tiananmen Square demonstrations, University of Maine, Presque Isle, Me., 20 April 1990.

13. Bitzer, "Rhetorical Situation," 8.

14. Stokely Carmichael, speech, Seattle, Washington, 19 April 1967.

15. Haig Bosmajian, *The Language of Oppression* (Washington, D.C.: University Press of America, 1983), 6.

16. *People's Daily*, 1.

17. *Ren Min Ribao*, editorials, several dates in April 1989.

18. Mikhail Bakhtin, *Rabelais and His World* (Bloomington, Ind.: Indiana University Press, 1984), 97.

19. Bitzer, "Rhetorical Situation," 8.

20. Ibid., 6.

21. Ibid., 7.

22. Ibid., 8.

23. Lloyd Bitzer, "Functional Communication: A Situational Perspective," in *Rhetoric in Transition: Studies in the Nature and Uses of Rhetoric*, ed. Eugene E. White (University Park: Pennsylvania State University Press, 1980), 21–38.

24. Shiang Shiaoji, "Symposium on Tiananmen Square."

25. Bitzer, "Rhetorical Situation," 8.

Chapter Nine

Ma Anand Sheela: Media Power through Radical Discourse

Catherine Ann Collins

Dan Clark and the Z100 FM Morning Zoo (a Portland, Oregon, radio station) released a song, "Shut Up, Sheela!!" labeling Ma Anand Sheela a "big-mouth" and "red disaster" (the Rajneeshees preferred wearing reds and pinks) and mocking her claims that Oregonians are "ignorant bigots."[1] The unflattering song indicates one response to the rhetoric of Ma Anand Sheela, whose inflammatory discourse fueled the controversy between the Rajneeshees and the rural Oregonians she ridiculed in the early 1980s. Sheela was president of Rajneesh Foundation International, supervisor of the worldwide religious activities of the Rajneeshees, and during the Bhagwan's self-imposed vow of silence, the authoritative voice for the Bhagwan's teachings and desires.

This chapter explores the relationship between power and discourse through an examination of the radical rhetoric of Ma Anand Sheela. Strategically generating controversy in her discourse, Sheela gained media attention, thereby securing power to promote the movement nationally. Her rhetoric illustrates the link between power and discourse, especially as it illuminates the appeals to and actualization of power occurring when the socially constructed realities of competing cultures collide.

THE RELATIONSHIP BETWEEN POWER AND DISCOURSE

Consider the relationship between power and discourse: Power is in some fashion desire manifest, the imposition of an individual's or group's will. Discourse is instrumental in that it may be a means to an end; through discourse, power may be articulated or achieved. However, in discourse, terms and values become embedded, sedimented, assumed. In this sense, discourse contains and reflects power relationships in its very form. Discourse is itself an act of power. Access to a public voice and adherence to discursive rules are themselves expressions of power. Discourse, then, relates to power in at least two distinct fashions. It may be both the means to the assumption of power and constitutive of power.

In this latter sense, discourse functions as a piety. Kenneth Burke describes piety as "a system-builder, a desire to round things out, to fit experiences together into a unified whole. Piety is *the sense of what properly goes with what*.[2] Piety is the normalizing or legitimizing of power. Piety generates orthodoxy, a devotion to an ordering. Piety implies what may be said and who may speak. Piety, thus conceived, is foundational to the orderings of the prevailing culture.

The prevailing culture's response to challenges to its pieties depends on the nature of the challenge. The response to protest may be an adjustment in some orderings within the orientation; the response to the radical, who rejects the fundamental orderings of the orientation by calling for new orderings, may be retreat to a more conservative position. This latter response is more likely when the radical employs discourse that mocks the mainstream orientation and offends the dominant culture's social proprieties.

To gain a public voice is to wrest power from the prevailing culture. Radical groups may attempt to linguistically usurp the fundamental authority of the ruling group by appropriating or devaluing the value symbols, the warrants and appeals of the predominant culture. In breaking apart the established links in the predominant culture's orientation, perspective by incongruity provides power.

Discourse that is socially or linguistically inappropriate challenges the prevailing culture's sense of the appropriate. Burke suggests that one way to attack a piety is through "methodical misnaming," a form of perspective by incongruity. In misnaming the values, sacred symbols, and life-style of the prevailing culture, the radical calls the orientation into question. In this case the power is manifest not in material gain but rather in the discourse itself. Surrounded and silenced by orthodoxy, the radical's merely gaining voice is an assertion of power.

Because the end is not material gain, the radical case need not be logical or consistent. Radical arguments need not lead anywhere. Their significance lies in the act of their articulation. The only necessary consistency is the challenge the radical offers to the status quo's power to define the terms and participants in public debate and the allocation of resources. Ma Anand Sheela's rhetoric serves as a case study of radical discourse.

An explanation of the context in which the conflict between culture and counterculture arose facilitates an exploration of Sheela's discourse.

THE CONTEXT

In 1981, Indian guru Bhagwan Shree Rajneesh led a worldwide movement of 350,000 *sannyasins* (followers). After experiencing political pressures in Poona, India, an assassination attempt, and personal health problems, the Bhagwan moved to the United States. After three months of medical treatment he moved to Oregon where, with several thousand of his followers, he settled in the desert of central Oregon on 64,229 acres that they named Rancho Rajneesh. On the ranch itself, they established the city of Rajneesh Puram, which encompasses 2,135 acres (three times the area of San Francisco).

The central Oregon residents saw the growth of the Rajneesh community as a threat to their way of life. Still, ranchers were initially tentative in their assessment of the commune, preferring to let the Rajneeshees do what they wanted on their own land. The Rajneesh takeover of the town of Antelope made the threat to the prevailing culture more pronounced. The interlopers represented a counterculture; but without polarizing rhetoric, the culture/counterculture clash might have simmered rather than boiled over into a statewide controversy. In the face of such rhetoric, the Oregon ranchers' initial tolerance gave way to fear and a perception that anything the Rajneeshees said or did, especially if it involved Ma Anand Sheela, was a threat to orthodox political and social order. The response was to seek media attention for their fears, urge the Rajneeshees to leave the state, and, failing that, find a way to remove them through the legal system. Pushed too far, the ranchers became emotional, petty, and vindictive. Neither side deescalated the conflict; both sides seemed to go out of their way, at times, to antagonize the other group.

Oregonians feared that the Rajneeshees had real political goals—radical changes—that were masked by Sheela's offensive rhetoric. These fears developed after the takeover of Antelope and centered on potential power plays in Wasco County, wherein Rajneeshees would employ their power to replace the existing order.

Rajneeshees, especially Ma Anand Sheela, initially denied having intentions to take over the county, arguing that they had no need to exercise power as it is traditionally exercised. This denial seemed contradicted by the homeless project they undertook. Several thousand homeless people from across the United States were given bus tickets to Rajneesh Puram. Under Oregon election law, with its twenty-day residency clause, the homeless would be able to vote in the elections almost immediately. In a county of 12,000, the homeless vote could radically change the outcome of land-use measures. The Rajneeshees denied any political motive, but Oregonians were convinced that the project was a power play designed to spoil *their* county, *their* way of life.

Sheela's use of national forums such as "Phil Donahue" and "Nightline" to launch verbal assaults on central Oregon locals and Wasco County officials further inflamed the controversy in central Oregon. Rumors abounded: Rancho Rajneesh was an armed military camp; the Rajneeshees were trying to poison residents in a nearby town; Rajneesh members were brainwashed and forcibly restrained from leaving Rancho Rajneesh.

All of this came to an end in mid-September 1985 when, with a group of powerful Rajneeshees, Sheela left the country. Bhagwan claims that she left with Rajneeshee money, that she had attempted the murders of at least three people, and that she was responsible for gross manipulations of power while in Rajneesh Puram. Sheela, in turn, aimed her firebrand rhetoric on Bhagwan. Headlines in *The Oregonian* proclaim, "Sheela brands Rajneesh 'liar'." When told of the charges Bhagwan had made against her, Sheela responded, "The hell with Bhagwan!"[3] The commune's response to Sheela's flight was equally antagonistic. Bhagwan claimed that Sheela was the author of the *Book of Rajneeshism* published under his name, which asserted that Rajneeshism is not a religion. Two thousand followers of Bhagwan burned the 5,000 copies of the book along with Sheela's robes. As she threw the robes on the flames, Bhagwan's new secretary said, "Sheela's desire for popedom!"[4]

Sheela's response was heard nationally November 3, 1985, on "60 Minutes," three years after the program's audience first heard from her. She accused Bhagwan of "exploit[ing] people by using their human frailty and emotions," and he accused her of being "drugged. She's on hard drugs."[5] Asked if the whole religion was just a con, Sheela replied, "absolutely."

At this point it becomes apparent that Sheela's discourse itself was a powerful instrument, serving to sustain and fuel the controversy between Oregonians and Rajneeshees and later between the Rajneeshees and herself.

COMPETING DISCOURSE

Once the Rajneeshees moved beyond Rancho Rajneesh and began to publicly challenge the status quo's discursive formation, their radical vision directly threatened the existing order. Ma Anand Sheela's polarizing rhetoric took the values and definitions of the establishment and subverted them, gaining a public voice for the Rajneesh cause. Confronted by distortions of their own words, values, and life-styles, central Oregonians lashed back. In so doing they accepted the Rajneesh (at least

Sheela's) rules for the encounter. Challenges to the legitimacy or appropriateness of Rajneesh rhetoric only gave Rajneeshees the public voice they sought.

The following examples illustrate the conflicting rhetoric that fueled media coverage locally and nationally.

Oregonians

"The press in general has simply taken them (the Rajneeshees) at face value. No matter what we've said, we've been taken for country bumpkins. You take what they say seriously and what we say is neglected or almost ridiculed."—Margaret Hill[6]

"This movement is a threat to our society and national security, both politically and economically. Something must be done to stop them before they get so rooted it will be difficult to do anything about it."—Rev. Charles Tatom[8]

"As a Christian, I believe this is a satanic force. . . . We're not just fighting our neighbors, we're fighting a satanic force."—Frances Dickson[10]

Rajneeshees

SHEELA: "In order for the Moral Majority and the mobs to understand Rajneesh, they will have to leave their mob mentality and their morality and become amoral. Right now they are living in the 16th century; it is about time that they grow up and move with the science. And become sophisticated as Rajneesh are."[7]

"It's like a person, having put on a monster head, looking in the mirror and being frightened by what they see. . . . They created that fear. They've created everything that's happened to them all the way along the line."— Krishna Deva[9]

"The more negative, hostile and ludicrous our opponents get, the more people get interested."—Ma Prem Sunshine[11]

On the Rajneesh side, the polarizing rhetoric offered perspective by incongruity, attacking the values and life-style of the prevailing culture and at times appropriating the terms and methodically misusing them. It was highly aggressive, accusing, mocking; when caught in a contradiction, the rhetor laughed or pushed further, avowing that he or she had no desire for power, or claiming that the comments were merely a joke and the Master said take advantage of any joke. Caught in an outright lie, the typical response was to assert that the predominant culture did not understand Rajneesh humor or was unaware of the events as they were happening. Through it all the rules seemed to be take the offensive, offend the public pieties and proprieties, gain publicity, and keep the prevailing culture off balance. The power roles reversed: The established culture was victim to the linguistically aggressive counterculture, whose power came from methodical misnaming of pieties and proprieties.

Prompted by Sheela's inflammatory rhetoric, Governor Vic Atiyeh suggested that the unpopular citizens should leave Oregon. "It is very clear that their presence has been extremely disturbing to the longtime residents. . . . Their presence is so different. If I moved into the neighborhood and they didn't really like me, I see no reason why I should stay."[12] This sentiment was shared by many rural Oregonians. *The Economist* reported the intensity of the local response when, in 1984, it noted: "The hostility is strongest among the conservative residents of Wasco County, who are mainly ranch people with a liking for guns, cowboy hats and traditional ways. . . . Most of them seem to have only the vaguest notion of what the commune stands for, but they do not want to be 'taken over.' Rather than accept that, they talk of shooting the commune off the map."[13] Sheela responded that Atiyeh's rhetoric just gave locals "support for their bigotry" and that if anyone should leave, it would be everyone but the American Indians; "[a]ll the rest are invaders."[14] In this fashion, Sheela's rhetoric provided its own legitimation. The Oregon response served only to substantiate Sheela's claims of intolerance of the orthodoxy.

The rhetoric that resulted because of the differences between these two groups was as harsh and barren as the land on which the two groups resided. Both factions developed discourse that symbolically attacked the other group's orderings and dissociated each group from the conflicting party. Some of the most controversial rhetoric, because it directly and irreverently attacked the prevailing culture's pieties, came from Ma Anand Sheela.

SHEELA'S DISCOURSE

One of Sheela's favorite attacks challenged the sexual mores of the prevailing culture. Having taken over the small town of Antelope, the Rajneeshees set aside an area of the small local park for nude sunbathing, a practice predictably offensive to the old community's standards. When the residents complained, Sheela initially labeled them fascist. Asked how the two groups got along, Sheela replied: "Pretty bad. Worse than we would be treated in Soviet Union. I don't call this state part of America, I call this state part of Soviet Union. It is fascist."[15] The association and label predictably inflamed the Oregonian distrust of the movement.

Sheela did not stop with name-calling, however. She linked intolerance to the sexual mores of the community. The reason the community was "uptight" about the Rajneesh movement was more a reflection of their repressed sexuality than any impropriety on the part of her people. Having accused the locals of spying on the nudists, Sheela explained: "Because all their lives they have suppressed sex, not even having orgasms with their own husbands. So many of the women have to make out with milkmen or whatever happens to come along."[16] Marriage was labeled a "license to make your wife or husband a whore."[17] Throughout this process, Sheela appropriated the values of the community and used them to critique orthodox pieties. Further, her explanation of Rajneesh philosophy expressed values cherished by the predominant culture. Thus, in large measure the two perspectives made use of the same premises. However, Sheela's subversion of pieties was, in fact, an attack on the orthodoxy itself.

Sheela claimed that her discourse and actions were not a means to the assumption of power. Political power as traditionally conceived was anathema. Early in 1984 an issue of *Bhagwan*, a Rajneesh magazine for general distribution, addressed the group's understanding of power. An interview between Swami Dhyan John and Sheela explains the counterculture's position:

John: Sheela, what is this thing called power?

Sheela: The way I understand power is as exploitation of people and situations. It is a habit, built for personal gain, whether it is for monetary, political or social reasons. Sometimes it even works as a habit for habit's sake, power for the sake of power. . . . Wherever there is competition there is the struggle for power.[18]

When asked if she had power Sheela answered no, she was just a housewife; but from what the Bhagwan had taught her about power, "when one has true power one never needs to show it, it expresses itself without any effort. It expresses itself in love, in kindness, in compassion."[19]

But for Oregonians, the fear remained, triggered by their memory of Sheela's March 1982 promise that the Rajneeshees "had no plans to take over Antelope,"[20] followed by the successful takeover of the town. The Rajneesh definition of power intertwined with love lost out to power confronting power when Sheela announced over the airwaves, "everybody's accusing me, telling me that I'm going to take over Wasco County so I say it's a good idea. Why not?"[21] The rationale she gave hinged on her conclusion that the county leaders were "bigots."[22]

A month later she reversed herself in a press release, claiming, "I am not a power seeker and what I have I am content with. I have no interest in any election and am not interested in the county. But unfortunately you don't understand my sense of humor."[23] The takeover of September was jokingly labeled a "spiritual" takeover. Accepting for the moment the arguments she made, one can call the tone of the first half of the press release neutral. However, the final part of the statement made it difficult to read her comments as other than aggressive. In explaining the project for busing in the homeless, she said that some people were promised return tickets, others signed papers saying it was a one-way fare; but they were adults and they were responsible for themselves, not the Rajneeshees, not the state of Oregon. She concluded, "And moreover, these people are helping the Salvation Army and the churches tremendously, because these do-gooders always need something so that they can use it as a ladder to heaven, and enjoy all that they have missed here."[24] The mocking conclusion changed the reading of the earlier explanation. Rather than a temporary truce, the conflict continued; one more group had been drawn into battle. Charitable actions were mocked, replaced by the Rajneesh order—give the homeless a place to live and work, give them human dignity rather than handouts and pious advice.

In a news account October 30, 1984, the *Statesman-Journal* reported: "Sheela, who often had used fiery rhetoric in repeated attacks on local politicians, said her earlier remarks were 'a joke.' She said she was not interested in 'anything smaller than the universe.' "[25] With a history of aggressive rhetoric and retractions, Sheela's remarks did not make Oregonians comfortable. The article itself ended with her conciliatory comments on the governor, the state, and the court system. What irritated most was the final comment—Oregonians "are perfectly average human beings"[26]—delivered in a superior tone that minimized Oregonians further. Apologies were not offered, conciliation was minimized, and Sheela's discourse fueled further headlines. It was not an effort to transcend the power friction between the two cultures, but as a rhetorical strategy for gaining media attention, the rhetoric was extremely effective; linguistic impiety draws audiences. Power, in turn, comes from gaining an audience for one's perspective.

As a guest on "Nightline," Sheela and her reputation for controversial rhetoric gained national attention. Again, her inflammatory discourse was not totally unprompted. The media, in this case ABC's "Nightline," fueled the controversy, thus gaining a further public hearing for the radicals. Koppel began with the Oregonian perspective:

Take an Indian guru, a crowd of chanting, smiling, devoted followers, put them down in North-Central Oregon and their neighbors get nervous. When the guru and his sect take over a whole town, the neighbors get even more nervous. And when the sect starts busing in hundreds of homeless people from all over the country just before a crucial November election, well, here's Nightline's Judd Rose to tell us what happened then.[27]

Rose described the "red dawn" in Antelope, the "big red machine" that he asserted "has its eye on the November election," and interviewed a woman who said, "The Rajneesh have taken over. They'll make the state red if somebody doesn't do something to stop them." Rose introduced Sheela, who responded, "By the year 2000, Oregon will be collapsed and city of Rajneesh Puram will be existing."[28] Rose then interviewed some of the homeless people who were bused into central Oregon. One new resident told the correspondent that he had been there over a week and had not been asked to register or vote in a particular way, that what he had found was a home. Rose sparked the conflict, "And to any of their neighbors who want to change that feeling, a warning." Sheela said, "They touch any of our people, I'll have for one of our person, I will have 15 of their heads. And I mean business."[29] The conflict was escalated; the context was established for the audience.

With Sheela and State Representative Wayne Fawbush as the guests, fireworks were all but assured. Koppel began by talking with Fawbush, who explained election law and the possibility that bringing the homeless into Oregon could make a difference. Koppel then turned to Sheela for the explanation of why the homeless were being brought in. Sheela began, "It is very simple. But Mr. Fascist at my right hand, Mr. Wayne the snake would not understand. Man who lusting for power would not understand."[30] Koppel probed the motives of the group. Sheela retreated to name-calling. "But after listening to people like Mr. Fascist next to me—." Koppel interrupted, "I'll tell you what Sheela. Do me a favor. You know, I'll see to it that nobody calls you any names and you don't call anybody any names." Sheela countered, "I'm not calling the name; I'm calling the fact." The interview continued until Fawbush, frustrated by Sheela's interruptions and, from his perspective, evasions, replied, "Ted, just look at what's happening. If we had any reliability that what these folks are saying we could believe, that would be one thing." Sheela interrupted, "Oh, you are full of shit. You don't know anything about what reliability is."[31] Koppel, Sheela, and Fawbush all tried to talk until Koppel warned Sheela that she would "forfeit any opportunity to speak" if she continued to use obscenities. Sheela tried to continue, but Koppel cut off her microphone and moved to the second topic of the evening. By letting her get to him, by cutting off her voice, Koppel increased Sheela's controversy and enhanced her potential for further media attention. Denied a public voice, Sheela still won—she forced the establishment to deal with her, largely on her terms. Denied a voice, she then claimed that the establishment had violated its own commitment to freedom of speech and thought, freedom of religion; the established orthodoxy must be flawed.

The Oregon press picked up on her labels of "snake" and "fascist" for Fawbush and explained that her charge that Fawbush was "full of shit" was not deleted because the tape was fed back live to the Oregon station. Over 1,000 people called the local affiliate to protest Sheela's latest charges, not so much to complain about the "language, but the tone of it and the Rajneeshees in general."[32] The response of fellow Rajneeshees only furthered the conflict and the media attention. The irreverence with which Rajneeshees treated the divisive discourse is apparent in public-relations specialist Ma Prem Isabel's interview with the press:

"Sheela's abrasive remarks were representative examples of the kind of straight-forward honesty practiced by followers of Bhagwan Shree Rajneesh," Isabel said.

"We have a different set of values," she said. "We aren't polite and we don't say what people want to hear. . . . I find it refreshing."[33]

The Rajneeshees methodically renamed conventional proprieties of language. The significance of the misnaming was captured, in part, by the warning that preceded the article: "EDITOR'S NOTE: This story contains language that may offend some readers."[34] The immediate effect on most in the predominant culture was to rise to the bait, to employ similar obscenities. To do so afforded the counterculture the power of definition. Fawbush commented after the "Nightline" experience, "I've dealt with her for three years and she's called me worse things before. . . . My main concern was not rising to take the bait of being called a fascist snake. . . . We're trying not to play into their hands by concentrating on this issue, but if we don't galvanize public opinion we're going to get run over."[35]

Sheela's reputation for linguistic controversy got her a slot on the "Phil Donahue" show. She did not disappoint those who wanted more controversy; her appearance on "Donahue" reinforced her image. The program was about cults: the Church Universal and Triumphant in Livingston, Montana, the Church of Scientology in Clearwater, Florida, and the Rajneeshees of Rajneesh Puram, Oregon. The Rajneesh controversy dominated the program. It was spurred on by the presence of Larryann Willis, a rancher from central Oregon, and Ma Anand Sheela.

Donahue began by asking Sheela to explain the homeless project; after several statements, he turned to Ms. Willis and asked her what she saw going on with the homeless project. In the middle of her second sentence, Sheela interrupted her, and Willis pointed out that Sheela had a pattern of interrupting. Donahue's attempt to smooth over the incident was ignored by Willis, who responded: "Every time anyone, who is on a talk show with Sheela, is about to make a point, she interrupts very rudely. I hope she will control herself in this."[36] A brief exchange between Donahue and Willis was interrupted by Sheela's laughter and an explanation of why Willis's comments were laughable. Donahue asked: "Sheela, why are you—Why—You do seem to be taking a kind of —joy of your, ah—the disdain you have for the people who are understandably anxious about this development. . . . You seem to be enjoying it. Almost giving them the finger when you do that."[37] Sheela ignored the criticism and explained that the people of central Oregon, Willis, and the legislators are like the merchants Jesus chased out of the temple. From name-calling on "Nightline" to mockery and methodical misnaming, Sheela had the other guests on her case at this point in the program. The "controversy" had not really begun, however. Mutual interruptions were brought to a halt when the screen showed Sheela wearing a gun. Donahue asked her why she was armed and she replied, "self-protection."[38] The audience laughed. Donahue probed the structure of the commune, the currency, the question of whether the commune was not, in a sense, a nation. When Donahue and Willis began to discuss a case pending before the Immigration and Naturalization Service, Sheela interrupted and continued to interrupt, thus preventing a discussion between Willis and Donahue. Donahue told her, "When you interrupt this much, you really do make it awfully difficult to take everything else you say seriously,"[39] at which point the audience applauded and Sheela interrupted yet another time. The pattern prevented dialogue and clearly focused attention on Sheela. Inappropriate behavior destroyed the discussion of the other guests and gained Sheela a forum. She may not have had their respect; but she got the airtime she sought. Impiety yielded power.

Donahue showed a clip of the Bhagwan, followed by his own secret service armed with machine guns. Sheela justified this by arguing that they were needed to protect the Rajneeshees from bigots, the bigots in Oregon and the bigots in the audience: "Yes, this audience and other audiences that would like to send all legal aliens out of this country and this, ah—Miss Piggy [referring to Willis] or whatever her name is . . . I don't remember her name. I think it's Miss Piggy. That's what they refer to her as in Oregon."[40] When Donahue suggested that this naming was inappropriate from a religion based on love and respect, Sheela argued that her use of language was not inappropriate, it was just a nickname. When pressed, she interrupted repeatedly, claiming she had not done anything wrong and that Willis had tried to hurt her to win the election. When Sheela did not agree with someone's characterization of the Rajneesh religion she was quick to claim, "That's a lie,"[41] regardless of the source of the information. She interrupted, laughed at the other speakers, accused the audience of being an embarrassment. When the audience responded negatively to her she accused them of being worse than the Soviet Union, of being bigoted. When Donahue asked if anyone who disagreed with her was a bigot, she argued for her freedom. She was intolerant when she was the one interrupted, and she tried to take the issue of freedom away from the mainstream culture, appropriating the value for her counterculture. When asked why, as an alien, she stayed in this country if the people were so bigoted, she talked about the Constitution and individual freedoms, about why she did not have to become a citizen to enjoy those rights. In short, what Sheela did on "Donahue" was dominate the conversation, express derision at the establishment, and hold out the prevailing culture's constitution and rights when her rhetoric so angered them that they resorted to the "well, if you don't like it why don't you leave" response. Her language pushed the audience and other guests beyond their ability to respond rationally, and once they stepped over the rational line, she used their emotionalism as an indication of the persecution she faced. The prevailing culture's intolerance and inability to actualize its values became the causal variable in Sheela's offensive rhetoric, a rhetoric of name-calling and methodical misnaming.

Speaking to a Portland, Oregon, audience after the program, Donahue described Sheela as a "rather unpleasant woman" and his studio audience's reaction as "absolutely upset with Sheela" in part because her rhetorical stance seemed to be "if you don't agree with her, there's something wrong with you."[42] His characterization of Sheela was well received as consistent with their own local experiences. The audience's disgust only served Sheela's cause. The more people were outraged by Sheela's rhetoric, the more the press gave her an opportunity to speak to a large group, the more her presence and her group's presence received national attention—the power to be heard and, ultimately, greater potential for actualized power, because the linguistic perspective by incongruity subverted the old order and forced awareness of the counterculture's orderings.

CONCLUSION

For three-and-a-half years, as the chief spokesperson, Sheela's linguistic impieties, mocking laughter, and inappropriate behavior were the symbols through which the group spirit of Rajneeshism was expressed. The symbolic expression did not change with her exodus from Oregon, even though the object of derision changed from Oregonians to the Bhagwan. Those same symbols were employed by the remaining members of the commune to mock and minimize Sheela. Paul Tillich argues that a symbol used by the ruling elite in any group, acquiesced to by the members, expresses not only "the power and justice of being of the group, it also expresses the communal spirit of the group, its ideals and valuations."[43] When an individual's or group's power is used for the minimization or destruction of the power of being of another, the exercise of power is an exercise of injustice. Contrary to Bhagwan and Sheela's expressed philosophy of individual freedom, of the true nature of power, Sheela's continued actions and the actions of Bhagwan and his followers after Sheela's flight were expressions of the unjust exploitative power they condemned in the prevailing Oregonian culture.

Throughout the exchange following Sheela's flight, Oregonians were vindicated in their distrust of the Rajneeshees. The attack on their pieties was seen as impropriety, as the unworthy challenges of petty, dishonest, irreverent outsiders. But for three-and-a-half years the radical strategy of perspective by incongruity, the methodical misnaming of the predominant culture's pieties, gave Ma Anand Sheela and, through her, the group a powerful opportunity to redefine the relationship between culture and counterculture. Linguistic impiety could not be ignored, especially when broadcast so extensively in the print and electronic media.

Sheela had succeeded in gaining a public voice for the movement by giving the media what it craved, controversy. First in the Oregon newspapers, later on "Nightline" and "Donahue," Sheela exercised power by adopting a discursive strategy that made hers the only voice heard. Interruptions, name-calling, laughter, loudness, and constant shifts in argumentative ground did not persuade, for persuasion was not the goal; rather, Sheela's linguistic strategy filled the space, not as rhetoric but as coercion. In effect, Sheela's public voice destroyed the concept of public discourse and her own forum.

Impiety, then, can be a powerful source for social change. But when the discourse goes beyond the creative potential of power encountering power and tries to destroy an individual's or group's power of being, it denies the fundamental freedom of the individual that the radical professes to seek. In the case of Ma Anand Sheela, the discourse wields the same exploitative power she condemned, a power exercised for personal, political, or social gain—"unenlightened" power. Sheela's rhetoric illustrates the link between power and discourse.

When culture and counterculture collide, a powerful force for change resides in the stability or instability of the culture's system of ordering. If the counterculture can first gain attention for its discourse and then successfully break the links in the predominant pieties by offering alternative orderings—perspective by incongruity—the counterculture gains power. The predominant culture's values, life-style, and sacred symbols are methodically misnamed. Impiety, especially linguistic impiety, is a powerful form of perspective by incongruity. The short-term effect is often the media attention that the radical seeks and that taboo language and behavior seem to guarantee. Impiety rends the links in the predominant culture's orderings, challenging the sense of what properly goes with what; it offers alternative orderings through a substitute set of pieties, not just offensively inappropriate behavior with shock value. When the radical's discourse is impious it challenges the valuations of the larger social order and breaks the monopoly on power held by the prevailing culture.

NOTES

1. Dan Clark and the Z100 Morning Zoo, "Shut Up Sheela!!"
2. Kenneth Burke, *Permanence and Change: An Anatomy of Purpose*, 3d ed. (Berkeley: University of California Press, 1984), 74.

3. Robert A. Ulrich, "Sheela, Others Quit Commune," *The Oregonian*, 17 September 1985, p. A1.

4. Sally Carpenter Hale, "Rajneeshees Dance, Burn Books," *Statesman-Journal*, 1 October 1985, p. B1.

5. "Bhagwan," transcript of "60 Minutes," vol. XVIII, no. 8, CBS Television Network, 3 November 1985, p. 14.

6. Alan Gustafson, "Antelope, Outpost of a Commune," *Statesman-Journal*, 4 July 1983, p. C1.

7. *USA Today*, 16 October 1984, p. 11A.

8. Kirk Braun, *Rajneeshpuram: The Unwelcome Society* (West Linn, Ore.: Scout Creek Press, 1984), 145–6.

9. Mike Stahlberg, "Rajneeshees Exult Though Others Simply See Red . . . ," *The Eugene Register Guard*, 25 November 1984, p. B2.

10. Gustafson, p. C1.

11. Stahlberg, p. B2.

12. Leslie A. Zaitz, "Commune Leader Says Atiyeh Fanned Flames of Bigotry," *The Oregonian*, 17 March 1982, p. B2.

13. "This Is the Place," *The Economist*, 29 September 1984, p. 28.

14. Zaitz, p. B2.

15. "Sheela Defends Rajneeshees' Philosophy and Life Style," *Statesman-Journal*, 16 October 1984, p. 5C.

16. Ibid.

17. Ibid.

18. Swami Dhyan John, "Sheela: The Power of Loving," *Bhagwan* 3 (1984): 23.

19. Ibid., 24.

20. Zaitz, p. B2.

21. "Sheela Says Rajneeshees Want Country," *Statesman-Journal*, 30 September 1984, p. 11A.

22. Ibid.

23. Ma Anand Sheela, press release, 29 October 1984, p. 1.

24. Ibid., 2.

25. "Sheela Calls Harsh Words Just a Joke," *Statesman-Journal*, 30 October 1984, p. 1A.

26. Ibid.

27. "Rajneesh Puram, Oregon/Frieda K.," ABC News "Nightline," no. 868, 19 September 1984, p. 2.

28. Ibid.

29. Ibid., 3.

30. Ibid., 4.

31. Ibid., 6.

32. Alan Gustafson, "Ma Sheela Stirs More Hot Words," *Statesman-Journal*, 21 September 1984, p. 1A.

33. Ibid., 13A.

34. Ibid., 1A.

35. Ibid., 13A.

36. "Donahue" transcript no. 10084 (Cincinnati, Ohio: Multimedia Entertainment, Inc., 1984), 5.

37. Ibid., 6.

38. Ibid., 8.

39. Ibid., 11.

40. Ibid., 12.

41. Ibid., 14.

42. Ron Cowan, "Donahue Finds Rajneeshee 'Unpleasant,' " *Statesman-Journal*, 7 October 1984, p. B1.

43. Paul Tillich, *Love, Power, and Justice* (London: Oxford University Press, 1954), 98.

ADDITIONAL REFERENCES

Two earlier papers provide additional information on the Rajneeshee experience in Oregon: Catherine Ann Collins and Christine Miller, "Rajneesh Rhetoric: A Comparative Ethical Appraisal," presented to the International Communication Association, Hawaii, 1985; and "Media Coverage of the Rajneeshees: A Dramatistic Analysis," presented to Northwest Communication Association, Idaho, 1986. Copies can be obtained by writing to the authors.

Chapter Ten

Understanding Fandom Rhetorically: The Case of "Beauty and the Beast"

Kari Whittenberger-Keith

On May 18, 1989, CBS canceled the television program "Beauty and the Beast," citing low ratings and poor demographics. By May 20, CBS headquarters had been inundated with over 4,000 telegrams protesting the cancellation; switchboards, too, were jammed with calls from angry fans. Companies that had advertised during "Beauty and the Beast" also received telegrams, letters, and calls asking for support of the program and the quality television it represented. By May 30, 1989, CBS had reversed its cancellation decision. Calling "Beauty and the Beast" a "rare treasure" important to CBS, then-president of entertainment programming Kim LeMasters announced that "Beauty and the Beast" had not been canceled, merely removed from the fall schedule for some "re-tooling" to make a good show even better. Twelve new episodes were ordered from Witt-Thomas Productions, and a new season of "Beauty and the Beast" was to wait in the wings as a midseason replacement series.

Such fan devotion itself justifies scholarly interest, but this kind of campaign is not unique. An examination of the "Beauty and the Beast" situation shows that much more is going on. This campaign was *not* the spontaneous, independent outcry of viewers; it was an attack planned by an entire community of fans. My purpose here is to explore this community of fans, and thus fandom more generally, through the analysis of fan-generated literature called (appropriately) fanzines.

Fandom represents a little-explored area of audience involvement with mass media. I define fandom as a collectivity of people who interact together on the basis of a specific media artifact (e.g., a television series or film). The distinguishing features of fandom include the intense involvement of the viewers/fans and the interaction of the fans not just with the artifact but with one another.

Fans and fandom are typically marginalized, both by the media establishment and by media scholars.[1] The fans themselves are aware of this bias in the media establishment. In the case of the campaign to save "Beauty and the Beast," fanzines advised fans not to identify themselves as such in writing to advertisers or the network; to do so would simply brand them as "crazies" to be ignored.

Within media studies, fandom has often been ignored, with researchers preferring to focus on wider audiences and the audience interaction with the program rather than fans' interaction with one another. For example, much audience research focuses on the active audience, but that activity is with the artifact rather than with other fans as related to the artifact.[2] Even the interpretative work done using fanzines has focused on the ways in which fans use the artifact to satisfy personal needs and desires rather than on the collectivity of fandom itself.[3]

Literary critical work has also looked at fandom as part of the research agenda regarding multiple readings of texts.[4] Again, the focus has been on the interaction between the reader and the text; the interaction of the readers with one another, although an important source of information on various textual interpretations, has, in and of itself, largely been ignored.

Although all this work adds greatly to our understanding of audiences and the ways in which people use mediated artifacts, a full understanding of fandom and its impact on people's use of the media cannot be achieved through such approaches. Rather, I contend that to understand fandom we must approach it rhetorically. Fandom represents a collective, people brought together for a joint cause, in this case the love of a television program. Although rhetorical scholars have not looked at fandom as such, research on social movements focuses on the same issues of building and sustaining a community.[5] However, social movement research, by definition, tends to focus on sociopolitical or religious movements or both, as well as on the development of "other voices" to battle the status quo. Although such research has some relevance to the group under study here ("Beauty and the Beast" fans "did battle" with CBS and "won" in the short run), it does not account for the long life of many series' fandoms (for example, the original "Star Trek" fandom is over twenty-three years old and still going strong) or the continuance of the fandom after the exigence has disappeared (i.e., after the program has gone off the air).

Yet rhetorical theory does provide the methods and perspectives by which to understand fandom. One purpose of rhetoric is to create and sustain community through the use of discourse and other symbolic forms.[6] Fandom represents such a community, brought together through an artifact, sustained through rhetorical forms. In this case, the primary rhetorical form is fan-generated literature, commonly known as fanzines. Through this literature, a new form of rhetorical life, where fans interact with one another as well as with the media artifact, is created through a community that involves people very deeply and affects their lives in very important ways.

I contend that it is only through such a rhetorical understanding of the community known as fandom that we can really understand fan involvement. Without such an understanding, fandom and the fans who participate can be quickly relegated to the "crazies" and the "unbalanced" in society. In order to make this case clear, I first provide a bit of the history about "Beauty and the Beast" and fandom. Second, through the analysis of fanzines, I identify the ways in which fans use fanzines to create and sustain their community. Finally, from this analysis, I draw some conclusions about fan communities and the rhetorical analysis of such communities.

BACKGROUND

The Program

"Beauty and the Beast" (henceforth referred to as "B + B") premiered in 1987 as a television adaptation of the children's fairy tale. In the fairy tale, the beauty falls in love with a seeming beast, who is actually a handsome prince as revealed by the beauty's kiss.[7] In the television adaptation, Catherine (actress Linda Hamilton) is the beauty who is saved, after an attack, by Vincent (actor Ron Perlman), a part-man, part-lion who lives under the streets of New York City as part of a utopian community of outcasts and misfits. Catherine and Vincent have both a deep, yet unconsummated, love and an empathic bond, allowing each to feel what the other is feeling; tunnel dweller and top dweller are thus united in various adventures throughout the city. Although never a ratings "hit," "B + B" early on developed a strong fan following (over thirty-five fan clubs and at least 350,000 members worldwide within the first two years), similar to that of the original "Star Trek." It is this fandom that saved "B + B" from its first cancellation; it is this fandom that, after the 1989 cancellation, worked to get the series picked up by another network. "B + B" fans were heavily involved with the program, involved enough to send telegrams, write letters, and call media people, sponsors, and CBS to save this program and to respond similarly after the second cancellation. This fandom remains strong, even though "B + B" is no longer in original production, with numerous fan clubs, publications, and conventions.

The Fandom

"B + B" has spawned a vigorous and well-organized fandom. The fans communicate primarily through fan clubs and fan-generated literature called fanzines. There are over thirty "B + B" fan clubs in the United States alone, with several more in Europe and Australasia; many fans belong to more than one fan organization. The majority of people actively involved with "B + B" fandom appears to be female (as is the case with many other fandoms); in the sample of fanzines under study here, 248 writers of letters of comment (LoCs) were female, 16 were male, and 14 had androgynous names. Fan-club activities include publishing fanzines, sponsoring conventions, and holding meetings to view, discuss, and share thoughts and feelings about "B + B."

Fanzines represent the most important tool of fandom. Fanzines began within science fiction (SF) fandom in the 1930s, originally distributed among members of SF clubs.[8] By the 1940s, many fanzines were mimeographed and sent to science fiction pulp readers, containing letters, debates, news of SF conventions, cartoons, and stories.[9] The late 1950s paper shortage killed most of the pulps and, with them, their fanzines.[10]

Within television fandoms, fanzines were adopted by the fans of the original "Star Trek" as a way of communicating with one another.[11] Fanzines of various types are now published about a variety of programs both in original production and in rerun syndication. Fanzines seem to spring up primarily around the science fiction/fantasy genre, hence the well-developed fan literatures surrounding such programs as the original "Star Trek," "Star Trek, the Next Generation," "Battlestar Galactica," and "Doctor Who." However, fanzines are not limited to the "out of this world"; active fan publishing occurs using such shows as "Miami Vice," "Starsky and Hutch," "The Equalizer," and "The Man from U.N.C.L.E." as their basis.[12]

Within the fanzine genre, several variations occur:

- *Fictionzines* are collections of prose, poetry, and original artwork based on the characterizations and contexts of the original series. They tend to take a variety of forms, from those exploring character to those dealing with erotic and homoerotic themes. (Penley, in her work on fanzines, concentrates on the "slash" fictionzines, so named because they are content coded in Datazine, the fanzine information clearinghouse, by a "/"; for example, K/S would tell a fan that that document dealt with homoeroticism involving the two main original "Star Trek" characters, Kirk and Spock.)[13]

- *Infozines* refer to hybrid documents that may include information about the actors and actresses who worked on the series; fan events, such as conventions and viewings; short stories and poetry; original artwork; and letters from fans discussing the series and their involvement in it.

- *Letterzines* are fan-generated publications that consists of fan letters about the program and their involvement with it. In a sense, letterzines act as a kind of paper-based computer bulletin board, where fans can share their thoughts and feelings with other fans across the country and around the world. (In addition, fans do use the new technologies. Not only do fanzines owe their existence to the photocopier and the personal computer for easy reproduction and type-setting, but several fan clubs meet via computer bulletin boards, with regular meeting times and "places.")

The focus of this analysis is on fan letters of comment (LoCs) in fan publications; therefore, I used only letterzines and infozines in my re-search (which I will refer to as simply fanzines). The fanzines I used for this study include *Passages, Once Upon a Time . . . Is Now,* and *Promises of Someday,* all letterzines; and *The Beauty and the Beast Newsletter,* an in-fozine. These publications cover the last half of 1988, all of 1989, and the first part of 1990.

Stylistically, fan LoCs take on many of the characteristics of oral dis-course. They are conversational in form; the letters sound as if writers are talking on paper. They use personalized forms of address and "talk" to specific fan letters from earlier editions. Nonverbals are incorporated typographically, as in using multiple exclamation points ("Vincent is so sexy!!!!"). The addressee of the letters also shifts, not only from letter to letter, but also within letters. Letters may be addressed to the fandom as a whole, to specific fans, or to characters on the program (many readers write specifically to Vincent). Other letters may address the actors, writers, and producers (interestingly, Ron Koslow and his writing team actually read the fanzines to get a sense of what the fans wanted from the program), as well as the CBS brass. In spite of these infor-malities, however, "B + B" fans do not write illiterate letters; these fans write critically and thoughtfully about a program that, for many, appears to have changed their lives.

These, then, are some of the general characteristics of the program, the fandom, and the fanzine. The fanzine is the glue that holds the fandom together, allowing fans to see themselves as a cohesive com-munity. The ways in which fanzines are used to create and sustain this sense of community thus become important to the rhetorical analyst. It is to this set of issues I now turn.

THE CREATION OF COMMUNITY

Fandom is different from other types of collectives in that it exists wholly as a rhetorical form. Fandom is created rhetorically through the medium of fanzines; although the series is important as a catalyst for community, it is the fanzines that provide the conduit for fan interaction and thus for community building. The process of "getting started" is therefore important; understanding what things motivate a fan to become involved in the community gives a sense of how fans use the media as well as the needs they have for human contact. Of course, we have no direct access to the needs and drives of individual fans, but we do have a record of both the rhetoric they create and the rhetoric they find convincing. In many ways, there is a stronger connection between this rhetoric and actions than in most rhetorical analysis, because the fans themselves are generating talk about what motivates them. In this section, I show that there are three primary types of rhetoric associated with creating the community of "B + B" fandom: an aesthetic rhetoric involving the quality of the show, a "fighting the good fight" rhetoric, and a rhetoric of personal fulfillment and satisfaction from belonging to the community. The following section of this chapter shows that although the aesthetic and community-oriented rhetoric carry through into the process of sustaining the community, the rhetoric of the "fight" tends to drop out.

The aesthetic rhetoric dominates many of the fanzine LoCs, and the relevant aesthetic dimensions here are two: the ethos of the characters, actors, and creators; and the "romance" of the show. In particular, many fans are attracted to the main characters, especially to Vincent, the "beast." Much of this attraction is clearly sexual, sensual, or both, and a great deal of discussion centers around the attractiveness of Vincent, both physically and intellectually/emotionally. For example, one fan writes:

Vincent is not a loner or a creature, there is nothing wrong with him, period! He is magnetically attractive. He possesses a noble spirit along with great intelligence and superior physical strength. He has the most beautiful and seductive voice I've ever heard and he knows how to talk to and treat a woman.[14]

As this LoC illustrates, Vincent is seen by many writers as the ideal male: a strong, masculine protector who still has the heart of a romantic, reciting poetry and commenting on the beauty of life with ease and grace. At the same time, Vincent's raw sexuality appears to be a major draw for many viewers; much discussion centers around seeing Vincent's "powerful thighs," his "well-developed chest," his "better than Paul Newman's" eyes, and hearing his gorgeous voice. For some fans, these all come together: "Yeah, he [Vincent] IS sexy, and anytime he wants to visit my dreams, I'm ready."[15] There is also a good deal of good-natured kidding among the fans about who is the "thigh" person, the "eye" person, the "chest" person, and so on. Many of the letters generally swoon over Vincent's sensuality; as readers attest when they chastise Catherine for not sleeping with Vincent, since the readers would "pounce" on him in a second. Although there is a contingent of Catherine lovers as well, the Vincent crowd is far and away in the majority. For many fans, Vincent *is* "B + B."

Much of the "conversation" in the fanzines centers on the actors as well as the characters. "B + B" fans are most respectful of the talents of the actors; Linda Hamilton (as Catherine) and Ron Perlman (as Vincent) receive especially high praise. During the two-and-a-half years of first-run programs, much time was spent either puffing these actors before the Emmys and other awards or decrying their loss of the awards after the ceremonies. Perlman's 1988 Golden Globe Award was especially appreciated by the fans; it signified that, finally, "the best show on television" was being recognized as such. In addition to recognition of the actors' talents in their roles, much talk also focuses on the actors as people. Although some talk centers on the actors' personal lives, such as praise for Linda Hamilton taking time off to be a full-time mother, or Ron Perlman and his wife expecting another child, most focuses on the actors as speakers in attendance at fan conventions (or "cons" in the parlance). Repeatedly, fans write in telling about their experiences with actors—how kind the actors were to "mere" fans, how entertaining, how willing to answer questions at convention sessions. This description of Roy Dotrice, who plays Father, the founder of the tunnel community on the series, when he appeared at a convention, is typical:

Roy Dotrice was an absolute joy! Unlike many celebrities new to [fan] conventions, Roy appears to be right in his element. Far from being frightened of the adoring masses, he seemed to be just as delighted to get a look at us as we were to get a closer look at him.[16]

Such fans are impressed with the cast and their willingness to "come down" to the level of the "little people." The fans see these actors as truly committed to the quality program that was "B + B" and go to great lengths to express their admiration for that dedication.

Some fans discuss their attraction to the program growing out of their previous experiences with fantasy/science fiction programs and particularly with the original "Star Trek." Some discussion, therefore, centers on the ways in which "B + B" exemplifies the values and morals of fantasy/science fiction, especially in terms of dealing with issues of power and diversity in human (and possible nonhuman) cultures. Interestingly, however, many fans also are brought to "B + B" with no previous experience in fandom; numerous letters begin with, "I have never been involved in fandom before but. . . ." One fan writes a typical "virgin's" letter:

This is also my first experience with "fandom" thanks to "Beauty and the Beast." I have never written a fan letter or written to a network about a show—until now. It's nice to know I'm not alone.[17]

Most letters reinforce the importance of not being alone and of finally having a group to talk with about "this marvelous obsession." There also appears to be a ritual connected with "the first letter"; fans preface it with that announcement, usually apologizing for what they are about to say.

In a particular contrast to many science fiction genres, "B + B" fans do not hesitate to position "B + B" within the Romantic tradition of aesthetics. They are quick to argue that it is "high art," on a par with Shakespeare or any of the Romantic poets. This type of letter is not at all uncommon:

To me, a work of art, that which really lasts, is something that lives. It lives in the excitement when it enthralls the viewer of the masterpiece or the listener of the concerto. It lives when it evokes a response from its audience and then the audience is moved to carry on the response and support the art work. Isn't this exactly what is happening with "Beauty and the Beast"? Don't we all have the desire to become part of the "family," don't we all want to carry it forth, support it, and see it survive?[18]

Some fans get even more enthusiastic about the quality and wonder of the program:

It's like we're witness to a modern day classic, as if something like Shakespeare is evolving right before our eyes. I feel like we can tell future generations about it! Vincent and Catherine will go down in history as one of the greatest love stories of all time![19]

(In a later section I show how this initial attraction to the arty qualities of the show becomes a rhetorical resource for sustaining the "B + B" community.)

In conjunction with their admiration for the program itself, during the period under study, many fans were drawn to fandom by the precarious position of the program in the CBS schedule; they wanted to "fight for what is right." From its first episodes, "B + B," both in the press and at CBS, was dubbed as a long shot. After all, the common wisdom went, who would want to watch a show about some woman and her love affair with some half-cat who lived in sewers? And, from the beginning, ratings were shaky. In its 8:00 Friday night slot, "B + B" did acceptably, but compared to other shows its rating and share were rather weak (a weakness not helped by frequent preemptions through both local affiliates and the networks). As the show developed during its second season (after a late start and several atypical shows due to the constraints of the writers' strike), its tenuous position became precarious. Audience fell off, especially among males aged 18 to 54. It consistently came in second behind the ABC competitors, and often came in third. And, as mentioned earlier, the program *was* canceled (only to be semi-renewed) in the spring of its second season.

Almost from the start, fans saw CBS as a potential beast with the power to deprive them of their "Beast." Much of the mail in the first season focused on "being supportive" of CBS through calls and letters and buying advertiser products. Fans were particularly irritated by the ratings system and the triumph of money over quality in terms of the program:

Poor ratings be damned. (And I can't understand why they are!) "Beauty and the Beast" has something for everyone—that's if they're willing to take the time to look. Yes, I realize CBS is in the business to make money, but must everything (quality, creativity, and class) be sacrificed to the almighty dollar?! There's already too many mindless shows on television and I never bought the notion that the American public was too stupid to understand anything other than murder, drugs, and rape (and all within the first 10 minutes no less!). To CBS, Kim LeMasters, Ron Koslow, Witt-Thomas Productions . . . thank you! Hang in there, guys; your dedication WILL pay off.[20]

As CBS's lack of support during the second season became clear, the fans turned downright nasty. Threats were issued; some thought that Vincent should "beast out" right at Black Rock; and CBS executives generally became the enemy that every "B + B" fan—and every supporter of quality television—should fight against. With the cancellation, many fans were adamant, writing that they would never watch CBS again, as revenge for the cancellation.

CBS was not the only organization reviled by the fans. The A. C. Nielsen Company was despised for its "biased and inaccurate ratings"; any critic, commentator, or talk-show host who made fun of "B + B"— the premise, the actors, the story lines, the viewers—was in for similar treatment. For example, John Lofton, columnist for *The Washington Times*, wrote an acerbic column about "B + B,"[21] which provoked equally hostile responses:

I have to make a comment on that vicious little review by John Lofton, columnist (or more aptly assassin) for the *Washington Times*. . . . What a puling, small minded, hateful review, obviously written by an insensitive cretin unable to appreciate the elevated qualities of human kindness, gentleness, and tolerance, which is what the show is really about. Does anyone have his address? I'd love to write him a letter. (I promise not to use plastic explosives, even though sorely tempted.)[22]

Such venom was not reserved for only "outsiders." The fans even attacked the show's creators and writers when they tried to retool the program (as per CBS instructions) and salvage the show for its third season. Writers and actors alike got hate mail and threats to their safety; finally, the set had to be closed to all outsiders to protect the cast and crew from angry and abusive fans.[23] And many fans were willing to cast as devils not just those in the media world but their families, co-workers, "friends," anyone who could not appreciate the value and quality of "B + B."

Beyond cathartic outburst, there was disciplined mobilization. Much space in the fanzines was devoted to practical methods for "saving our show." For example, fans were taught how to approach the network and advertisers to solicit support for the show (rule number one—*never* say you are involved in fandom). Lists of advertisers were provided, including addresses, phone numbers, and contact persons. Phone banks were set up nationwide (through local fan clubs) to remind friends, neighbors, and relatives to watch the show each week. Other suggestions included informing everyone one knew about "B + B" and how good it was, even the people standing in line at the grocery store. One fanzine went so far as to offer a "bounty" for influencing an actual Nielsen family (presumably a goal never achieved).

Perhaps the most powerful reason that people seemed to get involved in fandom is that "B + B" touched their lives in some very personal ways. In this sense, fandom empowers its members by allowing them to discover and exercise new parts of their personalities. The rhetorical form that dominates this motivation for joining the community is the testimonial. For many, "B + B" changed their lives. Numerous testimonials describe the ways in which viewing "B + B" helped fans make decisions to reevaluate their lives, explore the arts and their own hidden talents, and reestablish their faith in humanity (through the involvement with the utopian tunnel community). Some testimonials are particularly touching; one fan writes about "the biggest fan she knows":

This is a fan who was born with a noticeable speech impediment, who was forced to endure this situation throughout her life, ridiculed at an impressionable age, leaving her a very self-conscious, introverted person until "B + B." This is now a fan who takes it upon herself to promote this show and will actually, willingly, approach total strangers, asking if they watch the series, their opinion if they do, and is in total disbelief when she meets someone who . . . does not watch the show. . . . It is then, she believes her personal duty to inform this recruitee of all the aspects of this series. . . . This fan is not some lovesick, easily influenced individual who will outgrow this phase. This fan is my Aunt Vera; she is sixty some years young now that she has been reborn because of "B + B."[24]

In addition to changing lives, some fans have even credited "B + B" with saving their lives. Three fans wrote that they felt "B + B" had been sent by God to save them from suicide, which they were contemplating because of depression over bad relationships. As one fan wrote in empathizing with another:

As I mentioned before, your letter was wonderful. I identify with it because I went through something similar, only it was death that separated me from the two most important people in my life, and the medium the Lord used to rescue me from my slough of despondency was "Star Trek" and not "B + B." Perhaps, only because I wouldn't have lasted long enough to see "B + B." He uses whatever, and whoever, is to hand. His love is from everlasting to everlasting, something I used to doubt, but don't anymore.[25]

For that fan, it took "B + B" to make her a complete person again. In the same way that Eric Hoffer posits that true believers become involved in movements because they have been deeply hurt in some way, and need to be made whole by the movement, some "B + B" viewers see themselves as being made whole by this program.[26]

Fans also join fandom to gain the understanding and camaraderie of other believers. As was noted earlier, many fans attest to being fandom "virgins" who have never been involved in anything like organized fandom before. They express relief to know that "there are others like them," and that they "are not crazy." Fans, who are frightened by the intensity of their own involvement in this series, are helped to realize that they are not alone. Much of the talk in the fanzines is about the fan family that develops across the miles and across the oceans; fans who have never met put one another up at conventions, write long letters to one another about "B + B," and take "B + B" vacations visiting other fans along the way. Some fans even meet their soul mates through the fan network:

The greatest event occurred this year. One of my dear fellow correspondents and I have fallen in love with each other. I have never been more joyful in my life. My beloved and I will meet face-to-face in September in Miami. We will try to begin a life together, it may be difficult but there is nothing we can't overcome.[27]

Fans tend to see their fellow Beasties (or Beasters, BBs, or Beauties, depending on one's preference) as the chosen, because they are the people who can see the light about the quality and the wonder of this program. As one fan puts it:

We "B + B" fans hold ourselves so high above other fandoms because what we praise is of high quality. We praise courage, perseverance, strength, kindness, respect, compassion, humanism, and love. We pat ourselves on the back for admiring such uncommon and almost holy qualities and continue on our way.[28]

In this sense, "B + B" fans see themselves as special people, sensitive enough to appreciate this program. However, fans go beyond simple appreciation of the program's values; they enact these values in their everyday lives. Fans' lives have been changed because of this show. Repeatedly, LoCs tell stories of leaving abusive relationships, going back to school, changing careers, all directly attributed to the impact of "B + B" on their lives. Many fans have taken the causes of the show to heart, working for the homeless and the less fortunate in their communities. In particular, the "Lights of Winterfest" program (so named after the Winterfest celebration of the program) encourages local fan groups to donate both time and money to aid the homeless in their areas. In addition to local efforts, the Lights of Winterfest campaign has raised over $18,000 nationally, monies sent in by fans who have no local clubs through which to channel their energies.[29] Fans take the lessons and the ideals of "B + B" and make them a part of their daily activities; they see themselves becoming kinder, gentler, more tolerant people because of this series.

Interestingly, such activism does not, for most fans, extend to involvement in other programs. Although a significant number (approximately 30%) of "B + B" fans have been involved in other fannish activities (including "Star Trek" old and new), most fans have not been involved in other programs and do not foresee involvement in other programs.[30] In fact, with the cancellation of "B + B," many vowed never to be involved with any kind of television program again; for these fans, the end of "B + B" was simply too painful to endure again.

Thus, a number of forces drew fans to "B + B" and its fandom, including such aesthetic forces as the quality of the program, an attraction to the characters and the actors, and an attraction to the fantasy/science fiction genre; pragmatic forces involving fighting CBS to keep the show on the air; and personal forces involving the impact "B + B" has on individual lives. Although these forces draw people into fandom, keeping them there is quite another story. At some point, as with most communities that develop around a cause, the devil is no more (in this case, CBS canceled the program, thus defeating the fans), the actors may go on to bigger and better things, and something is needed to keep the fandom intact. In the case of "B + B," several rhetorical features seem to assure the health and well-being of its fandom for years to come. It is these features I discuss in the next section.

SUSTAINING COMMUNITY

Just as it is rhetorically constructed, the "B + B" community is rhetorically sustained. The techniques for sustaining a far-flung network of "B + B" fans through the medium of fanzines boil down to interpretative

interaction with the show, comparison of the "B + B" utopia with ac-
tualizing possibilities for real utopias, and community self-examination
for unifying values. It is through these means that fans perform two
crucial rhetorical functions of community: rehearsing and reaffirming
cherished values, and holding back divisive factors that threaten the
community.

As I noted in the previous section, "B + B" fans are drawn to the
program because they perceive it to be quality television of the highest
order. This perception of quality keeps them active in fandom. Program
quality, especially with regard to the depth and the complexity of the
issues dealt with on the shows, keeps fans involved and interested over
several years and multiple viewings. Much of the space in the LoCs is
devoted to the critical interpretation of the program. Some of these
interpretations are rather technical, as in this interpretation of Vincent's
dream about entering Catherine's apartment:

My interpretation [of the "Nor Iron Bars a Cage"] dream sequence is more
Freudian than anything. I see Vincent's inability to enter Catherine's apartment
as very sexual. My interpretation sees Catherine's apartment as an extension of
her *physical* body: Vincent *enters* her apartment in his dream, and the subsequent
"exploration" of the intimate objects there (notice the way he touches her book,
looks at her bed, picks up her brush?) which leads to the "climax" of the scene:
seeing the image of Catherine by the window, waiting for him. It is at this point,
as he is moving toward her, that she fades away. Why? One possible explanation
may be that Vincent's lack of previous experience with physical intimacy prevents him from completing the dream. He doesn't *know* how to end it.[31]

Other interpretations are less technical:

Remember folks, we're dealing with an archetype here, fraught with lots of
symbolic importance. "Beauty and the Beast" is an archetype of integration; the
whole point is that Beauty needs the Beast as well as vice versa. Catherine and
Vincent are the means of reconciliation, of integration—their task is to build a
bridge between their worlds.[32]

In a very real sense, fans act as naive critical theorists; although not
trained in interpretative analysis, they perform multiple readings
through detailed and often insightful interpretations of the show.

Many of these readings act to rhetorically recreate the program as a
romantic fantasy. The focus of "B + B" fans is on the beauty and the
romance of Vincent and Catherine's undying love and bittersweet romance; LoCs focus on the readings of poetry and the possibilities of
consummating this love. Yet the program itself resembles a modified
cop/hero drama in the tradition of "Ironside." Catherine is an assistant
district attorney, Vincent protects her through the strength of their bond,

and many episodes focus on the crime of the week, with Vincent acting as both Catherine's savior from trouble and the ultimate punishment for any bad guys (getting mauled by a lion man is no fun). In a sense, there is a strong air of the postmodern about "B + B." It contains many unresolved and unresolvable contradictions: beauty versus beast, human versus nonhuman, light versus dark, above versus below, reality versus utopia, love versus violence. These contradictions are not superficially introduced in dialogue; they are built into the very fabric of a narrative in which, unlike its fairy-tale counterpart, a kiss cannot make the contradictions disappear.

But fans have a different sense of the contradictions. Fans readily overlook most of the blood and violence of the program; for example, one fan writes that:

I've decided not to write about anything I find less than pleasing in "B + B." During the first season, I ignored the parts of "B + B" related to criminals, etc., and only focused on the love, gentleness, beauty, etc. Now, in my LoCs I'll ignore awkward lighting, slow pacing, etc. I don't watch and love "B + B" because it is perfect in all areas . . . it isn't. I feel about it as I do because of the many glorious things I get from it that don't exist anyplace else in this combination . . . a symbolic candlelit dinner . . . a loving couple dancing—first shown as shadows on a wall, then in slow motion in the flesh. There are few places in the world concerned with beauty, love, elegance, romance, friendship, etc. . . . let alone on weekly TV.[33]

Taking this focus on art and elegance a step further, many fans recommend that "B + B" be required school viewing to teach children about the higher values in life.

Other readings focus on the agreement between "B + B" and Christian doctrine. Although some viewers might see the love story between a human woman and a beast as unchristian and unholy, many viewers give long and detailed explanations about the ways in which the program reflects and integrates Christian principles. For example, one LoC gave a detailed analysis of the ways in which Vincent exemplified Jesus Christ, from his position as an outcast to his propensity to speak in a very poetic and ethereal style. Another fan interprets the principles of the program biblically and applies them to her own life:

So many of the themes explored in the show have set my mind on scriptural principles, made me *think*. I thank God for this show every day. He has used it to have such an impact on my life. I have changed, and I like it. I pray for everyone involved in the show all the time, and for the third season renewal. The most precious thing the Lord has shown me through V and C's love for each other is a reflection of his love for us. Many times, in His Word, He compares himself to a bridegroom and us, those who love Him, as the bride, seeking her, coming to get her, saving her, protecting her, loving her. Seeing this ideal man/woman relationship . . . helped me realize my relationship to Him. I now know the type of man I should seek and pray for, my human bridegroom should have these qualities Vincent has. A prayerful, Godly man who values honesty, and love above all else.[34]

Fan readings also spend a good deal of time deifying "B + B" relative to the current cultural landscape. This current landscape is defined by television, thus leading to the conclusion that "B + B" is the greatest program in television history; in the words of more than one fan, "Even the worst episode of "B + B" is far better than the best episode of any other program on television." "B + B" is, for these fans, art of the highest form; it seeks to move their emotions and lift their spirits through its messages of hope and good triumphing over evil. Some fans focus on the difficulties of viewing great art; for example:

"B + B" causes me so much pain so often to watch. Sometimes I do not want to think so hard or feel so deeply. Sometimes, I wish to sit back and relax and let my spirit be salved with the opiate of mindlessness that most TV is, but the way to grow is to "confront our fears" and our pain and THINK. I salute you, "Beauty and the Beast," for forcing one to think, and to feel, just as the finest novel, play, or poem does. Keep it up.[35]

Other fans exalt themselves and degrade others for not appreciating "B + B"; one viewer writes that "Unfortunately, I think we all know that 'B + B' is analogous to Beethoven on MTV; most American viewers used to junkfood TV can't understand the subtlety and the depth of this classy show."[36]

These acts of interpretation, whether of the program's religious content, its cultural value, or its romantic character, do not occur in a vacuum. Rather, the purpose of such interpretation is to help viewers express, clarify, and explore higher values and ideals. Therefore, "B + B" fandom also sustains itself through its exploration of the philosophical issues surrounding the series. Much like the original "Star Trek," "B + B" is felt to examine issues of diversity, of minorities and oppressed peoples, and of the future of the nation and of humankind. One viewer sums up this position when he writes:

One of the things that has really impressed me about "Beauty and the Beast," and that seems to have impressed others as well, is the high ideals expressed in the show. Over and over in letters to this and other fan publications people mention them:

-not judging others by appearances
-the caring for one another exhibited by the Tunnel Dwellers
-the peaceful "live and let live" philosophy of the tunnel dwellers . . .

and last, but certainly not least, Catherine and Vincent's love for one another, in which each tries extremely hard to live up to the high ideals they feel the other expects and deserves.

These are pretty high ideals. We can all do that kind of reaching for ideal within ourselves, and be better people for it, even if we don't always attain them.[37]

The series itself deals with these issues explicitly. It continually examines the contrasts between the above world of New York City, portrayed as grimy, gritty, hard, and dangerous, and the tunnel world, filmed in soft focus, lit by candles and gaslights, warm and glowing with books on every wall and Victorian era furnishings (all, conveniently, cast off by the people above). Although the tunnel world is portrayed as a utopian community, it is one always threatened from above; intruders constantly disturb and endanger the safety of the outcasts. This, in turn, reflects an ancient narrative theme: Wandering exiles find a new place, and the formerly despised become the moral elite. This same journey is carried out in the LoCs of those who discover this program and join its band of elite viewers.

Many fans feel a part of the tunnel community because they see themselves as outsiders. All the members of the tunnel community are, first and foremost, outcasts from the world above. Vincent, the lion man, lives with Father, the founder (and, as the name implies) father figure of the community, a physician who was persecuted unfairly during the McCarthy era. Other community members include children rescued by Catherine and Vincent from an abusive foster home, a young deaf woman abandoned by her parents as an infant, and a pregnant former prostitute taken in to have her baby and make a new life for herself. The series continually deals with the issues of outsiders and outcasts from society, issues that fans follow up in their LoCs. Many fans are deeply touched by the humanity of these outcasts and, because of what they have seen on the program, devote themselves to helping the less fortunate. "B + B" fan clubs sponsor food drives and do volunteer work with the needy; other fans write about the children they have adopted, the shut-ins they visit, or the foster children they care for, as a result, they say, of their involvement with this program.[38]

Fans also use "B + B" as a springboard for discussions of utopian societies and of other worlds. In this way, "B + B" functions similarly to both the original and the new "Star Trek" as well as other science fiction programs. It offers a vision of another way of being, a vision that fans find involving and fascinating. Fans are particularly fond of the safety and warmth of the tunnels; more than one fan has written about their use of the tunnels as a psychological escape from the difficulties of daily life. Generally, the higher values "B + B" deals with provide much fodder for fans and represent part of the continuing attraction of the series. In this way, one might link these interests with the post-modern quest for community, which represents an attempt to ground community in art rather than in previous social or religious institutions.

As with any community, that of "B + B" is not all sweetness and light. Although the devil in the form of CBS is no more, this fandom contin-ually reinvents itself through the splintering and reunification of the fan community. Of course, whenever things get organized, conflicts erupt and splintering occurs; whether it is the civil rights movement, the wom-en's movement, or organized political parties, factions form. And "B + B" fandom is no different; with over thirty-five fan clubs and thousands of people actively involved in fandom, factions will develop, and have developed. But "B + B" may have more difficulty than other collectivities in dealing with such a natural process, for "B + B" fandom does not value unity for the sake of unity; unity is an integral higher value within the philosophy espoused by the show. So fans must develop the rhe-torical resources to deal with this continuing challenge. These resources have taken two basic forms. One is that appeal to the values and to the program itself as a uniting factor. For example, during the tense period of "what if" regarding cancellation, fans wrote many letters like this:

I think of my new friends . . . and all the moments we have already shared. I think of all the other kindred spirits out there that I have yet to reach out to touch and explore. I think upon trust and honor and brotherhood (expressed by this show) that our world desperately needs. I think upon the crystal and the rose and what they symbolize. I think upon love, romance, and THE voice reading poetry and I just can't walk away. . . . Reading the letters in the 'zines and corresponding with new "B + B" friends has somewhat renewed my faith in my fellow man. I know that there are many of us who desire to live at peace in a community with each other. There are those of us who truly desire to reach out in brotherhood; who want to share the joys and the sorrows of others with true concern, compassion, and understanding. I no longer feel like a lone voice.[39]

As this letter illustrates, regardless of the disagreement, fans remind one another that "we are all in this together; we are all in this for the beauty and the wonder of this show."

The other appeal is far more pragmatic. Using the original "Star Trek" as their example (a fandom rife with factionalism and splinter groups), "B + B" fans remind one another that "we have to remain open minded, tolerant, and respectful of one another; otherwise, we could end up like Trekkies." This letter is typical:

This last part may be ill-advised of me, but I'll open my heart about it anyway. I hope against hope that "B + B" fandom stays as amicable as it is right now. Warring factions have a way of cropping up over the most bizarre points of contention. . . . The backbiting and constant feuding that developed in "Star Trek" fandom just took all the joy out of it for me, and I [got away from it all] for a long time from fandom in general. If my fantasy isn't yours, please don't feel that we can't be friends and please, *please* don't feel I am rejecting you if I can't share yours.[40]

As this letter argues, fandom needs to remain united, not become "a house divided." Thus, factionalism becomes more than a difference between interpretations or ideologies; factionalism becomes a creeping cancer that threatens to destroy both the values and the realities of "B+B" fandom. The effort to overcome this tendency, and to keep fandom together, tends to bind people closely and continually to the fandom.

The "B+B" community sustains itself through a number of rhetorical means, including both the aesthetic and testimonial resources of the creation phase and forces unique to the sustaining process: the interpretative interaction with the program, the comparison of the show's world to reality, and the struggle to maintain a united community. Through these means, the fandom both reaffirms its values and belief system and establishes its unique character against the rest of the world.

CONCLUSIONS

What, then, does this analysis of "B+B" fandom tell us about fandom more generally? First, in contrast with most audience-centered research, the role of the media here is not so much that of *object* as *instrument* of the fandom. Fans use the artifact as a "gathering point" in the creation of community: The basis of the community is not simply in reaction to the media artifact. Although it remains the focus of discussion and debate, fandom can develop and grow in the absence of the media that spawned it; witness the continuance of "Star Trek" fandom after almost thirty years of "the same old shows." Although many social movement researchers have succumbed to the temptation of separating ideas (or ideologies) from their instantiation in social practice, the study of fandom provides a useful corrective to this approach. Within fandom, as within any community, ideas and practices evolve together and are inextricable.

This points to another conclusion about fandom. The creation stage of fandom is one in which the artifact does play a primary role; people become involved because of the program, and their early letters focus on the show. However, the sustaining stage focuses more on the people; as fans become involved, far more space is given to talking about what the fandom has meant to them: the friends, the support, the importance of community. Again, although the show is necessary as an instrument of organization, it becomes secondary to the community as fandom develops.

Thus, fandom cannot be understood merely as a result of viewer interaction with the artifact. An audience-centered approach is too narrowly focused, because it examines the viewer relation to the artifact but generally excludes viewer interaction with other people. Thus, the tools of rhetorical analysis seem appropriate to the analysis of fandom, to capturing its true nature, and to better understanding the process of community building. The rhetorical forms of fandom also reinforce this conclusion; due to the "paper trail" fans leave, the analyst has the materials for analysis readily available.

Fans are not crazies, if crazies are people that do not belong to the community or have one of their own. Instead of marginalizing their community because of its origins in a media situation, we should respect it for its resemblance to other communities we cherish. These are people who are deeply committed to both a "cause" (their media artifact) and their community. By better understanding fandom, in all its richness and all its complexity, we can better understand the rhetorical process of building and sustaining any community.

NOTES

1. For commentary on fandom and its treatment by outsiders, see Henry Jenkins III, " 'Star Trek' Rerun, Reread, Rewritten: Fan Writing as Textual Poaching," *Critical Studies in Mass Communication* 5 (June 1988): 85–107; R. Jewett and J. S. Lawrence, *The American Monomyth* (Garden City, N.Y.: Anchor Press, 1977); C. Leershen, " 'Star Trek's' Nine Lives," *Newsweek*, 22 December 1986, pp. 66–73; Robin Wood, *Hollywood from Vietnam to Reagan* (New York: Columbia University Press, 1986).

2. Kevin M. Carragee, "Interpretative Media Study and Interpretative Social Science," *Critical Studies in Mass Communication* 7 (June 1990): 81–96; John Fiske, "Television: Polysemy and Popularity," *Critical Studies in Mass Communication* 3 (December 1986): 391–408; John Fiske, *Television Culture* (London: Methuen, 1987); Jenkins, " 'Star Trek' Rerun, Reread, Revisited," 85–107; David Morley, *The "Nationwide" Audience* (London: British Film Institute, 1980); David Morley, "The 'Nationwide' Audience: A Critical Postscript," *Screen Education* 39 (1981): 3–14; Linda Steiner, "Oppositional Decoding as an Act of Resistance," *Critical Studies in Mass Communication* 5 (March 1988): 1–15.

3. See, for example, Jenkins, " 'Star Trek' Rerun, Reread, Rewritten," 85–107; Constance Penley, "To Boldly Go Where No Woman Has Gone Before: Feminism, Psychoanalysis, and Popular Culture," paper presented at the Cultural Studies Now and in the Future conference, University of Illinois, Champaign-Urbana, April 1990.

4. Janice Radway, *Reading the Romance: Women, Patriarchy, and Popular Literature* (Chapel Hill, N.C.: University of North Carolina Press, 1984).

5. Robert S. Cathcart, "New Approaches to the Study of Movements: Defining Movements Rhetorically," *Western Journal of Speech Communication* 36 (Spring 1972): 82–88; Charles Conrad, "The Rhetoric of the Moral Majority: An

Analysis of Romantic Form," *Quarterly Journal of Speech* 69 (May 1983): 159–70; Richard Gregg, "The Ego Function of Protest Rhetoric," *Philosophy and Rhetoric* 4 (Spring 1971): 71–91; Leland M. Griffin, "On Studying Movements,"*Central States Speech Journal* 31 (Winter 1980): 225–32; Roderick P. Hart, "The Rhetoric of the True Believer," *Speech Monographs* 38 (November 1971): 249–61; Herbert W. Simons, "Requirements, Problems, and Strategies: A Theory of Persuasion for Social Movements," *Quarterly Journal of Speech* 56 (February 1970): 1–11; Charles J. Stewart, "A Functional Approach to the Rhetoric of Social Movements," *Central States Speech Journal* 31 (Winter 1980): 298–305.

6. Ernest Bormann, "Fantasy and Rhetorical Vision: The Rhetorical Criticism of Social Reality," *Quarterly Journal of Speech* 58 (December 1972): 396–407; Ernest Bormann, *The Force of Fantasy: Restoring the American Dream* (Carbondale, Ill.: Southern Illinois University Press, 1985); Roderick P. Hart, "The Functions of Human Communication in the Maintenance of Public Values," in *Handbook of Rhetorical and Communication Theory*, eds. Carroll Arnold and John Waite Bowers (Boston: Allyn and Bacon, 1984), 749–91; John Louis Lucaites, "Constitutional Argument in a National Theater: The Impeachment Trial of Dr. Henry Sacheverell," in *Popular Trials: Rhetoric, Mass Media, and the Law*, ed. Robert Hariman (Tuscaloosa, Ala.: University of Alabama Press, 1990), 31–54; Michael Calvin McGee, "The 'Ideograph': A Link Between Rhetoric and Ideology," *Quarterly Journal of Speech* 66 (February 1980): 1–16.

7. Edward Gross, *The Unofficial Tale of Beauty and the Beast* (Las Vegas: Pioneer Books, 1980); Betsy Hearne, *Beauty and the Beast: Visions and Revisions of an Old Tale* (Chicago: University of Chicago Press, 1989); Iona Opie and Peter Opie, *The Classic Fairytales* (New York: Oxford University Press, 1974), 179–95.

8. *The Science Fiction Encyclopedia*, ed. Peter Nichols (Garden City, N.Y.: Doubleday, 1979), 215, s.v. "fanzine."

9. *The New Encyclopedia of Science Fiction*, ed. James Gunn (New York: Viking, 1988), 160–2, s.v. "fandom"; Joe Siclari, "Science Fiction Fandom: A History of an Unusual Hobby," in *The Science Fiction Reference Book*, ed. Marshall B. Tymn (Mercer Island, Wash.: Starmont House, 1981), 87–129.

10. Andrew King, personal correspondence with author, January 1991.

11. Jenkins, " 'Star Trek' Rerun, Reread, Revised," 85–107.

12. *Datazine*, a bimonthly publication of Datazine Publications, serves as a clearinghouse for fan-related publications and merchandise; it focuses primarily on television and film fandoms.

13. Penley, "To Boldly Go."

14. *Beauty and the Beast Newsletter* 2 (September 1989): 22.

15. *Promises of Someday* 1 (November 1989): 18.

16. *Passages* 8 (December 1989): 3.

17. Ibid., 8.

18. *Promises of Someday* 1 (July 1989): 21.

19. *Passages* 18 (August 1989): 5.

20. *Promises of Someday* 1 (March 1989): 22.

21. John Lofton, "Strangest Beast He Ever Saw . . . on TV," *The Washington Times*, 30 November 1988.

22. *Passages* 10 (February 1989): 13. Note that this response directly contradicts the values of understanding and tolerance for diversity espoused by the pro-

gram. This lack of tolerance on the part of fans appeared to contribute to the factionalization of the fandom, especially with the changes in the retooled third season.

23. *Beauty and the Beast Newsletter* 2 (September 1989): 12–14.

24. *Once Upon a Time . . . Is Now* 8 (February 1989): 2.

25. *Passages* 18 (August 1989): 3.

26. Eric Hoffer, *The True Believer* (New York: Harper, 1951); see also Hart, "The Rhetoric of the True Believer," 249–61.

27. *Beauty and the Beast Newsletter* 2 (December 1989): 15.

28. *Beauty and the Beast Newsletter* 2 (September 1989): 38.

29. Dorothy Sconzo, personal correspondence with the author, December 1990.

30. These figures represent preliminary results of a survey mailed to 235 LoC writers. Of the 165 who responded, 50 (30%) had been involved in fandom for other programs (primarily "Star Trek"), and 115 (70%) had not been actively involved in fandom previously. Interestingly, most fans who had not been involved previously said that, because of their disappointment over the cancellation of "Beauty and the Beast," they would not get involved in fandom in the future.

31. *Passages* 9 (January 1989): 11.

32. *Promises of Someday* 1 (March 1989): 24.

33. *Promises of Someday* 1 (November 1989): 21.

34. *Passages* 16/17 (July 1989): 9.

35. *Beauty and the Beast Newsletter* 2 (September 1989): 29.

36. *Passages* 12 (April 1989): 10.

37. *Passages* 8 (December 1988): 17–18.

38. *Promises of Someday* 2 (January 1990): 3.

39. *Promises of Someday* 1 (September 1989): 21.

40. *Promises of Someday* 1 (November 1989): 11. It is interesting to note that fandoms have historically been rife with factionalism. See Siclari, "Science Fiction Fandom," 87–129.

Chapter Eleven

Purchasing Identity: Advertising and the Embrace and Celebration of Self

Charles Urban Larson

The world is too much with us . . . getting and spending.
William Wordsworth

In their 1982 book, *Channels of Desire*, Stuart and Elizabeth Ewens trace the development of American consumer-oriented culture. They work from a Marxist perspective in which the central concept is the alienation of the individual in any capitalistic society. They argue that alienation is at the base of consumerism, and that consumption serves as but a momentary balm for feelings of worthlessness, isolation, and personal estrangement.[1] Numerous other critics of consumerism (and especially of advertising as a tool of capitalist consumerism) hold similar positions.[2] The Ewenses maintain that the isolation and estrangement arise because workers are separated from the end results of their labors. Not having an opportunity to take pride in the end product, and being isolated from fellow workers on the assembly line, workers seek meaning for their lives by linking the perceived value of their work with a continuous chain of purchasing goods and services. Such purchases are usually not made out of any need for the products; they are not the basics of life; in fact, frequently the goods are frivolous. Instead, according to the Ewenses, purchases are made for highly symbolic reasons that are tied to feelings of isolation and the need for a sense of community. These purchases (coupled with easy credit and mass advertising) force the worker into an endless cycle of wage slavery and symbolic substitutes for the feelings of self-worth that were once tied to pride in the end product of one's work.

This chapter argues along similar lines but without embracing the Marxist critique on which the Ewenses base their argument. Instead, the claim here is that although the consumption of products and the advertisements for them do relate to self-identification, the motive behind the purchase can as plausibly be argued to stem from either a need for or a *celebration* of the self and one's reference groups. This identification or celebration of self premise can be demonstrated in several ways: (1) by tracing the rise of consumerism; (2) by examining a variety of advertising research methods; and (3) by offering a non-Marxist reading of several elements in contemporary advertising that demonstrate how varying degrees of self-identity are offered (e.g., in product names, ad slogans, pictorials, and ad copy). The remainder of this chapter explores these three means of demonstration.

THE RISE OF CONSUMERISM: 1860–1940

The significant rise of American consumerism in the years between the Civil War and World War II is linked to the simultaneous development of capitalism, the industrial revolution, and most importantly to the large-scale emigrations from Europe and Russia in the latter decades of the nineteenth century and the early decades of the twentieth. Today we are witnessing similar emigrations from Mexico, the Caribbean basin, Southeast Asia, the Soviet bloc, and elsewhere. The more recent immigrants come for the same reasons as their predecessors—a chance to improve their lot in life and a recognition of the United States as a country offering not only opportunity but an abundance of consumer goods. These floods of immigrants provided two critical elements needed for the emergence of consumerism. First, the new immigrants were cheap labor for American industry, which was thus able to provide the middle classes with inexpensive goods and services that had previously been enjoyed by only the wealthy. Second, the new immigrant class began to earn and accumulate capital—sometimes by having several or all the members of a family working, sometimes by having several families share living quarters, and frequently by doing both. Having money to spend, the immigrants soon developed into potential consumers for the many new and inexpensive products coming off the assembly lines.

In earlier times, the word *consumption* carried with it highly negative connotations: "to consume was an act of pillage" that meant "to take up completely, devour, waste and spend," and "it meant to destroy, to use up, to waste, to exhaust." The Ewenses compare these connotations to the older usage of the word, when it was associated with the disease we call tuberculosis, which wastes away the diseased individual.[3]

With industrialization, the idea of using things up (e.g., raw materials, energy, space) became linked with prosperity. The words *consumption* and *consumer* gradually came to be neutral and then even self-congratulatory. In fact, in contemporary American culture, Americans proudly refer to themselves as consumers without a second thought or blush of shame. Today we find columns in newspapers offering advice to consumers, consumer protection organizations, consumer advocates, consumer rating services, corporate consumer relations departments, and even monthly consumer periodicals offering advice on making wise purchase decisions.

The new immigrants were not initially prime targets for a consumerist philosophy of life. They were people of the land—peasants, hired hands, and sharecroppers—who were not accustomed to waste. In the old country, the home and not the factory was the production center for what the family wore, ate, and used until it was worn out and then usually recycled in some way. Old clothing was repaired or refitted for another family member or perhaps found its way into a patchwork quilt or the rag bag; a broken shovel was reshaped into a hoe; garbage was fed to the livestock; irreparable furniture became fuel for the fireplace. The new country was quite something else. Advertisements aimed at recruiting new immigrants depicted America as a vast and wonderful bazaar where they might find marvelous goods in great abundance, ready made, inexpensive, and easily available with little effort. A classic recruitment ad for encouraging Italian immigration to America depicted "a mill on one side of the street and a bank on the other—and a parade of workers trooping from one to the other carrying bags of money under their arms," stacking up their bankrolls.[4] "Work hard!" was the advice, "and you might be able to make a purchase of land—in your homeland or better yet, here in America!" For the immigrants of the eighteenth and nineteenth centuries (and for many of today's new arrivals), money or currency was to be distrusted. It could be devalued by the government; it might not be accepted if it was not a hard currency; banks might fail. In short, paper money or balances in bank accounts were "false estate." Land, on the other hand, rarely became worthless; it yielded produce; it could be sold or traded. In short, land was "real estate." Little wonder that the immigrants placed such a high priority on home ownership and, later, on the accumulation of things. These possessions were central emblems of their new self-identity, proclaiming to all of society who and what the immigrants had become.[5] The acquisition of possessions thus became a means of identifying and celebrating individual success.

But the easy wages, success, and plentiful goods were not without cost. The first generation of immigrant children were frequently embarrassed by their origins and tried to divorce themselves from identification with the old country, its customs, and its ways. They camouflaged themselves using proper speech and diction, stylish dress, and middle-class behavior in order to "fit in." They became experts at role-playing, the use of various masks, and "impression management." In the desperate rejection of their ethnic identities and in embracing their consumer identities, they became "unreal." T. J. Jackson Lears claims that this sense of unreality coupled with the vision of plentiful goods, labor-saving conveniences, and the importance of social status sometimes had deleterious effects on the self.[6] He notes that:

The decline of autonomous selfhood lay at the heart of the modern sense of unreality. Without a solid sense of self to deny or control, standards blurred and Victorian moral boundaries grew indistinct. Yet, the internalized injunction to "produce" remained. The result was anxious busyness.[7]

The resulting sense of "dis-ease" required a "cure" or a "therapeutic ethos," to use Lears's words. The therapies ranged widely, including patent medicines, formulas for religious salvation, and self-help psychological "growth" systems as well as health foods, hypnosis, stylish dress, and conspicuous consumption, all offered in aid of a life-long search for reality, "true" experience, and the discovery of self. Vance Packard, in his classic expose *The Hidden Persuaders*, quotes an advertiser who expresses the "therapeutic ethos" and defines the "cure":

The cosmetic manufacturers are not selling lanolin; they are selling hope.... We no longer buy oranges; we buy vitality. We do not buy just an auto; we buy prestige.[8]

Lears notes that during the 1920s, symbolic advertising claims rapidly displaced the largely informational and/or substantive claims of earlier times:

The clearest illustration of this change appeared in automobile advertising. Pre–World War I advertisements were nearly all based on straightforward presentation of technical details. By the twenties, they were virtually devoid of information; instead they promised style, status, or escape to an exotic "real life" far from the reader's ordinary experience. The earlier ads assumed a knowledgeable, rational audience; the latter ones offered therapeutic fulfillment for nonrational longings.[9]

Lears's example of the ultimate advocate of the therapeutic ethos (whether in marketing self-help and religious panaceas or in advertising products that promise or celebrate identity) was Bruce Barton, one of the co-founders of the highly successful advertising agency Batten, Barton, Durstine and Osborn (B.B.D.&O.). Barton was a popular motivational speaker and the author of such religious self-help books as *The Young Man's Jesus* (1914) and *The Man Nobody Knows*, which proclaimed

Jesus as the "founder of modern business," who Barton claimed "was also the most successful advertising man in history—a master self promoter who created 'big stories.' "[10] In addition to illustrating the therapeutic aspects of consumerism, Barton was also an excellent copywriter, originating such classic slogans as "A man may be down; but he's never out." Lears maintains that Barton's life and work illustrate most clearly that "the therapeutic ethos often stemmed from personal quests for selfhood in an ambiguous moral universe."[11] It is interesting to note that Barton's agency also skillfully developed the first true political advertisements when it handled the advertising in Dwight D. Eisenhower's presidential campaign of 1952. In Lears's opinion, Barton's "enthusiasm for a therapeutic culture of consumption arose not only from his class interests but also from his half conscious effort to realize a secure and independent sense of selfhood."[12]

In any case, Barton provides us with a capstone example of the rise of the consumer culture, whether motivated by the need for a therapeutic ethos or a celebration of self-identity. The growth of the consumer culture from 1860 to 1940 and its focus on providing goods in place of therapy, or identity in place of salvation, set the stage for modern advertising practice and its focus on consumer research, which followed World War II and continues up to the present day.

ADVERTISING RESEARCH METHODS AND SELF-CELEBRATION

Prior to World War II, advertising agencies did not devote many resources to conducting consumer-based research. What research was done tended to be survey research to determine audience preferences for a given package design, slogan, jingle, or product attribute. Frequently, this research was misleading. For example, Packard reports the experience of a brewery that brewed two types of beer—light and regular. In consumer interviews, respondents overwhelmingly reported that they preferred the *light* variety by a margin of three to one. The brewery, however, knew that it had been producing and selling a greater amount of the *regular* beer by a ratio of nine to one. The brewery concluded that by asking which beer a person preferred, it was "in effect asking: Do you drink the kind preferred by people of refinement and discriminating taste, or do you just drink the regular stuff?"[13]

In another case, identical products were packaged in two different containers. One had an illustration of the product on the front panel, and the other had a coat of arms. Consumers consciously *said* that they preferred the one with the illustration because they could see what was in the package. However, subsequent research on the unconscious level produced opposite results—the consumers associated the coat of arms with high quality and associated the illustration with shoddy goods, and they *purchased* the quality image.[14] Because of a number of similar cases, interview and survey research was displaced in the 1950s by a new, consumer-driven, and highly Freudian approach called "motivation research." A major guru of motivation research, Louis Cheskin, director of the Color Research Institute, summed up the basic assumption of this approach:

Research conducted on the assumption that people can tell how they are affected by an image, a color or a design should not be honored with the name research. Modern psychology and psychoanalytic findings in particular have demonstrated that people are motivated unconsciously. The real motivations are hidden deep in the subconscious.[15]

The subconscious motivations of consumers increasingly became the focus of attention among advertisers and advertising agencies in the 1950s and early 1960s. World War II had brought the sophisticated means of mass production that was capable of production levels that far outstripped long-range demand. In spite of the pent-up postwar demand for consumer goods and the increased discretionary income available to consumers, producers feared a slowdown. As Packard notes:

Production now became a relatively secondary concern. Executive planners changed from being maker-minded to market-minded. The president of the National Sales Executives in fact exclaimed: "Capitalism is dead—consumerism is king!"[16]

Equally important was the introduction of the television medium to the nation in the late 1940s and especially in the 1950s. Almost anyone with a memory of those years can recount what it was like to shop for a television set and how truly amazing even the most naive kinds of programming and advertising seemed. The advertising industry adapted quickly from the dominance of print as an advertising medium and, not surprisingly, began to apply motivation research to television advertising in various kinds of consumer research—research that would soon be criticized by Packard and others as exploitative of the self-identity needs of the American consumer.[17] The promotional material for Packard's best-selling *The Hidden Persuaders* put it this way:

In this book you'll discover a world of psychology professors turned merchandisers. You'll learn how they operate, what they know about you and your neighbors, and how they are using that knowledge to sell you cake mixes, cigarettes, soaps and even ideas. . . . Motivation research . . . seeks to learn what motivates people in making choices. It employs techniques designed to reach the subconscious mind because preferences generally are determined by factors of which the individual is not conscious.[18]

Some of the more sensational and dramatic findings of motivation research as reported by Packard include the downsizing of a candy bar into "bite-sized" pieces (presumably to reduce guilt feelings over self-indulgence) and a corresponding boom in sales of cough drops because a cough drop represented a guilt-free substitute for consumers with a sweet tooth.[19] There was a surprising finding that consumers preferred to borrow from loan companies rather than banks because they felt more virtuous than workers from loan companies but less virtuous than bank officers, who were sometimes seen as surrogate parents examining the frivolous spending habits of a careless child.[20] In order to gain doctors' approval, shrewd pharmaceutical firms deemphasized the value of their drugs in curing various ailments so that doctors got credit for the cure, thus reinforcing the physician's self-image as a healer.[21] Removal of dried milk and eggs from cake mixes allowed homemakers to feel that they were adding something of themselves in the "gift" of the cake to their families, thus reinforcing a nurturing identity.[22] Most men bought sedans instead of convertibles because they thought of themselves as family men (symbolized by the sedan) who would never take a mistress (symbolized by the convertible).[23] Similarly, cigar smoking reassured males of their machismo.[24] Houses represented a symbolic mother to males and extensions and expressions of self-identity to females.[25]

Although motivational research fell into disfavor in the late 1960s, the tendency to focus on the consumer's self-identity needs has continued to the present day, albeit in different forms.

"Positioning" a product based on "psychographic" variables in the minds of the target audience was the dominant advertising strategy touted in the 1970s and early 1980s. The major argument of positioning theorists was that, in a highly cluttered marketplace, advertisers needed to place their products in a *creneau* or niche that had "top of the mind awareness" within a product category.[26] "Empty" niches were usually well identified using either or both of two consumer-based research techniques:

1. *Focus group interviews.* During focus group interviews, groups of potential consumers would discuss product attributes, slogans, alternative uses, and sample storyboards. Participants often triggered one another's unstated motives for their preferences. The skilled focus group leader would then follow up or focus on these topics until it became clear which aspects of the product category (e.g., price, product claims, gender preferences, benefits) were not being filled by an existing product category. This "hole" or niche in the marketplace was then used to target a market segment, thus "positioning" the product in the consumers' minds in relation to competing products.

Sometimes these motivational associations even provided statements that could be directly used for ad copy, in effect making consumers their own copywriters.

2. *Psychographic questionnaires.* Psychographic questionnaires were used to identify consumer life-styles or A.I.O. profiles—what kinds of *activities* they pursue, what their *interests* are, and what their *opinions* are regarding the product or service. In other words, what self-identity did they pursue? The results were used to mesh preferred life-style with ad copy.

For example, consumer responses were used to position Listerine as a stronger mouthwash than Listermint. Listerine's bad taste was what a "truly clean" person expected. Typical responses identified the "truly clean" market through responses such as: "Odors in the house embarrass me"; "Everyone should have a deodorant"; "The kind of dirt you can't see is worse than the kind you can see"; "I do not feel clean without a daily bath." Purchase of the product, then, became equivalent to a celebration of cleanliness.[27]

Perhaps the classic marketing story related to the use of focus groups and psychographics to identify a life-style or preferred identity concerns a traditional staple in the family cupboard—Arm and Hammer baking soda. Since the product already had a 97 percent market penetration in 1971, its only growth strategy was to induce increased usage.[28] This was dramatically accomplished by convincing consumers to put a box of baking soda in the refrigerator, supposedly as an air freshener. The campaign resulted in a 72 percent increase in sales in test markets. In fact, a nationwide rollout had to be delayed because test market results indicated that Arm and Hammer would not have sufficient production capability to meet the projected nationwide demand. New facilities were built; the campaign was rolled out nationally; and the rest is history. How does this case relate to consumer celebration of self-identity?

The focus group and psychographic research results used in Arm and Hammer's consumer research provided the first major clue that odorless refrigerators were a benchmark of being "truly clean" for many housewives. The idea of putting some in the refrigerator was nothing new—it had been a usage suggestion on the side of the Arm and Hammer box for years, and baking soda was a widely accepted mild cleanser for the refrigerator. The theme of sweetening and freshening came up in focus groups repeatedly, and so it was pursued further using a number of psychographic questions:

When we put the proposition to the respondents directly—"Your refrigerator smells, and baking soda will cure that"—it didn't go over at all. . . . But when we came in through the back door and worded the proposition in such a way that it didn't imply the woman was a lousy housekeeper, they showed a lot of interest in the idea.[29]

Further psychographic testing revealed:

Some women feel guilty that they do not clean their refrigerator as often as they think they should. Putting a box of baking soda inside at least cleans the air and that alleviates some of the guilt—and no work is required.[30]

Tapping into the name of a popular television quiz show, advertisers created the "I've Got a Secret—in the refrigerator" campaign, which hailed the product as a means of identifying and celebrating one's own cleanliness.

Most recently, consumer-based research has been geodemographic in nature. Its premise is that people live in neighborhoods that express their values, identities, and preferred life-styles. In other words, "birds of a feather flock together" and "you are where you live." In this approach, the advertiser identifies communities having demographic characteristics that are associated with a preferred life-style and runs advertising to reach persons clustering in those targeted communities. Such media variables as television viewing habits and preferences, preferred radio formats (e.g., all news versus country versus easy listening), preferred times of day for using various media, and others all give the advertiser not only a target market segment but data on the best way and time to communicate with the segment. These kinds of data have led to the rapid growth in the importance of "media planning" in most up-to-date advertising agencies, which promises to be the consumer research methodology of the 1990s.

The development of geodemographic audience research is reported in Michael J. Weiss's book *The Clustering of America*.[31] Weiss chronicles the work of Jonathon Robinson, a computer scientist who devised a complex target-marketing tool that wedded census data, consumer survey data, and zip codes. The tool (PRIZM—Potential Rating Index for Zip Markets) sorted America's 36,000 zip codes into forty distinct "life-style clusters," each of which identified a unique profile of its inhabitants.[32] Robinson set up his own corporation, calling it "Claritas" (Latin for clarity), and began to market his cluster system using clever descriptive names for each of the forty clusters. One can sense the presence of self-identity in the clusters as Weiss describes the dynamics of PRIZM:

From Beverly Hills to the Bronx, the nation resembles a patchwork quilt of lifestyles. . . . In "Coalburg and Corntown," a cluster of small towns in heartland America, locals socialize in American Legion halls and approach the Fourth of July with a sense of history (while) "Bohemian Mixers" smoke pot with their kids. . . . In "Blue Collar Nursery" neighborhoods composed of child-rearing suburban families, parents petition to build more schools for their children. In "Pools and Patios," subdivisions with older, empty nesting households, residents vote to cut school tax. . . . Study the clusters and you'll discover . . . why one marketer will hawk a product via Hal Holbrook and another will hire Max Headroom.[33]

What are the implications of the clusters for self-identity? PRIZM helps explain why identical market strategies succeed in some zip codes but fail miserably in others. It also pinpoints persons seeking the same kinds of self-identity. Finally, it explains why brand loyalty may shift as one's franchise ages. A few examples may clarify the point:

- When Buick downsized the Electra in 1985, it had to market the vehicle to "Young Influentials" instead of its traditional market cluster, "Money and Brains." As a result, its media plan shifted ads from the evening news to "St. Elsewhere."[34]
- Although the Marines had the best recruiting success in urban minority clusters, the Army found its recruits in rural and small-town clusters like "Shotguns and Pickups," "Mines and Mills," "Blue Collar Nursery," and "Coaltown and Corntown."[35]
- *Adam and Eve*, a catalog for erotic novelties, lacy lingerie, and sex toys, presumed that its target market was "Bohemian Mix." Cluster analysis revealed that the real market was "Money and Brains"—a cluster typified by Coral Gables, Florida, and populated with lawyers, doctors, and other professionals consuming all sorts of adult luxuries, including "speedboats or strawberry love oil."[36]
- The "Young Influentials" cluster is typified by Glendale, Colorado, where you observe "women professionals in running shoes on the way to work; men riding mopeds instead of motorcycles; everyone wired to Sony Walkmans and carrying squash racquets tucked into Gucci bags. Corner shopping plazas are sprinkled with Haagen-Dazs ice cream stores and Porsche repair shops."[37] These folks subscribe to consumption periodicals—*Gourmet* and *Architectural Digest*—drink vintage wines, speculate in mutual funds and investment property, and are into foreign travel. They "have to have. . . . They must be able to show some of the trappings of success."[38]

It is clear that geodemographic consumer research such as that utilizing PRIZM and similar systems focuses as much on the emblems of embracing and celebrating self-identity as did the earlier motivation research, positioning, and psychographic research. The final section of this chapter explores several advertising appeals in an attempt to demonstrate the day-to-day applications of the strategies of self-celebration.

STRATEGIES OF SELF-CELEBRATION

There are undoubtedly many strategies of advertising that promote self-celebration, but for our purposes, we will consider only three— product names, product slogans, and advertising pictorials and accompanying copy. The following brief examples serve merely to demonstrate how a range of appeals in these strategies invites various kinds of consumers to embrace or celebrate a certain identity. The examples were chosen to give the reader a sense of the diversity of the types of self-identities offered in contemporary advertising appeals.

Product Names

Product names are frequently "distillation symbols" for the kind of identity being offered by the product. For example, consider the implications of these men's fragrance products—Brut, English Leather, Polo, Jaguar, le 3e Homme de Caron, and Obsession For Men. One quickly senses the nature and variety of the "powers" implied by the product names. Brut, for example, suggests raw physical power, and English Leather suggests mature economic power and status. Polo and Jaguar also suggest economic power but are clearly aimed at a younger male than is English Leather. Both le 3e Homme de Caron and Obsession For Men suggest sexual power. A similar range of product name identities is apparent in the women's cosmetic product category. For example, consider the names of several eye and complexion treatment creams—they fall into three identity categories. The *French identity*, for example, includes Lancôme's Progres Eye Creme, Clarin Masque Absorbant, and Lotion De'manquillante and Evian's Brumisateur Mineral Water Spray. Then there are those that promise significant *medicinal identity*, such as Eyewear's Prescriptives, Elizabeth Arden's Carmide Time Complex Capsules, René Guinot's Liftosome, and L'Oréal's Plentitude Action Liposomes. Finally, there is the *cleanliness identity*, which includes Revlon's Pure Skin Care, Estée Lauder's Advanced Night Repair, Neutrogena's Clean Pore Advantage, and Clinique's Exfoliating Scrub.

So product names can promise the acquisition or celebration of self-identity across a range of possibilities within product categories.

Product Slogans

Product slogans can also suggest a range of identities. Sometimes comparing the slogans of various products in the same category can demonstrate the range of self-identity being appealed to. One can sense clear and distinct status identity appeals in the following set of automobile slogans, meant to appeal to consumers who think of themselves as adventuresome, cared for, or perfectionists:

• "The Relentless Pursuit of Perfection." (Lexus)
• "We Build Excitement." (Pontiac)
• "The Heartbeat of America." (Chevrolet)

- "Precision Crafted Performance." (Acura)
- "Putting Quality on the Road." (Cadillac)
- "I Love What You Do For Me." (Toyota)
- "Engineered Like No Other Car in the World." (Mercedes)
- "Welcome to the Smart Lane." (Hyundai)
- "Quality is Job # 1." (Ford, Lincoln, Mercury)
- "It Just Feels Right." (Mazda)

In a service product category—overnight accommodations—a similar cross section of identities is ordered for embrace or celebration, aimed at consumers who consider themselves as hard-hitting business executives, friendly neighbors, or smart shoppers:

- "Hit the Roof!" (Red Roof Inns)
- "We'll Leave a Light on For Ya." (Motel 6)
- "The Right Place. The Right Price." (Great Western)
- "The World Is Waking Up to Us." (Day's Inn)
- "The Sign of a Good Night's Sleep." (Excel Inns)

Or consider the following airline slogans promising exciting, cared for, or professional identities:

- "Fly the Friendly Skies." (United)
- "We Did It First; We Do It Better." (TWA)
- "We Love to Fly and It Shows." (Delta)
- "Something Special in the Air." (American)
- "Our Spirit Will Lift You." (Midway)

Thus slogans represent another invitation for customer identity.

Advertising Pictorials and Copy

Advertising pictorials and ad copy work together to offer self-identity to various kinds of consumers. Take, for example, the following description of an eight-page, four-color print ad for Revlon lipstick that ran in *Self Magazine*. It promises a "sensuous and unique" identity. The first page features three simple sentences in large print on a white background. They accompany a small four-color pictorial of a perfect pair of female lips with a subdued red lipstick on them. At the left corner of the model's mouth is a small brown birthmark. Some female consumers will identify this mouth as belonging to top fashion model Cindy Crawford. The three alliterative sentences appeal to the senses: "Nothing Looks Like It." "Nothing Feels Like It." "Nothing Lasts Like It." The opposite four-color page features large tubes of Revlon lipstick superimposed on one another with Revlon's slogan at the bottom: "The most unforgettable women in the world wear Revlon." On opening the ad to the center two pages, one sees an entire page dominated by Crawford's face. Her high-fashion red velvet lip color and matching earrings, her perfect complexion, her minimally made-up eyes, and her perfectly manicured nails (painted "Plush Red") arrest the attention. The ad copy focuses on the senses of touch and sight:

Revlon introduces Velvet Touch Lipstick. Imagine a sultry velvety finish. Imagine a sumptuous velvety feel. Imagine colors so potent—they last for up to 6 glorious hours. You've just imagined the most luxurious lipstick ever created. Red Velvet Touch Lipstick. What more could two lips ask for!

Three of the four inside pages are devoted to Crawford's face, cape, jewelry, and nine of her ten fingernails, each now painted a different color. Her shade of lipstick has been altered to "Softshell Pink." The headline and ad copy for the fourth page accompanies seven bottles of nail polish. It reads:

Revlon Nail Enamel. More Shine. More Colors. More Lasting. Now Revlon creates Nail Enamel that dries faster than ever. To a mirror bright shine. In 85 luscious colors. With a tough, long-lasting finish that resists chipping, peeling and fading. It's U.S. Patent No. 4,832,944—your guarantee of the truest color from start to finish.

Clearly the ad and the products offer the opportunity to embrace and celebrate a sensuous, unique, and creative feminine identity. Crawford's famous birthmark began that theme, which is featured throughout the pictures and copy: the specific names of the lipsticks and nail polishes, the reference to the wide variety of hues—eighty-five shades of color— and specific patent number all signal uniqueness and individuality.

In an advertisement for Rolex wristwatches for men, the verbal and visual appeals promote a stylish macho identity for celebration or embrace. The visual depiction includes a photograph of Frederick Forsyth, the best-selling author of such intrigues as *The Day of the Jackal, The Odessa File, The Dogs of War,* and *The Devil's Alternative,* at the top and an enlarged photo of a gold Rolex. Forsyth is posed in front of a stand of snow-covered pines shading his eyes from the winter sun. He is dressed in an expensive fur-trimmed jacket. The headline reads, "Frederick Forsyth's Rolex is like his novels. Tough, accurate and very stylish."

The ad copy informs us of Forsyth's economic and literary successes. We learn that his first three books have appeared as "successful feature films" and that he is a master craftsman whose storytelling is "superb." We are also told that he has lived a life as adventurous as his characters' as a frontline war correspondent, and the ad copy further describes the watch he is wearing—a "Rolex Oyster Day-Date in 18 kt. gold with matching President bracelet." Forsyth testifies to its quality and macho durability, for he avers that he never needs to remove it, "even to use a chain saw." Finally the copy tells us that Forsyth is particularly pleased with his leather jacket. When he spied it in an exclusive London shop he was told by the shop assistant that the fur collar came from a jackal.

Clearly, the photo of Forsyth dressed in an exclusive leather jacket and standing in the snow in a wilderness area offers an initial invitation to embrace and celebrate a stylish macho identity. The copy that refers to Forsyth's books and resulting films reinforces the stylish and successful elements in the identity. The references to Forsyth's experience as a war correspondent initiates the invitation to the macho element in the celebrated identity. The references in the copy to the durability of the Rolex (even when using a chain saw) reinforce the tough image. Finally, the revelation that the fur collar is from the predator that is the name of the novelist's most famous character rounds out the celebration of machismo and self-promotion.

A final example of how ad pictures and copy promise identity can be seen in a recent ad for Shimano fishing reels. The ad celebrates a slightly different kind of macho image—the dedicated outdoorsman—that the consumer can embrace or celebrate by purchasing a Shimano. The ad pictorial occupies the upper two-thirds of a two-page spread and shows the silhouette of a high-powered bass boat on a quiet lake at twilight; the setting sun is in the background. A pair of fishermen are seated on pedestal fishing seats quietly casting and retrieving their lines—and thinking. Fishing gear is lying all over the boat. The headline, which takes up about half of the remaining space, reads: "Give a Man a Fish and You Feed Him for a Day. Teach Him to Fish and He Forgets About Eating." The brief ad copy and a visual of two Shimano reels take up the rest of the page. Fishing becomes an enactment of mastery and power as you "grab the long shank" of the "twin power handle" and "dig the lure down deep." The ad tells you that you are the kind of fisherman who is always after "one more fish. Just one more." The image and copy provide a curious reversal, playing on the cliche about teaching people to fish so that they can provide for themselves for years instead of for a single day. The macho man of the copy is interested in process, not in fishing. It is a way of acting and living that he affirms. The fishing scene is a mere synecdoche, a fragment of a larger machismo life-style.

These three examples are representative of the way ad pictorials and ad copy combine to offer consumers particular kinds of self-identity to embrace and celebrate.

CONCLUSION

In conclusion, a major function of contemporary advertising is to offer consumers an opportunity to embrace and/or celebrate a preferred self-identity through the purchase of goods and services. This motivation to embrace and/or celebrate the self is as plausible an explanation of consumerism (and its tool of advertising) as is any Marxist-driven critique. This chapter demonstrates that plausibility by examining explanations for the rise of consumerism, by exploring the development of several schools of consumer-based advertising research, and by interpreting the offers made in specific advertising techniques used to invite customers to engage in the embrace and celebration of self.

NOTES

1. Stuart Ewens and Elizabeth Ewens, *Channels of Desire* (St. Louis: McGraw Hill, 1982).

2. See, for example, Gillian Dyer, *Advertising as Communication* (London: Routledge, 1988); Judith Williamson, *Decoding Advertising* (London: Marion Boyers Publishers, 1978); Richard Wrightman Fox and T. J. Jackson Lears, *The Culture of Consumption* (New York: Pantheon Books, 1983); and Michael Schudson, *Advertising, the Uneasy Persuasion: Its Dubious Impact on American Society* (New York: Basic Books, 1984).

3. Ewens and Ewens, *Channels of Desire*, 1–7.

4. Ibid., 7–9.

5. Ibid., 11–14.

6. T. J. Jackson Lears, "From Salvation to Self Realization: Advertising and the Therapeutic Roots of the Consumer Culture, 1880–1930," in Fox and Lears, *Culture of Consumption*, 1–38. See also Lears's *No Place of Grace: Anti-modernism and the Transformation of American Culture, 1880–1920* (New York: Pantheon Books, 1981).

7. Lears, "From Salvation to Self Realization," 9.

8. Vance Packard, *The Hidden Persuaders* (New York: Pocket Books, 1964), 5.

9. Lears, "From Salvation to Self Realization," 27.

10. Ibid., 29–31.

11. Ibid.

12. Ibid., 37.

13. Packard, *Hidden Persuaders*, 9–10.

14. Louis Cheskin, *How to Predict What People Will Buy* (New York: Liveright Publishing Corporation, 1957), 41.

15. Ibid., 33.

16. Packard, *Hidden Persuaders*, 15.

17. Ibid.

18. Ibid., 5.

19. Ibid., 51–53.

20. Ibid., 56–57.

21. Ibid., 63–64.

22. Ibid., 65–66.

23. Ibid., 73–74.

24. Ibid., 76–78.

25. Ibid., 79.

26. Al Reis and Jack Trout, *Positioning: The Battle for Your Mind* (New York: McGraw Hill, 1986).

27. Michael Robinson, *Advertising: From Fundamentals to Strategies* (Lexington, Mass.: D. C. Heath, 1987), 55–56.

28. Jack Honomichl, *Marketing Research People: Their Behind-the-Scenes Stories* (Chicago: Crain Books, 1984), 5–22.

29. Ibid., 9.

30. Ibid., 9–10.

31. See Michael J. Weiss, *The Clustering of America* (New York: Perennial Library, 1989).

32. Ibid., xi–xvi.

33. Ibid., 2–3.

34. Ibid., 15.

35. Ibid.

36. Ibid., 17.

37. Ibid., 40.

38. Ibid.

Chapter Twelve

A Critical Look at the Postmodern Future

Andrew King

The burden of my argument is that postmodernism has taken its weapons and thrust them into the hands of its opponents. The abandonment of the abstract "world" of modernity for membership and participation in a more humane and intimate "life-world" is an illusion. The return to a world of practical discourse and grounded identity is the latest version of the journey to the Golden Age or the voyage to the Happy Isles. But it has not brought the deep insight that Dante's journey brought to him nor even the world-weary satisfaction of the long-suffering Odysseus. The results are more like the sense of isolation that the seeker felt in *My Dinner With Andre*. Many of the so-called, self-styled culture groups are ersatz creations. They are aesthetic constructs without genuine economic, social, and political roots. Their manufactured quality is even more visible than that of the nation-state, an entity with the benefit of a bogus past lovingly created by folklorists, dramatists, and historians. In brief, the margin as well as the center suffers from homelessness and anomie.

THE FLIGHT FROM THE CENTER

The great theme of Western literature has been the journey to the center: the Greek hero's journey to the lower world; Aeneas's journey to the new motherworld, Rome; Dante's journey to the Axis Mundi. Since Conrad we have had a reversal of the heroic quest. The questing hero flies to the heart of darkness and discovers that a nihilistic carnality has taken firm possession of both periphery and center. Beginning with Conrad we see the demythologization of the journey. In the secular society, community is drained of its mystery and defined as a form of exchange.

The fullest expression of the flight from the center is Graham Greene's *A Burnt-Out Case*. The man called Querry, Europe's greatest religious architect, flees metropolitan Europe to settle in a remote leper colony in equatorial Africa. He is one of Greene's de profundis men, an intellectual who has plumbed the depths. Querry has been at the center of the great Western mission where faith and reason, art and science, community and the individual soul are joined, and has found only a deep void. In the first chapter of the book he stops at a combination fueling station and seminary, where he witnesses African novitiates gambling for matchsticks with fierce enjoyment. He longs to experience "the innocence and immaturity of isolation."[1] But if Querry is denied the enjoyment of simple things he is also denied the ennobling experience of painful sacrifice:

"I no longer know what suffering is. I have come to the end of that too."
"Too?"
"Like all the rest. To the end of everything."

Ultimately arriving at a Congo leper colony, Querry works to serve the community. He is beyond pride, almost beyond hope. Thus it is that Europe's greatest cathedral architect takes up the humble task of designing a chair for a man with elephantiasis, constructing a rehabilitation station, and building a native hospital. The resident physician, Dr. Colin, pronounces him "a burnt-out case," the psychological counterpart of a leper who has reached a stage of mutilation so severe that he or she can no longer feel pain. But as Querry hurls himself into the work, feeling gradually begins to return. Once again he knows regret, love, and friendship. When his assistant, a fingerless leper named Deo Gratias, flees into the bush during a night of terror, Querry tracks him down. He comforts the leper, covers him with his own body to shield him from the rain, and finally persuades him to return to the colony. This incident, which echoes the deeds of medieval saints, is magnified by the local European officials and soon draws the attention of the international press. It proves to be Querry's undoing.

From Deo Gratias he learns the word "pendele." At first its meaning is not clear, but through a variety of contexts the word is revealed to mean one's birthplace or the point of origin of one's clan. In a still more general sense it means the beginning of things, the source of happiness and grace. Querry's flight from the center becomes fraught with irony. The farther he retreats the more he engages the questions that lie at the center of Christian European civilization.

The same irony is seen in D. H. Lawrence, who left Europe to find the vitality that the West had lost. He found the same anxiety and lack of spirit everywhere. Similarly, Garcia Lorca turned to gypsies in the hope of discovering an arcane wisdom, but found only more of the sickness of Europe.

The postmodern quest—ironically styled as the quest of those who set off to live rather than to know—abandons a guiding moral tradition and substitutes local practice or personal impulse. But does the pretense that history no longer speaks with an authoritative voice or that moral messages do not transcend time and culture really throw us upon pragmatic calculations? Are we really left to choose our course on the basis of the relative cash value of our ideas? The literature of the twentieth century suggests that the pentecostal ideal of finding the center dies very hard. It is even apparent in the work of the brilliant critic Michael McGee, who asks us to let go of the inherited categories of things so that we may truly see their inner nature.[2]

POSTMODERN IRONY

In particular, the case studies in this book reveal two pillars of postmodern irony. First they temper our enthusiasm for the potency of the rhetorical act. Perhaps our most beguiling illusion has been the illusion of communicative action. Groups may renounce the tyranny of the ethnocidal or ethnophobic secular culture, but as one of our authors so eloquently put it, they are, in effect, left with their rhetoric while the dominant groups go on running the world. They are left in the unenviable position of William Buckley, Jr., who often debates powerful generals, statesmen, and captains of industry. He wipes the floor with them, challenging their evidence, punching holes in their logic, exposing their dubious assumptions, and shredding their false conclusions. However, the next day all these people are back at the job of running the world and Buckley is left with his show. The inability to change the dominant view of the world encourages a feeling of separation between language and action and between ideas and social praxis, the very condition that the rejection of modernity was supposed to heal. A community that cannot perform its own metaphors is a bogus community incarcerated in its niche. Like the yuppie watching a "craftsman" distress his furniture to provide the illusion of rustication and a country gentry past, groups content themselves with a nostalgic and aesthetic resolution of their problems. Emblematic of the postmodern identity is the spectacle of fourth-generation white ethnics taking university courses to "discover" their identities. The aesthetic domain has always served as an arena where unresolved conflicts can be addressed, but in the information society the line between merely addressing an issue and actually coming to grips with it is increasingly blurred.

A DECENTERED UNDERSTANDING

What is a decentered understanding? According to Jürgen Habermas, postmodernism's decentered understanding of the world "presupposes that relations to the world, claims to validity, and basic attitudes have become differentiated."[3] This means that the student of discourse ought to shift his or her attention away from the discovery of universal appeals to the particular topoi of particular groups. Discourse is understood contextually, as a product of "traditions," "group membership," and "socialization."

According to Habermas, these arenas provide both resources and meaning for human utterance in the world of everyday life.[4] But this decentered understanding, far from ending the isolation of citizens from genuine public dialogue, further incarcerates them in subgroups. It does nothing to heal the balkanization of discourse. As persons become increasingly aware of themselves as members of groups, and of their interests and claims in relation to other groups, they do nothing to wrest public discourse from its monopolization by experts and professional groups. Have civil rights groups opened up legal discussion to ordinary citizens, or have they surrendered to the particular logics, rhetorics, and perspectives of lawyers?

Nor is the group necessarily a more open arena than the larger society. Small groups may be as stratified, as repressive, and as unenlightened as the small towns and rural areas so many Americans fled during the early and middle years of the twentieth century. In fact, persons like me from rural areas recognize in the rhetoric of many subordinate groups a mythology very like that of the village and the farm. Warmth, belonging, and participation are the other sides of the coins of coercion, public shame, and provincialism. The movement back to the small town may also be seen as a symptom of the feeling of loss of control. Such retreats to the margin may "play into the hands of managers and bureaucrats" who remain on the scene.[5]

In this sense, the movement to the margin parallels that of another fin de siècle civilization, the Austro-Hungarian Empire. In the last quarter of the nineteenth century, the fears about the loss of Germanic hegemony and the threats to political coherence appeared just as Austrian society experienced its most brilliant cultural flowering.[6] The exuberant self-confidence of the great merchants faded, and the most powerful portion of the citizenry turned its attention from external to internal affairs. As the future seemed less certain, they invented a storied past, transforming parts of Vienna into a stylish Greco-Roman museum piece. The children of politicians and generals hurled themselves into the arts and in their experimentalism expressed a deep pessimism about living an integrated life of public action and private virtue. Everywhere one saw the retreat from outer to inner. Schorske and a host of scholars have pointed out the significance of the Austrian intellectual journey from Goethe to Schnitzler and from Marx to Freud. Convinced that the general population could no longer hear them, group after group returned to the personal, the familial, and the artistic. The reader will remember that the major contribution of the 1890s to the social sciences was Conflict Theory, a belief that human creativity, material progress, and individual mobility was bought at a heavy cost. These costs were social alienation, constant struggle, and conquest of one group by another.

Although the European moral tradition was not discarded, the fin de siècle Austrians used it in haphazard, unreasonable, and disorderly ways. As the Austrian elite withdrew from public life, the loss of the old center left a void. The withdrawal evoked three predictable responses from formerly subordinate groups. The first response of the successor groups was a slavish imitation of a successful formula that had already been abandoned by the elite. Like Japan versus the West in the twentieth century, they hoped to beat the elites at their own game. The second response was a retreat into the regional and local traditions of the mosaic of national groups. The third was frenzied experimentalism. Perhaps the best literary rendering of the sense of helplessness and anomie is captured in Robert Musil's enduring work of the time, *The Man Without Qualities*.[7]

GAINS FOR THE STUDENT

Whatever the fortunes of the postmodern devolution, it has signaled clear shifts in critical perspective. In closing, I list the most important of these shifts:

1. *A different locus for the study of discourse.* A postmodern perspective *is* a clear gain if it broadens the standard conception of political community. It invites us to see political discourse outside formal institutions and to examine political discourse as ordinary people practice it. This means less concentration on political decision making and political consequences and a greater concern with the origin and production of political discourse prior to its institutional packaging.

2. *A broader understanding of the nature and variety of political discourse.* By examining political discourse within the context of subordinate groups we gain a better appreciation of the breadth of political discourse and its covert meanings. Thus, we see that "playing the dozens" in the black community is more than a form of edifying street theater or the exhibition of individual verbal prowess. Its origins lie in "training for self-control" in a setting in which emotional discipline is necessary for survival and in which one is "expected" to absorb insult without reacting physically.[8] We thus gain a greater under-

standing of the political functions of folktales, ritual gestures, rumor, gossip, and other traditional weapons of the weak.

3. *A greater awareness of the role of power in ordinary discourse*. It has been said that the postmodern impulse reduces all ideas to their political utility (power dimension). This is clearly an overstatement. The postmodern critic does not believe that ideas are reducible to their power dimensions, but he or she does believe that most ideas can benefit from being looked at in this way. At the very least, human needs constantly transcend desires for effectiveness and domination.

CONCLUSION

And so our small volume is done. In closing, it may be interesting to speculate on the "future" of postmodernism. Some scholars say that we are already standing in its twilight (it lacks the moral grandeur to make a good sunset). Several contributors to this volume expressed the belief that the reign of postmodernism would be brief, and that like modernism it contained the seeds of its own destruction. One recounted a tale by Jorge Luis Borges in which a third-century Lombard warrior, Droctulft, laid siege to Ravenna, deserted to the Roman side, and died defending the city he had previously attacked.[9] Like existentialism, postmodernism is a mood rather than a doctrine, and its advocates exhibit the same volatile temper. Another writer spoke of the exquisite sensitivity of the movement as an attack of proud flesh, an unhealthy self-consciousness. She posed a variant of Graham Greene's old question: "Which of us knows the architect of Chartres cathedral? Whoever it was labored with faith, not for greed or brutal self assertion. And I don't expect the builder viewed this service as a form of humiliation or slavish clientage."[10] Nor could she imagine that the anonymous architect viewed God as a strategic or provisional concept instead of an actual supreme being. Finally, one of the authors told me that thinking about the survival of humane study had itself become a marginal activity, almost a solitary vocation. I do not believe it. For the first time in human history there are hundreds of thousands, perhaps even millions, who have faith in the importance of ideas and the intellectual humility to see that civilization is a fragile plant that is always in danger of being trampled or uprooted. We hope that the aftermath of postmodernism will produce exciting surprises for all. The future, if it is to be won at all, depends on the application of organized knowledge to social and material problems. That is to say, it depends on the central institutions of society. Most postmodernists have grown up in the cocoon of the academy. To them, civilization seems a solid thing. But civilization *is* fragile; it has been in danger of disappearing more than once from the onslaughts of the Vandals and the Goths. Today it is in danger of being trivialized by mass media and buried by anomic individualism. That is why I predict that the next great flowering will take place in the most unexpected, perhaps the most benighted and reviled of places. In the midst of Eliot's Wasteland, lost amidst stonecrop and blasted hopes, the Renaissance is already dawning. A new set of centering terms has begun to inform our lives. Region replaces nation; community replaces state. Lombardy replaces Italy, and a new cultural flowering begins in North America's reviled South.

NOTES

1. Graham Greene, *A Burnt-Out Case* (London: Penguin Books and William Heinemann Ltd., 1965), 38.

2. Michael Calvin McGee, "Text, Context, and the Fragmentation of Contemporary Culture," *Western Journal of Speech Communication* 54 (Summer 1990): 284.

3. Jürgen Habermas, *Moral Consciousness and Communicative Action*, trans. Christian Lenhardt and Shierry Nicholsen (Cambridge, Mass.: MIT Press, 1990), 138.

4. Ibid., 135.

5. William Corlett, *Community Without Unity: A Politics of Derridean Extravagance* (New York: Delta Press, 1989), 42.

6. Carl E. Schorske, *Fin-de-Siècle Vienna* (New York: Knopf, 1980), 103.

7. Robert Musil, *The Man Without Qualities*, trans. Eithne Wilking & Ernst Kaiser (New York: Putnam Capricorn PB, 1965).

8. James C. Scott, *Domination and the Arts of Resistance* (New Haven, Conn., and London: Yale University Press, 1990), 136–7.

9. Jorge Luis Borges, *A Personal Anthology* (New York: Grove Press, 1967), 170.

10. Greene, *A Burnt-Out Case*, p. 58.

Selected Bibliography

BOOKS

Ablon, Joan. *Little People in America: The Social Dimensions of Dwarfism*. New York: Praeger Publishers, 1984.

Alinsky, Saul. *Rules for Radicals: A Practical Primer for Realistic Radicals*. New York: Random House, 1971.

Anderson, Frances I., and David Noel Freedman. *Hosea: A New Translation with Introduction and Commentary*. Vol. 24 of *The Anchor Bible*. eds. William Foxwell Albright and David Noel Freedman. Garden City, N.Y.: Doubleday, 1980.

Arac, Jonathon. *Postmodernism and Politics*. Minneapolis: University of Minnesota Press, 1986.

Armstrong, Paul B. *Conflicting Readings: Variety and Validity in Interpretation*. Chapel Hill, N.C.: University of North Carolina Press, 1990.

Bakhtin, Mikhail. *The Dialogic Imagination: Four Essays*. ed. Michael Holquist. Austin, Tex.: University of Texas Press, 1981.

———. *Rabelais and His World*. Bloomington, Ind.: Indiana University Press, 1984.

Bataille, Georges. *Visions of Excess: Selected Writings, 1927–1939*. ed. Allan Stoekl. Minneapolis: University of Minnesota Press, 1988.

Bayrd, Edward. *The Thin Game*. New York: Avon Books, 1978.

Black, Edwin. *Rhetorical Criticism: A Study in Method*. Madison, Wis.: University of Wisconsin Press, 1965.

Borges, Jorge Luis. *A Personal Anthology*. New York: Grove Press, 1967.

Bormann, Ernest. *The Force of Fantasy: Restoring the American Dream*. Carbondale, Ill.: Southern Illinois University Press, 1985.

Bosmajian, Haig. *The Language of Oppression*. Washington, D.C.: University Press of America, 1983.

Braun, Kirk. *Rajneeshpuram: The Unwelcome Society*. West Linn, Ore.: Scout Creek Press, 1984.

Brueggemann, Paul. *The Prophetic Imagination*. Philadelphia: Fortress Press, 1982.

Burke, Kenneth. *Permanence and Change: An Anatomy of Purpose*, 3d ed. Berkeley: University of California Press, 1984.

———. *A Rhetoric of Motives*. New York: Prentice Hall, 1950.

Carroll, Robert. *When Prophecy Failed*. London: SCM Press Ltd., 1979.

Chapkis, Wendy. *Beauty Secrets*. Boston: South End Press, 1986.

Chavez, John R. *The Lost Land*. Albuquerque: University of New Mexico Press, 1984.

Chemetzy, Jules. *Our Decentralized Literature*. Amherst, Mass.: University of Massachusetts Press, 1986.

Chernin, Kim. *The Obsession: Reflections on the Tyranny of Slenderness*. New York: Harper Colophon Books, 1981.

Cheskin, Louis. *How to Predict What People Will Buy*. New York: Liveright Publishing Co., 1937.

Cohen, Stanley. *Folk Devils and Moral Panics*. London: Macgibbon and Kee, 1972.

Cornford, F. M. *From Religion to Philosophy: A Study in the Origins of Western Speculation*. New York: Harper and Row, 1957.

Dodds, E. R. *The Greeks and the Irrational*. Berkeley and Los Angeles: University of California Press, 1968.

Eliade, Mircea. *Cosmos and History: The Myth of the Eternal Return*. New York: Harper Torch Books, 1959.

Ewens, Stuart, and Elizabeth Ewens. *Channels of Desire*. St. Louis: McGraw Hill, 1982.

Erikson, Erik. *Childhood and Society*. New York: Norton, 1950.

Erikson, Kai T. *Wayward Puritans: A Study in the Sociology of Deviance*. New York: Wiley, 1964.

Fisher, Walter R. *Human Communication as Narration: Toward a Philosophy of Reason, Value, and Action*. Columbia, S.C.: University of South Carolina Press, 1987.

Fiske, John. *Television Culture*. London: Methuen, 1987.

Folger, Joseph P., and Marshall Scott Poole. *Working Through Conflict*. Glenview, Ill.: Scott, Foresman and Co., 1984.

Geslick, Lorraine. *Centers, Symbols and Hierarchies: Essays on the Classical States of Southeast Asia*. New Haven, Conn.: Yale University Press, 1988.

Glassner, Barry. *Bodies: Why We Look the Way We Do and How We Feel About It*. New York: G. P. Putnam's Sons, 1988.

Goffmann, Irving. *The Presentation of the Self in Everyday Life*. Garden City, N.Y.: Doubleday, 1959.

Goggio, Silvio. *Modern/Postmodern*. Philadelphia: University of Pennsylvania Press, 1972.

Gonzales, Rodolfo. *I Am Joaquin*. New York: Bantam Books, 1972.

Graff, Gerald. *Professing Literature: An Institutional History*. Chicago: University of Chicago Press, 1987.

Gross, Edward. *The Unofficial Tale of Beauty and the Beast*. Las Vegas: Pioneer Books, 1988.

Gunn, James. *The New Encyclopedia of Science Fiction*. New York: Viking, 1988.

Habermas, Jürgen. *Moral Consciousness and Communicative Action*. Trans. Christian Lenhardt and Shierry Weber Nicholsen. Cambridge, Mass.: MIT Press, 1988.

Hall, Stuart, and Thomas Jefferson. *Resistance Through Rituals: Youth Subcultures in Post-War Britain*. London: Huchinson & Co., 1976.

Hearne, Betsy. *Beauty and the Beast: Visions and Revisions of an Old Tale*. Chicago: University of Chicago Press, 1989.

Heschel, Abraham J. *The Prophets*. 2 vols. New York: Harper and Row, 1969.

Hoffer, Eric. *The True Believer*. New York: Harper, 1951.

Isserman, Maurice. *If I Had a Hammer?* New York: Simon and Schuster, 1987.

Jamieson, Kathleen. *Eloquence in an Electronic Age: The Transformation of Political Speechmaking*. New York: Oxford University Press, 1988.

Janeway, Elizabeth. *Powers of the Weak*. New York: Morrow Quill Paperbacks, 1982.

Jewett, R., and J. S. Lawrence. *The American Monomyth*. Garden City, N.Y.: Anchor Press, 1987.

King, Andrew. *Power and Communication*. Prospect Heights, Ill.: Waveland Press, 1987.

Lears, T. J. Jackson and Richard Wrightman Fox. *The Culture of Consumption*. New York: Pantheon Books, 1983.

———. *No Place of Grace: Antimodernism and the Transformation of American Culture, 1880–1920*. New York: Pantheon Books, 1981.

Lowe, David M. *A History of Bourgeois Perception*. Chicago: University of Chicago Press, 1982.

Lyotard, Jean François. *The Postmodern Condition: A Report on Knowledge*. Minneapolis: University of Minnesota Press, 1988.

Marin, Christine. *A Spokesman of the Mexican-American Movement: Rodolfo "Corky" Gonzales and the Fight for Chicano Liberation, 1966–1972*. San Francisco: R and E Research Associates, 1977.

Martinez, Elizabeth Sutherland, and Enriqueta Longeaux y Vasquez. *Viva La Raza!* Garden City, N.Y.: Doubleday, 1974.

Mayer, Jean. *Overweight: Causes, Costs, and Control*. Englewood Cliffs, N.J.: Prentice-Hall, 1974.

Meyrowitz, Joshua. *No Sense of Place: The Impact of Electronic Media on Social Behavior*. New York: Oxford University Press, 1985.

Millman, Marcia. *Such a Pretty Face: Being Fat in America*. New York: Berkeley Books, 1981.

Morely, David. *The "Nationwide" Audience*. London: British Film Institute, 1980.

Musil, Robert. *The Man Without Qualities*. New York: Putnam/Capricorn PB, 1965.

Patterson, Orlando. *Slavery and Social Death: A Comparative Study*. Cambridge, Mass.: Harvard University Press, 1982.

Radway, Janice. *Reading the Romance*. Chapel Hill, N.C.: University of North Carolina Press, 1984.

Schorske, Carl E. *Fin-de-Siècle Vienna*. New York: Knopf, 1980.

Scott, James C. *Domination and the Arts of Resistance*. New Haven, Conn., and London: Yale University Press, 1990.

Shapiro, Ian. *Political Community*. Berkeley: University of California Press, 1990.

Spitzak, Carole. *Confessing Excess: Women and the Politics of Body Reduction*. Albany, N.Y.: State University of New York Press, 1990.

Stallybrass, Peter, and Allon White. *The Politics of Transgression*. Ithaca, N.Y.: Cornell University Press, 1986.

Stewart, Charles J., Craig Allen Smith and Robert E. Denton, Jr. *Persuasion and Social Movements*, 2d ed. Prospect Heights, Ill.: Waveland Press, 1989.

Stich, Stephen P. *The Fragmentation of Reason; Preface to a Theory of Reason*. Cambridge, Mass.: MIT Press, 1990.

Styron, William. *The Confessions of Nat Turner*. New York: Random House, 1966.

Turner, Victor. *The Ritual Process: Structure and Anti-Structure*. Chicago: Aldine, 1969.

Wheelwright, Philip. *The Burning Fountain: A Study in the Language of Symbolism*. Bloomington, Ind.: Indiana University Press, 1954.

ARTICLES, CHAPTERS, AND PERIODICALS

Baumgartner, M. P. "Social Control from Below." In *Toward a General Theory of Social Control*, Vol. 1, edited by Donald Black. Orlando, Fla.: Academic Press, 1984.

Berman, Paul. "Don't Follow Leaders." *The New Republic* 10 and 17 August 1978.

Bitzer, Lloyd F. "Functional Communication: A Situational Perspective." In *Rhetoric in Transition: Studies in the Nature and Uses of Rhetoric*, edited by Eugene E. White. University Park, Pa.: Pennsylvania State University Press, 1980.

———. "The Rhetorical Situation." *Philosophy and Rhetoric* 1 (1968):1–14.

Black, Donald. "A Strategy of Pure Sociology." In *Theoretical Perspectives in Sociology*, edited by Scott G. McNall. New York: St. Martin's Press, 1979.

Bormann, Ernest. "Fantasy and Rhetorical Vision: The Rhetorical Criticism of Social Reality." *Quarterly Journal of Speech* 58 (December 1972):396–407.

Bourdieu, Pierre. "Social Space and Symbolic Power." *Sociological Theory* 7 (1989):14–25.

Browning, Daniel R. "8 Sanctuary Defendants Found Guilty; 3 Acquitted." *Arizona Daily Star*, 2 May 1986, final ed.

Came, Barry. "A Growing Menace." *Maclean's*, 23 January 1989.

Carragee, Levom. "Interpretive Media Study and Interpretative Social Science." *Critical Studies in Mass Communication* 7 (June 1990): 81–96.

Cathcart, Robert S. "New Approaches to the Study of Movements: Defining Movements Rhetorically." *Western Journal of Speech Communication* 36 (Spring 1972):82–88.

Clarke, John. "The Skinheads and the Magical Recovery of Community." In *Resistance Through Rituals: Youth Subcultures in Post-War Britain*, edited by Stuart Hall and Thomas Jefferson. London: Huchinson & Co., 1976.

———. "Style." In *Resistance Through Rituals: Youth Subcultures in Post-War Britain*, edited by Stuart Hall and Thomas Jefferson. London: Huchinson & Co., 1976.

Conrad, Charles. "The Transformation of the 'Old Feminist' Movement." *Quarterly Journal of Speech* 67 (1981):285.

Cullinan, Thomas, O.S.B. "The Church as an Agent of Social Change—From the Edge." *Agenda for Prophets: Toward a Political Ideology for Britain*, edited by Rex Ambler and David Haslam. London: Bowerdean Press, 1980.

Fiske, John. "Television: Polysemy and Popularity." *Critical Studies in Mass Communication* 3 (December 1986):391–408.

Foucault, Michel. "Nietzsche, Genealogy, History." In *Language, Counter-Memory, Practice: Selected Essays and Interviews*, edited by Donald Bouchard. Ithaca, N.Y.: Cornell University Press, 1977.

———. "The Subject and Power." In *Michel Foucault: Beyond Structuralism and Hermeneutics*, edited by Hubert Dreyfus and Paul Rabinow. Chicago: University of Chicago Press, 1982.

Fox, Kathryn Joan. "Real Punks and Pretenders." *Journal of Contemporary Ethnography* 3 (1986):344–70.

French, John R. P. Jr., and Bertram Raven. "The Bases of Social Power." In *Group Dynamics: Research and Theory*, edited by Dorwin Cartwright. Ann Arbor: Michigan Institute for Social Research, 1959.

Glassner, Barry. "Fit for Postmodern Culture." In *Symbol Interaction and Cultural Practice*, edited by Howard S. Becker and Michial M. McCall. Chicago and London: University of Chicago Press, 1990.

Gregg, Richard B. "The Ego Function of Protest Rhetoric." *Philosophy and Rhetoric* 4 (Spring 1971): 71–91.

Haase, Andrew. "Body Shops: The Death of George Bataille." In *Body Invaders: Panic Sex in America*, edited by Arthur Kroker and Marilouise Kroker. New York: St. Martin's Press, 1987.

Hammerback, John C., and Richard J. Jensen. "Cesar Estrada Chavez: Labor Leader and Minority Activist." In *American Orators of the Twentieth Century*, edited by Bernard K. Duffy and Halford R. Ryan. Westport, Conn.: Greenwood Press, 1987.

———. "A Revolution of Heart and Mind: Cesar Chavez's Rhetorical Crusade." *Journal of the West* 27 (April 1988):71.

Hart, Roderick P. "The Functions of Human Communication in the Maintenance of Public Values." In *Handbook of Rhetorical and Communication Theory*, edited by Carroll Arnold and John Waite Bowers. Boston: Allyn and Bacon, 1984.

———. "The Rhetoric of the True Believer." *Speech Monographs* 38 (November 1971): 249–261.

Heath, Robert L. "Dialectical Confrontation: A Strategy of Black Radicalism." *Central States Speech Journal* 24 (Fall 1973): 173.

Hebdige, Dick. "Reggae, Rasta, and Rudies." In *Resistance Through Rituals: Youth Subcultures in Post-War Britain*, edited by Stuart Hall and Thomas Jefferson. London: Huchinson & Co., 1976.

Huntington, Samuel. "Political Modernization: A Study in Metaphor." *Daedalus* (Summer 1966):769.

Ignatieff, Michael. "Modern Dying." *The New Republic* 28 (November 26, 1978):28.

Jenkins, Henry III. " 'Star Trek' Rerun, Reread, Rewritten: Fan Writing as Textual Poaching." *Critical Studies in Mass Communication* 5 (June 1988):85–107.

Jensen, Richard J., and John C. Hammerback. "No Revolutions Without Poets: The Rhetoric of Rodolfo "Corky" Gonzales." *Western Journal of Speech Communication* 46 (Winter 1982):75.

Lears, T. J. Jackson. "From Salvation to Self Realization: Advertising and the Therapeutic Roots of the Consumer Culture." In *The Culture of Consumption*, edited by Richard Wrightman Fox and T. J. Jackson Lears. New York: Pantheon Books, 1983.

Leershen, C. " 'Star Trek's' Nine Lives," *Newsweek*, 22 December 1986, 66–73.

Leo, John. "A Chilling Wave of Racism." *Time*, 25 January 1988.

Lucaites, John Lewis. "Constitutional Argument in a National Theater: The Impeachment Trial of Dr. Henry Sacheverell." In *Popular Trials: Rhetoric, Mass Media, and the Law*, edited by Robert Hariman. Tuscaloosa, Ala.: University of Alabama Press, 1990.

McGee, Michael Calvin. "The 'Ideograph': A Link Between Rhetoric and Ideology." *Quarterly Journal of Speech* 66 (February 1980):1–16.

———. "In Search of the People: A Rhetorical Alternative." *Quarterly Journal of Speech* 61 (October 1975):235–49.

———. "Text, Context, and the Fragmentation of Contemporary Culture." *Western Journal of Speech Communication* 54 (Summer 1990):272–89.

Morley, David. "The 'Nationwide' Audience: A Critical Postscript." *Screen Education* 39 (1981):3–14.

Norman, Ronald Lippitt. "The Dynamics of Power." *Human Relations* 5 (1952):37–64.

Penley, Constance. "To Boldly Go Where No Woman Has Gone Before: Feminism, Psychoanalysis, and Popular Culture." Paper presented at the Cultural Studies Now and in the Future Conference, Champaign-Urbana, Ill., April 1990.

Philp, Mark. "Michel Foucault." In *The Return of Grand Theory in the Human Sciences*, edited by Quentin Skinner. Cambridge: Cambridge University Press, 1985.

Rabin, Chaim. "Discourse Analysis and the Dating of Deuteronomy." In *Interpreting the Hebrew Bible: Essays in Honour of E. I. J. Rosenthal*, edited by John A. Emerton and Stefan C. Reid. New York: Cambridge University Press, 1982.

Sears, Eva. "Skinheads: A New Generation of Hate-Mongers." *USA Today*, May 1989.

Siclari, Joe. "Science Fiction Fandom: A History of an Unusual Hobby." In *The Science Fiction Reference Book*, edited by Marshall B. Tymn. Mercer Island, Wash.: Starmont House, 1981.

Simons, Herbert W. "Requirements, Problems, and Strategies: A Theory of Persuasion for Social Movements." *Quarterly Journal of Speech* 56 (February 1970):5–6.

Simons, Herbert W., Elizabeth W. Mechling, and Howard N. Schreier. "The Functions of Human Communication in Mobilizing Action from the Bottom Up: The Rhetoric of Social Movement." In *Handbook of Rhetorical and Communication Theory*, edited by Carroll C. Arnold and John Waite Bowers. Boston: Allyn and Bacon, 1984.

Spitzak, Carole. "The Obese Person as a Subject in American Culture." Paper presented at the annual meeting of the Speech Communication Association, Washington, D.C., November 1983.

Steiner, Linda. "Oppositional Decoding as an Act of Resistance." *Critical Studies in Mass Communication* 5 (March 1988):1–15.

Stewart, Charles J. "A Functional Approach to the Rhetoric of Social Movements." *Central States Speech Journal* 31 (Winter 1980): 298–305.

Towner, W. Sibley. "On Calling People 'Prophets' in 1970." *Interpretation* 24 (October 1970):492–509.

Weber, Max. "Class, Status, Party." In *From Max Weber: Essays in Sociology*, edited by Hans Gerth and C. Wright Mills. New York: Oxford University Press, 1946.

Wolff, Hans Walter. "Prophecy from the Eighth Century through the Fifth Century." *Interpretation* 32 (January 1978):17–30.

Index

Ablon, Joan, 37, 44, 45
agrarians, 25
Alinsky, Saul, 73–74
avant garde, 66

Bakhtin, Mikhail, 49
Barton, Bruce, 156–57
Batanille, Georges, 50
Bhagwan Shree Rajneesh, 115, 117, 118, 121, 124–26
Bitzer, Lloyd, 99, 104, 108, 111–12
Black, Edwin, 75, 76, 81
Bobbitt, David, 3
bricolage, 62
Burke, Kenneth, 74, 78, 79–80, 100, 102, 116
Burkeian method, 73, 81

Chavez, Cesar, 93–96
Cheskin, Louis, 157
conflict theory, 173
Conrad, Charles, 86
Conrad, Joseph, 15, 169
consumer, 154–62
consumerism, 153–58
Corbett, Jim, 71–72
Crawford, Cindy, 165

Deng Xiaoping, 101, 103, 105, 112
Derrida, Jacques, 14, 16

disassociative pairs, 102
Duncan, Hugh, 9

Eliade, Mircea, 16
El Plan de Aztlan, 89, 92–93, 96
empowerment, 74
enlightenment, 7, 13, 26
Euroman, 13, 28

Fabrey, William, 39, 41–43, 47
fandom, 131–37, 140–49
fans, 131–48
fanzines, 132–38, 148
focus group interviews, 159–60
Foucault, Michel, 14, 31, 33–36, 43, 50

Glassner, Barry, 32–33
Gonzales, Rudolfo, "Corky," 88–92
Graff, Gerald, 28
Greene, Graham, 170, 174

Habermas, Jürgen, 18, 27, 172
hegemony: condition of, 106–8; of groups, 3, 4, 7; of sites, 7; in speech, 3, 12

Ignatieff, Michael, 31–32
interpersonal dyad, 59

Jamieson, Kathleen, 6
Janeway, Elizabeth, 58–60

Koppel, Ted, 122–23

La Raza, 91
Lawrence, D. H., 170
Lears, T. Jackson, 156
Leff, Michael, 1
legitimacy: conditions of, 3–4, 9–10, 26, 33, 48; crisis of, 18, 60, 74, 102, 116
LoCos, 135–36, 142–46
Long, Huey, 8
Lorca, Garcia, 171
LPA, 32, 38, 44–52

magic, 60
Marx, Karl, 66, 173
Marxism, 133, 154
McGee, Michael, 1, 171
Moore, Barrington, 4
myth, 60

NAAFA, 32, 38–52
narrative, 7, 76–79, 146
Nicgorski, Darlene, 75–81
Nietzsche, Friedrich, 15, 31
nonverbal tactics, 86

Packard, Vance, 157–59
Plan of Delano, 88, 93–96
positioning, 139
postmodern: as a characteristic, 7, 13, 28, 47, 144, 171, 173, 174; critic, 2, 3; as discourse, 1, 27; as an ism, 7,

10, 13–18, 69, 100; as quest, 171; rhetoric, 40; scholarship, 6, 7; voice, 2
power, 7, 10, 13–17, 20, 33, 49, 51, 57–62, 64, 67–72, 81, 85–87, 92–95, 102, 115–18, 126–28, 137, 163, 166, 174
powerlessness, 58, 60, 65
PRIZM, 162–63
product: names, 162–63; as slogans, 163
psychographic questionnaires, 160

rhetorical situation, 99, 104, 108–9
Rousseau, Jean-Jacques, 14

Sanctuary Movement, 72–74
Sartre, Jean-Paul, 9, 14, 15
Scott, James C., 4, 7, 46
self-identity, 155, 163
Simons, Herbert, 87
social identity, 57, 58, 64
Spitzak, Carole, 35, 36, 37
Styron, William, 8
subaltern voice, 1, 2
supernatural, 61

Tillich, Paul, 125
Turner, Victor, 38

utopia, 85

Wander, Philip, 17
Washington, Booker T., 8
Weaver, Richard, 35
Williams, Raymond, 57

Zhao Ziyang, 103

About the Editor and Contributors

ANDREW KING is Professor and Chair of the Department of Speech Communication at Louisiana State University. He has authored two previous books. King's academic interests lie in the areas of communication and power as well as medieval and Renaissance rhetorical theory.

WILLIAM BAILEY is Director of Undergraduate Studies in the Department of Communication at the University of Arizona. Bailey has been recognized as an outstanding critic and academic stylist. His most concentrated work has been in the area of dyadic communication.

JEANNE E. CLARK is Associate Professor of Communication at Willamette University. Trained in Anthropology as well as in Communication, her work centers the role of media in political communication. Dr. Clark is also interested in the communication practices of bureaucracy.

CATHERINE ANN COLLINS is Professor and Chair of the Department of Speech Communication at Willamette University. Her work has centered in political communication. Lately, she has worked in the area of international communication.

JOHN C. HAMMERBACK is Professor of Speech Communication at California State University, Hayward. A past president of the Western Communication Association, Hammerback is both a social theorist and a rhetorical critic.

RICHARD J. JENSEN is Professor of Communication at the University of New Mexico. He is the author of numerous books and articles on Chicano and regional and ethnic communication styles. His best-known work is in the area of protest rhetoric.

CHARLES URBAN LARSON is Professor of Communication Studies at

Northern Illinois University. He is the author of *Persuasion: Reception and Responsibility*, a best seller nationally and internationally, now in its seventh edition. He has authored numerous articles, and serves as a consultant to politicians and to the business community.

CALVIN MORRILL is Associate Professor in the Department of Communication at the University of Arizona. Morrill's work spans sociology, semiotics, linguistics, and criticism. He is interested in problems of communication and culture.

KENNETH C. PETRESS is an Assistant Professor of Communication in the Division of Humanities, University of Maine, Presque Isle. His research has ranged from marital communication to iconography. His principal interest is in Asian rhetoric.

KARI WHITTENBERGER-KEITH is an Assistant Professor in the Department of Communication, University of Louisville. She has spent much of her research time studying a tradition that flowered originally during the Renaissance. Her work deals with politeness and social constraints in communication encounters.

KENNETH ZAGACKI is Associate Professor of Speech Communication at Louisiana State University. He has published numerous articles on the rhetoric of foreign policy. His present work centers on the study of communication practices within the scientific community.